Underground Spaces Unveiled

ice
Institution of Civil Engineers

publishing

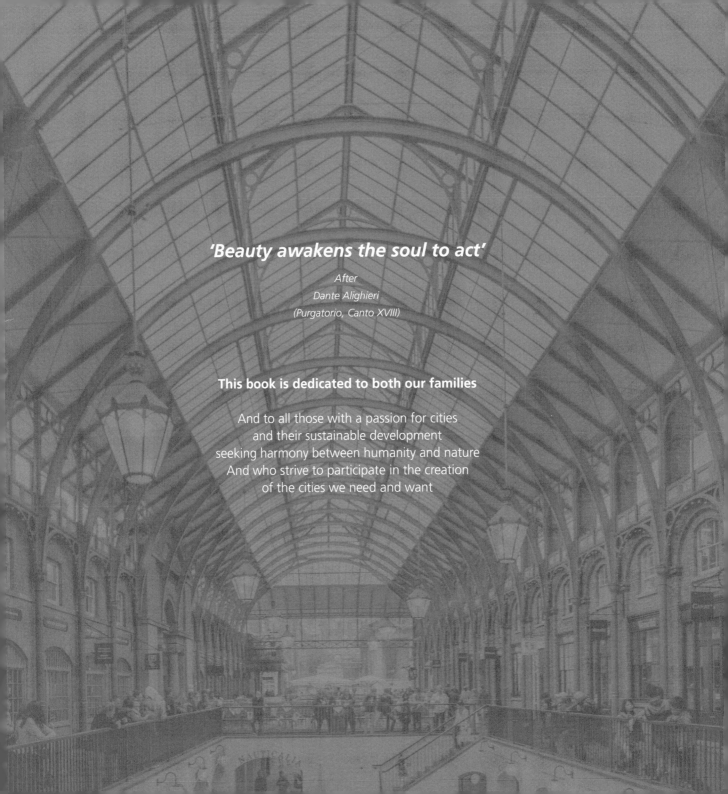

'Beauty awakens the soul to act'

*After
Dante Alighieri
(Purgatorio, Canto XVIII)*

This book is dedicated to both our families

And to all those with a passion for cities
and their sustainable development
seeking harmony between humanity and nature
And who strive to participate in the creation
of the cities we need and want

Underground Spaces Unveiled

Planning and creating the cities of the future

GEORGE GREEN LIBRARY OF
SCIENCE AND ENGINEERING

Han Admiraal
BSc CivEng, MBA
Enprodes Management Consultancy BV

Antonia Cornaro
BSocSc, MA Urban Planning
Amberg Engineering AG

Published by ICE Publishing, One Great George Street, Westminster, London SW1P 3AA.

Full details of ICE Publishing representatives and distributors can be found at:
www.icebookshop.com/bookshop_contact.asp

Other titles from ICE Publishing:

- *Conceptual Structural Design, Second edition*
  O. Popovic Larsen. ISBN 978-0-7277-6110-1

- *Rethinking Masterplanning*
  H. AlWaer and B. Illsley. ISBN 978-0-7277-6082-1

- *The Railway Metropolis*
  M. Schabas. ISBN 978-0-7277-6180-4

www.icebookshop.com
A catalogue record for this book is available from the British Library

ISBN 978-0-7277-6145-3
© Thomas Telford Limited 2018

ICE Publishing is a division of Thomas Telford Ltd, a wholly-owned subsidiary of the Institution of Civil Engineers (ICE).

Commissioning Editor: Amber Thomas
Development Editor: Maria Inês Pinheiro
Production Editor: Madhubanti Bhattacharyya
Market Development Executive: Elizabeth Hobson

Designed and typeset by Kneath Associates, Swansea
Index created by Laurence Errington
Printed and bound in Great Britain by TJ International, Padstow

Table of contents

	Foreword by Dominique Perrault	vii
	Foreword by Dr Joan Clos	ix
	Preface	xi
	Acknowledgements	xiii
	About the authors	xv
Chapter 1	The subsurface as the final urban frontier	
	1.1. Introduction	01
	1.2. The city we need	02
	1.3. A modern-day struggle	04
	1.4. A new approach – spatial dialogue and beyond	13
	1.5. This chapter's core ideas	18
	References	20
Chapter 2	Achieving harmony between humanity and nature – urban underground sustainability	
	2.1. Harmony between humanity and nature	23
	2.2. Human interventions below the surface	24
	2.3. Subsurface ecosystem services	27
	2.4. An ecological approach	30
	2.5. Towards a model for determining sustainable underground development	35
	2.6. This chapter's core ideas	39
	References	40
Chapter 3	From yaodong to the third dimension – historical approaches to underground urbanism	
	3.1. The yaodong – natural subsurface habitats	43
	3.2. The 19th century – revolutionary engineering and unrivalled optimism	46
	3.3. The 20th century – underground urbanism	49

Contents

	3.4. This chapter's core ideas	56
	References	57
Chapter 4	Spatial design – creating a new urban tissue	
	4.1. Beyond the urban service layer	59
	4.2. From the yaodong via contemporary to future designs	63
	4.3. Privately owned public open underground spaces	70
	4.4. Urban underground corridors	74
	4.5. This chapter's core ideas	81
	References	82
Chapter 5	Policy building and urban planning	
	5.1. Policy building	85
	5.2. Planning methodology for the underground	96
	5.3. Underground urban planning cases	104
	5.4. The need for data	108
	5.5. Urban systems integration	110
	5.6. This chapter's core ideas	110
	References	111
Chapter 6	Future cities – resilient cities	
	6.1. Resilience as a concept	115
	6.2. The threatening subsurface	117
	6.3. Challenges for urban areas	118
	6.4. Meeting the challenges using underground space	120
	6.5. This chapter's core ideas	125
	References	126
Chapter 7	Building for people – valued underground spaces	
	7.1. Loveable spaces	129
	7.2. Comfortable spaces	135

	7.3. Safe and secure spaces	142
	7.4. This chapter's core ideas	148
	References	148
Chapter 8	Governance and legal challenges of underground space use	
	8.1. Oversight and insight	151
	8.2. Land ownership	152
	8.3. Easement and right-of-way compensation	156
	8.4. The principle of tort	157
	8.5. Building codes	159
	8.6. Environmental control	163
	8.7. Managing the subsurface	164
	8.8. This chapter's core ideas	167
	References	168
Chapter 9	Investing in underground space is all about value capture	
	9.1. The cost conundrum	171
	9.2. Creating societal value	172
	9.3. Capturing created value	177
	9.4. Investing in underground space	182
	9.5. Political will empowers	185
	9.6. This chapter's core ideas	188
	References	189
Chapter 10	How disruption is creating new paradigms for an urban underground future	193
	References	199
	Index	201

Foreword by Dominique Perrault

Among many cultures, the underground world holds strong symbolic meaning. For some, it is where evil dwells; for others, it has long represented a natural shelter against elements. Although mindsets tend to change, the work of enthusiasts such as Han and Antonia represents a significant leap forwards in the progress of a global culture of 'groundscapes'.

This summer, I was delighted to meet Han again in Lyon, France, for a seminar. Han, Antonia and I have a strong interest in underground space, or groundscapes, and their potential value for future cities. We share the belief that building underground is not just a conceptual temporary architectural trend but holds long-term potential, especially for dense urban environments.

Cities now attract the majority of the world's population. In extremely dense cities, decision-makers are being challenged to find balance between sustainability and public space availability, between liveability and price control.

Han and Antonia have both developed incredible expertise in their own fields and in underground construction, eventually joining their efforts in developing underground space use as the chair and vice-chair of the International Tunnelling and Underground Space Association's Committee on Underground Space (ITACUS). Whereas Antonia focuses on how underground spaces can play a role in urban planning and public space development, Han concentrates on combining engineering, organisational expertise, economics and social management.

They not only have had crucial roles in major underground projects around the world but also dedicate time to educating current and future engineers, architects, urban planners and decision-makers about every aspect of underground space use.

'Justification can only be obtained through dialogue.' Inclusive dialogue is key to Antonia and Han's approach to underground construction project management. Their book is the result of their vision and a step towards nurturing dialogue through educating current and future decision-makers. It features an ideal balance between technicality and accessibility, between a comprehensive approach to the matter and in-depth case studies that will help the reader translate its new knowledge into the real world.

An important feature of this book is that it plays an integral part in raising awareness on groundscape. Although its focus is urban planning and urban design, it aims at giving a wide overview of the subject to the reader, regardless of their experience.

In having such a comprehensive approach to underground construction, Han and Antonia participate in a larger global culture that was reborn during the 20th century in our modern societies: the culture of appreciating the potential of the underground. This has started developing as a type of 'network' of knowledge, of people, of technologies, of education and of urban experiments through the practical vanguard work of architects such as Edouard Utudjian and the visionary design of Archigram and Superstudio.

Today, what was only an echo is ready to emerge as the groundscape of our cities.

As various major cities now grasp the extent of the potential that their underground spaces hold, I'd like to invite you to seize the value of this book.

Dominique Perrault

Foreword by Dr Joan Clos

Underground Spaces Unveiled: Planning and Creating the Cities of the Future is an enriching analysis of underground space that comes at a crucial moment in the implementation process of the New Urban Agenda, the outcome document of Habitat III, adopted in Quito (Ecuador).

The quest for compact, energy-efficient, resilient and liveable cities has led to an increasing emphasis on planned urbanisation. The character and image of a city, too, are defined and framed by its streets and public spaces, whether boulevards or neighbourhood roads, squares or neighbourhood gardens or children's playgrounds. Urban centres that have limited public space on the surface or face severe weather conditions, such as Montreal and Helsinki, are starting to turn their attention to the underground, from subterranean parks to shopping malls and shopping arcades.

However, the potential of underground spaces is typically overlooked or neglected in planning processes. Most cities have limited understanding of the potential of underground space, and there is little clarity on the importance of a planning approach to this space. Traditionally, cities have made use of underground space for transport (particularly rapid rail transport), services and parking. In some cases, such as Hong Kong, Singapore and, lately,

London, areas of public space, with commerce and entertainment, as well as pedestrian connectivity, have been developed successfully. However, such spaces often follow the layout of surface public space, as the circumstances and even the legal status below private plots remain unclear, and underground spatial planning or design strategies – where they exist – may not provide adequate guidance in this regard. Indeed, the effective use of underground space poses specific challenges, including geology and underground ecology, as well as legal barriers and governance constraints in its planning and management. Without a vision, a strategy and appropriate legal and fiscal instruments to address these challenges, its use would remain ad hoc and chaotic.

A growing interest in underground space is clearly driven by the need and opportunities for the location of services and waste management, as well as energy-related infrastructure for production and distribution. In addition, locating other functions underground (such as transportation, cinemas and shopping facilities, as well as museums and cultural spaces – as in the case of Athens) will create more space above ground for recreation and other social activities. Building underground can improve our urban environment by relieving the pressure on the surface, developing better public transport networks, reducing noise, and leaving more green areas intact above ground.

The use of underground space can help cities remain compact, be energy efficient or find the space needed to include new functions in the existing city landscape. Underground spaces can play a critical role in cities, connecting spaces, people and goods, and thereby facilitating commerce, social interaction and mobility, creating new urban tissue, which can also contribute to the liveability and character of cities.

Planning the underground space coupled with the development of legal frameworks will require planners and decision-makers to work together with new knowledge and understanding of the specific constraints and opportunities of this important space. This book occupies an important niche and significantly advances the discussion in this area.

Joan Clos
Under-Secretary-General, United Nations
Executive Director, UN-Habitat

Preface

Humanity is facing enormous challenges as it moves into the Anthropocene – the era where human intervention is influencing the Earth's natural systems. We are part of a transition that requires us to seek a new balance between nature and humanity and between ourselves. It is about harmony among human beings and between humanity and nature. This transition requires us to look for new paradigms that question the past and show new ways forward. Some look to outer space for the future of humanity. We believe that in the interim before we can leave this planet in search of other worlds, we should look at what underground space has to offer.

Our fascination with underground space lies in the stark contrasts it delivers, from the raw, dark utilitarian uses of 19th-century Paris sewer systems designed by Haussmann to the modern architecture of Perrault, manipulating the soil and welding surface and underground together in poetic forms of stunning beauty that enhance the urban fabric and create loveable public spaces. It is the task of the urban planner to unveil these invisible spaces. By unveiling and making these spaces visible, they will contribute to our cities of the future. Cities that are sustainable, resilient, inclusive and, above all, liveable for their citizens. Becoming aware, understanding and appreciating the role of the subsurface is vital, as it plays a critical role in the existence and development of smart cities. Participatory, integrated and sustainable planning and management are the means to achieve this.

With this book, we hope to contribute to a greater understanding of underground space. It comes forth from a journey of discovery that turned from fascination to real passion. According to the philosopher John Rawls, we all form our opinions and decisions while remaining behind a veil of ignorance that refuses us other views. We truly hope that this book helps in unveiling the underground space for you and to shift the veil of ignorance that covers its existence.

Han Admiraal and Antonia Cornaro

Acknowledgements

The authors would like to extend their gratitude to Joan Clos and Dominique Perrault for writing the forewords to this book. We are extremely fortunate to have found supporters in them to convey our message. Each in their unique way has shaped the urban landscape and left a legacy for years to come.

We are also grateful for the continuing support we receive from the International Tunnelling and Underground Space Association (ITA). We thank its current president Tarcisio Celestino, and its past-presidents, in particular Søren Eskesen, Martin Knights and Harvey Parker, who understood the importance of unveiling underground space to a broader audience. We also want to express our gratitude to Olivier Vion, the ITA executive director, for his support for our work and the work of the ITA Committee on Underground Space (ITACUS). Without our fellow steering board members, the members of the advisory board and, indeed, the committee members, we would not have found the inspiration to write this book. The support we receive from the International Society of City and Regional Planners (ISOCARP) has been an immense help to us in ensuring that we focus on the subject of urban planning as instrumental to creating the cities of the future. Their receptiveness of our message has been incredible. We thank Ric Stephens, ISOCARP's current president, and past vice-presidents Shipra Narang Suri, Manfred Schenk and Piotr Lorens, who have always supported and inspired us.

Writing a book takes time, and we would like to thank our families for standing by us as we wrote. Their support was without a doubt what kept us on course.

Our employers, Amberg Engineering of Switzerland and Enprodes of the Netherlands, have given us and are continuing to give us ample opportunities to explore underground space and put into practice what we preach.

A special word of thanks goes to Prof. Dr. em. Ray Sterling. Together with John Carmody, he was most assuredly one of the pioneers who picked up the topic in the 1970s and attempted to revive underground urbanism. Ray inspired us in many ways and was always a staunch supporter, both as a member of the ITACUS Steering Board and as a past-president of the Associated Research Centers for Urban Underground Space (ACUUS).

Last but not least, our sincere gratitude and appreciation go to the Institution of Civil

Acknowledgements

Engineers and ICE Publishing. They had the foresight to ask us to chair a conference that led to our former editor Amber Thomas asking us to write this book. Also, a special word of thanks to our current editor Inês Pinheiro, who was professional and refreshing to deal with in our monthly online book progress meetings and supported us throughout the writing process.

With this book, we aim to provide the context and impetus to make underground space part of urban planning and urban development. As such, we feel it's about unveiling opportunities to a broad audience – an audience that will help to create the cities of the future. Cities that this world so desperately needs.

Start to 'think deep' and unveil all those underground spaces that will further shape and enhance the cities we need.

About the authors

Han Admiraal

Han, a civil engineer (University of Applied Science, Rotterdam), is co-chair of the International Tunnelling and Underground Space Association's Committee on Underground Space (ITACUS) and a member of the Urban Planning Advisory Group of the United Nations Office for Disaster Risk Reduction (UNISDR), advising the special representative. As president of the Dutch-Flemish Pipeline Industry Guild, he promotes underground freight transport as a sustainable and economically efficient mode.

Over the course of his career, Han has worked for the National Department of Public Works and Water Management, acting, among other positions, as the project manager for the first machine-excavated (TBM-driven) tunnel in soft soil in the Netherlands. Later, as the executive director of the Netherlands Centre for Underground Construction (COB) he implemented visionary concepts on underground construction, and was part-time professor of underground space at Zeeland University of Applied Science. Since 2008 he has been the owner and managing director of Enprodes Management Consultancy in Delft, consulting in the fields of underground space and road tunnel safety.

He is passionate about urban planning and interdisciplinary dialogue between various stakeholders and professional disciplines dealing with urban and underground development. Having published numerous articles on this topic, this is his first book.

Antonia Cornaro

Antonia studied at New York University, where she earned her MA in Urban Planning in 1996.

She has over 20 years' experience of working as an urban and transport planner from the public and private sector in New York City, London, Vienna and Zurich, having worked for DCP in New York, Parsons Brinckerhoff (PB now WSP) in London, the Austrian Institute of Regional Planning (ÖIR) in Vienna, and the Zurich-based multi-disciplinary engineering consulting firm EBP.

In her current work as the business development manager for Amberg Engineering – an internationally active Swiss firm specialising in underground infrastructure design and management – she focuses on urban underground space with the aim of increasing the mobility, liveability and resilience of urban areas (from 2010 to date). This focus is also central to her work as co-chair of ITACUS.

Antonia is passionate about cities and global and sustainable development, and has presented and published extensively on this subject, often jointly with Han Admiraal. This is her first book.

Chapter 1

The subsurface as the final urban frontier

1.1. Introduction

Whenever we talk to people about underground space we hear exciting and enthusiastic stories. But we also meet desperation from trying to cope with the enormous complexity of the subsurface. There is a struggle in trying to comprehend what the subsurface is about and how to plan it. Using underground space is but a small part of a much larger puzzle that planners and geologists are trying to comprehend. However, people are pressing ahead, just like frontier pioneers from earlier times – as they see enormous opportunities and feel it is the only way forward as far as our cities are concerned.

In this introductory chapter we will start by challenging the thinking that the development of underground spaces is only for cities that need to cope with a scarcity of land for future development and are facing an enormous growth in their population. We will argue that the new urban paradigm that is required for the cities we need cannot afford to overlook the use of underground space.

It will also be shown that although many successful projects have been constructed worldwide, these often remain isolated cases. As such, they are part of a culture of mono-development that stems from solving one-dimensional problems. The danger is that these projects could eventually block further development as the subsurface becomes crowded and projects start to impact each other. Therefore, a new approach is required, one that positions the sustainable exploration of the subsurface firmly within a multi-dimensional approach. As such, urban planning, urban design and architecture are required as domains that work together with other areas, such as civil engineering and geology, to bring about a spatial subsurface dialogue.

In this chapter, we will briefly examine the importance of planning and managing the use of the subsurface. To illustrate this, conceptual models of the subsurface will be presented, and we will show that the resource 'space' is just one of several resources contained within the subsurface.

The themes we touch on in this chapter will be expanded on later in the book. The overall aim of this introduction is to paint you a picture – one that includes the macro level of considering our cities' future, as well as highlighting the micro level of projects themselves. We will take you on a journey that examines all aspects of underground space development within the wider context of the subsurface itself. It will be a journey of exploration, as the subsurface could very well prove to be the final urban frontier waiting to be explored. As Édouard Utudjian (1952) so poignantly phrased it nearly 100 years ago: 'It is necessary that the urban planner thinks deep and that underground development of cities is done not through random necessities, but according to a definite commitment, legislation and a predetermined plan.'

It is this call for definite commitment that is the basis of our philosophy. We firmly believe that there is a need to start to 'think deep' – as only in this way can society move towards an urban underground future as part of the cities we need. We see the 'final urban frontier' as a metaphor that encapsulates the spirit of humankind's exploration of extra-terrestrial space as immortalised by the science fiction series *Star Trek*. It also captures the spirit of the early settlers of the 'Wild West' claiming terrestrial space by hitting a stake in the soil, thereby affirming their stake in land settlement. When it comes to subterranean space, we are all stakeholders, as life at the surface is supported by it and indeed, in many ways, depends on it.

We hope to show in this book that sustainable use of the subsurface is possible and therefore not science fiction; we also hope to show that claiming underground space based on a 'first-come, first-served' basis as in the 'Wild West' is not the way to move forward. Time has come to 'think deep'.

1.2. The city we need

The use of underground space can contribute to making our cities liveable, sustainable and inclusive. As such, we believe that the real reason why this final urban frontier should be explored lies in the need to choose what kind of cities we want to live in. Many authors have been concentrating on the inevitable fact that our planet's population is ever growing and that we are witnessing a mass migration to urban areas. Mega-cities are becoming a norm rather than an exception. We feel, however, that taking this viewpoint leads to looking at the subsurface and at underground space from a defensive point of view. The final urban frontier becomes that last piece of space that we can still occupy, and it starts with placing all users who do not necessarily have to be at the surface, below it. Although this argument has been made for the past 150 years as being the rationale for exploring the subsurface, it has not brought about a major exploration of the possibilities below the surface. This defensive stance of using underground space as a spatial relief valve will be explored in later chapters. For now, it suffices to say that a more pre-emptive approach, looking at the needs of urban areas, and developing from the potential that the subsurface has to offer to match those needs, is a more planning-based approach. Urban planning is about the needs of citizens, it is about how to deal with the large influx of people into urban areas, but it is also about how to deal with the unprecedented sprawl of cities and how to balance this in such a way that our cities become the cities we need.

In 2012, the UN Secretary-General Ban Ki-Moon sent a letter to the *New York Times* titled 'The future we want'. It was written on the eve of the Rio+20 conference. Twenty years earlier the goal was set to develop sustainably towards the future. Ban concluded that in those 20 years nothing much had changed and that the challenges had only grown. He also highlighted the fact that for the first time in history human activities are fundamentally changing the Earth's dynamics. Indeed, some scientists identify our current era as a new geological epoch. Ban called on everyone to contribute to a future for all, the future we want: 'This is a moment for world leaders and their people to unite in common purpose around a shared vision of our common future – the future we want' (Ban, 2012).

What is interesting is his observation about human activities fundamentally changing the Earth's dynamics. When looking at the sustainable exploration of the subsurface, this is something that clearly needs to be considered. It will be discussed later in Chapter 6.

Four years on, the Habitat III conference took place in Quito, Ecuador, in 2016. The World Urban Campaign published a brochure as preparation for the road to Quito. In *The City We Need* the authors stated clearly that 'the battle for a more sustainable future will be won or lost in cities' (World Urban Campaign, 2014). They are convinced that the way we 'plan, build, and manage our cities' will inevitably determine the future of cities. Cities of the future develop sustainably, are resilient against the challenges they face and are, above all, liveable and inclusive cities. As the authors of *The City We Need* put it:

The cities we want should be engines of economic development and lie at the core of a new urban era where people can find freedom, innovation, prosperity, and resilience. Public, private, and civil society organizations offer thousands of important solutions both small and large.

It is for this reason their call to action is for a new urban paradigm to be shaped.

This is where the main challenge lies when considering underground space. It is not just about the ever-growing population on this planet or the mass immigration from rural areas to urban areas, it goes beyond that. The key question is: how will the use of underground space contribute to the city we need? How will it create the future we want? This is what an urban underground future is about: enabling cities to develop sustainably and be resilient, liveable and inclusive. Only seen in this context can there be a place for underground space within urban development. It does, however, entail us to demonstrate that underground space can only come about if it is shown to be part of a sustainable exploration of the subsurface.

Having identified that there is no reason not to use the subsurface as part of urban development (indeed, it should come about with the same urgency as other developments), a second key question would seem to be: why is it taking so long? This question will be explored in Section 1.4, as we start building the whole picture. For now, it suffices to say that part of the answer could lie in the fact that moving towards an urban underground future could be quite complicated. It is not just about deciding on what is required from a planning perspective,

there is an absolute need to consider the
geology on which the city is built, and to look
at future scenarios. Underground spaces do not
come about by themselves – excepting naturally
formed caves – but once they are there, they
are there to stay. Demolition of buildings at the
surface level has no comparison with buildings
or other facilities below the surface. The urban
underground future requires a new urban
paradigm as much as cities themselves need
it. The fact that for the first time in history we
are actively pursuing this and realise that we need
to pull together all resources to survive might
just prove to be the momentum required – a
momentum that historically, as we will discuss in
Chapter 3, was lacking. This momentum is here
now; it can be used, and it will lead to further
exploring the final urban frontier.

1.3. A modern-day struggle

1.3.1 The Rush to Oklahoma

In many ways, the exploration of the subsurface
shows a remarkable resemblance to the way that
early settlers laid claim to property in the 'Wild
West' or 'Old West' frontier of the USA. This
quote is taken from the introduction to an eye-
witness account that was published in *Harper's
Weekly* (Howard, 1889), less than a month after
the 'Rush to Oklahoma', and illustrates how the
town of Guthrie came about in less than a day:

> Congress had failed to provide for any
> form of civil government. Although the
> area had been surveyed into the standard
> system of 6-mile square townships and
> mile-square sections of 640 acres each,
> no sites for towns had been designated

let alone laid out in streets and lots. The
rules simply provided that at noon on
April 22 persons gathered at the Arkansas
or Texas borders would be permitted
to enter, seek a parcel of unclaimed
land, and file a claim of ownership in
accordance with the applicable Federal
laws governing the disposal of the
public domain. Federal marshals, railroad
personnel, and other persons lawfully in
the territory before the opening ('legal
sooners') were prohibited from filing
land claims – a provision that was more
violated than observed.

The account goes on to illustrate the sheer
disappointment of early would-be settlers to
find that all the best plots had already been
claimed by legal sooners, as the following
exchange demonstrates:

> 'We're done for', said a town-
> site speculator, in dismay. 'Some one
> has gone in ahead of us and laid out
> the town.' 'Never mind that,' shouted
> another town-site speculator, 'but make
> a rush and get what you can.'

'Get what you can' is an excellent description
of the way the development of the subsurface
has taken place, and indeed still is taking place
below many cities. Even in cases where this has
not been the intention, development without
taking future development into account has
led to underground occupation being based
on 'space available' rather than on 'space
laid out'. To further explore this, we will take
a look at how subsurface development has
come about.

1.3.2 The physical underground landscape

Subsurface development has come about in a variety of ways. Although there are exceptions, as we will see in Section 1.4.4, the majority can be placed in two categories: objects and networks. The physical underground landscape consists of objects (often in the shape of basements or box-type constructions) and networks (varying from cables and pipes to tunnels) in the landscape. Networks are most often found in the horizontal plane. Nevertheless, the placement of pipes in the vertical plane is becoming more common, and we will treat these as objects. Both categories, objects and networks, have in common that access from the surface is always required. Although this may seem obvious, the fact that subsurface structures cannot exist without physical access to the surface is an inherent aspect of these structures. It also means that a new urban tissue below the surface will always by definition be part of the urban fabric.

A further distinction to make when viewing the physical underground landscape is between public and private uses. It will allow us to not only further analyse the relationship between the various uses but also to qualify the use in terms of contributing to the city we need.

This leads to the model of the physical underground landscape shown in Figure 1.1.

1.3.3 Private objects in the underground landscape

When looking at underground space development worldwide, the authors can only conclude that in the majority of cases this has come about in a haphazard, unplanned and often autonomous way. It is the individual actions of developers

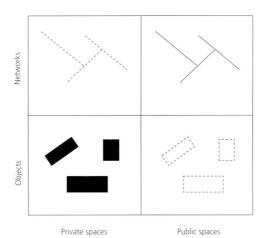

Networks

Objects

Private spaces   Public spaces

Figure 1-1 The physical underground landscape

that are increasingly pressing local authorities to answer questions in terms of planning the subsurface. Let's illustrate this by taking a closer look at two examples: underground thermal storage and basement developments.

The use of the underground for thermal energy storage is increasingly seen as an attractive way to reduce the carbon footprint of residential areas and office blocks. The geology of, for example the Netherlands, consists of many aquifers between impermeable strata that allow large-scale application of aquifer thermal energy storage (ATES) schemes (Dutch ATES, 2017). This technology requires pipes running vertically into the subsurface to access an aquifer. The system runs in a seasonal mode: cold water is extracted to cool homes or offices during summer, and the heated water is stored to heat buildings during winter. One of the issues these schemes face is that of thermal interference. Placing two wells too close to each other reduces efficiency or potentially leads to cancelling out the thermal difference. Conversely, placing wells too far apart leads to sub-optimal use of the aquifer capacity. This has now become a real problem, with the number of ATES systems growing – for example, increasing in the Netherlands from five in 1990 to 2740 in 2012 and predictions of 20 000 by 2020. At a macro level, ATES systems will provide a new sustainable energy supply and, as such, are deemed to be contributing to sustainable development; at the micro level, new planning and regulatory requirements are needed to protect existing systems and to ensure an optimal use of existing resources. In the absence of national guidance, municipalities now have 'underground energy' sections in their master plans and provide zoning maps (Figure 1.2) to ensure correct placement of ATES system wells.

In the Arnhem Master Plan 2020–2040, a paragraph is devoted to the subsurface (Gemeente Arnhem, 2012, p. 77, translated from Dutch by the author):

> The Arnhem subsurface is inseparably linked with the surface urban fabric. The subsurface contains hundreds of kilometres of cables and pipes, building foundations, occupational uses (Water Museum, University for Dance and Music, supermarkets, etc.), car parks and infrastructure for underground waste disposal systems. It also contains ground water (vital for humans and nature), rich archaeological deposits, contamination and explosives from WWII. In short, we can speak of 'subsurface congestion', whereby balancing surface and subsurface interests requires specific attention. By including the subsurface early in our urban plans, opportunities can be exploited, uses protected and challenges during development avoided.

It is important to note that it was the rapid growth of ATES systems in relation to other underground developments that drove the city to include the subsurface within its urban planning process.

A second example of autonomous scattered objects in the physical underground landscape are the so-called 'iceberg mansions' in London. In a comparison study between the underground space development in London and New York, Reynolds and Reynolds (2015) showed how planned basement developments beneath houses in the City of Westminster and the Royal Borough of Kensington and Chelsea forced these local authorities to develop

Figure 1-2 Underground space zoning map for the ATES system beneath the Waarderpolder industrial estate in the City of Haarlem, the Netherlands

Uses

⬜	Water management, specific – cold
⬛	Water management, specific – warm
▨	Water management, specific – influence zone

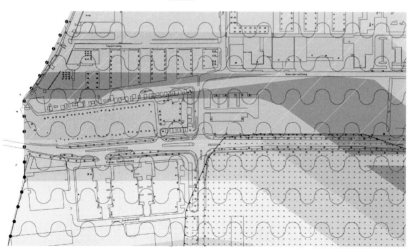

specific regulations to cope with these planned developments in 2013. The Royal Borough of Kensington and Chelsea published a more in-depth approach – its Basements Planning Policy – in January 2015 (Royal Borough of Kensington and Chelsea, 2015).

The term 'iceberg mansion' was first used by *The Daily Mail* in 2012 for extensive basement extensions proposed and built by 'today's billionaires' who often found their Victorian properties to be too cramped for their activities (Ostler, 2012). In 2014 *The Guardian* reported on the 'deep concerns' that these basement improvements were causing (Dowling, 2014). Interestingly, the concerns are more to do with the nuisance related to construction, such as noise and traffic issues. These concerns are also recognised in the Basements Planning Policy, as is illustrated in Box 1.1, which also gives the policy restrictions. The local authority does recognise the benefits of basement development:

> Basements are a useful way to add extra accommodation to homes and commercial buildings. Whilst roof extensions and rear extensions add visibly to the amount of built development, basements can be built with much less long term visual impact – provided appropriate requirements are followed.

The royal borough mentions some other concerns: for example, the importance of rainwater run-off and the impact that the extensions can have on trees.

As Reynolds and Reynolds (2015) also observed in the case of the two local authorities within the Greater London Area, and what we

The Council will require all basement development to:

a not exceed a maximum of 50% of each garden or open part of the site. The unaffected garden must be in a single area and where relevant should form a continuous area with other neighbouring gardens. Exceptions may be made on large sites;

b not comprise more than one storey. Exceptions may be made on large sites;

c not add further basement floors where there is an extant or implemented planning permission for a basement or one built through the exercise of permitted development rights;

d not cause loss, damage or long term threat to trees of townscape or amenity value;

e comply with the tests in national policy as they relate to the assessment of harm to the significance of heritage assets;

f not involve excavation underneath a listed building (including vaults);

g not introduce light wells and railings to the front or side of the property where they would seriously harm the character and appearance of the locality, particularly where they are not an established and positive feature of the local streetscape;

h maintain and take opportunities to improve the character or appearance of the building, garden or wider area, with external elements such as light wells, roof lights, plant and means of escape being sensitively designed and discreetly sited; in the case of light wells and roof lights, also limit the impact of light pollution;

i include a sustainable drainage system (SuDS), to be retained thereafter;

j include a minimum of one metre of soil above any part of the basement beneath a garden;

k ensure that traffic and construction activity do not cause unacceptable harm to pedestrian, cycle, vehicular and road safety; adversely affect bus or other transport operations (e.g. cycle hire), significantly increase traffic congestion, nor place unreasonable inconvenience on the day to day life of those living, working and visiting nearby;

l ensure that construction impacts such as noise, vibration and dust are kept to acceptable levels for the duration of the works;

m be designed to safeguard the structural stability of the existing building, nearby buildings and other infrastructure including London Underground tunnels and the highway;

n be protected from sewer flooding through the installation of a suitable pumped device.

can learn from the case of the City of Arnhem, that although these random objects in the underground landscape do cause regulatory interventions at the local or micro level, any implications for future developments of the subsurface are not taken into account. In the case of the Royal Borough of Kensington and Chelsea, future development of new underground networks could be severely hindered by massive basement extensions. The same holds true for ATES systems, which by their nature run down hundreds of metres into the subsurface.

The two cases examined identify a use limited to an individual or at most a group of individuals, and a development cut off from the public domain. They represent a mono-functional use of the subsurface; the use is limited to providing heating and cooling or it provides more housing space. On a map, the development would be indicated by a spot or an area at most. The connection to the surface is not open to the public and is contained within the confines of the building at the surface.

1.3.4 Public objects in the underground landscape

Similarly to the above, we can identify objects in the underground landscape that are open for public use and are part of the public domain even though their ownership could well be in private hands.

A prime example, expanding on the 'iceberg mansion' concept, is the Carrousel du Louvre in Paris. It is an underground development, essentially beneath the courtyard of the Louvre Palace, the famous museum housing, among other masterpieces, the *Mona Lisa*. The development itself is a mix of shopping mall, meeting facilities and public space, and it provides access to the Louvre museum. Importantly, it can be accessed from the surface and is linked to the Palais Royal – Musée du Louvre underground metro station. The Carrousel du Louvre is a prime example of how the use of underground space can complement a historical building, preserve its heritage, and provide additional public space that is functional and attractive and creates added value.

There is another characterisation that this case brings, which is linkage. Any use of the subsurface requires by definition a connection to the surface (as observed before). This linkage can take on many forms. In the case of the Carrousel du Louvre it is not just the connection to the metro station or the stairs linking to the surface. The Pyramide du Louvre (Figure 1.3) has become a landmark in its own right. Designed by Chinese American architect Ieoh Ming Pei (Agence France-Presse, 2017), it provides a visual interface between the subsurface and the surface. It is more than just a feature; it successfully integrates the underground development into the urban fabric. As we will see in Section 1.4.4 and later, when looking at the use of underground space as a means to create the city we need, the connections between the various forms of underground space developments are critical for creating a new urban underground tissue. A final observation in this case is that it is an example of mixed use and is versatile in that it can adapt to changes – the space created can be reused for other purposes should the need occur in future.

A second case that incorporates some of the features above is the Covent Garden Market Hall in London. Although not generally mentioned as a prime example of underground space development, this site offers everything we would like to see when envisioning an urban underground future. Originally designed by Charles Fowler in the neo-classical style of the period, the building was erected in 1828-30, and was restored by the Greater London Council in 1978 (Covent Garden Area Trust, 2017). The building is a single open public space containing shops, sitting areas and provision for open-air music (Figure 1.4). The former cellars were converted to basement shops during the restoration of the market hall in the 1980s, when a mezzanine level was created by opening up the basement and creating new spaces.

Figure 1-3 The Pyramide du Louvre as seen from the subsurface | Courtesy of Viq111, reproduced under CC BY-SA 2.0

What makes the Covent Garden Market Hall an interesting example is the way that the mezzanine level has been created by opening up the underground space and integrating this into the surface development. The canopies that were added during the Victorian era create a feeling of enclosure despite all the sides remaining open for access.

Comparing both these cases, it is easy to see how the use of underground space has enhanced the previously existing buildings. In the case of Covent Garden, it has literally created a new lease of life by reusing the former storage basements beneath the building. In the case of the Louvre, new space was created below the existing historical building, giving new vitality to the national treasure at the surface.

As with the earlier examples of objects in the physical underground space landscape, these examples are represented by a spot or an area on a map. The difference in these latter cases is the fact that the developments are very much mixed use and open to the public and have connections to the surface that are open to the public.

1.3.5 Private underground networks

When looking at underground networks we meet the concept of the tunnel. Tunnels vary in both length and diameter. On a map, they are typically represented by a line. Underground networks range from very small diameters for cables to larger diameters for pipes and sewers to the even larger diameters of tunnels. It comes as no surprise that most subsurface cable and pipe networks are not accessible other than by the owners of the network. In that sense, they are part of the private domain even if they are owned by public companies or serve a public use as is the case with utilities.

A big example of a private underground network is the Large Hadron Collider (LHC), which is owned by CERN. Lying at a maximum depth of 175 m below the surface, the tunnel alignment runs for 26.7 km in a circular configuration. The tunnel has a gradient of between 45 and 170 m, following the geologically attractive Leman basin molasse, and has a diameter of between 2.20 and 3.80 m (Baldy *et al.*, 2009). Interestingly, the tunnel runs beneath both France and Switzerland. Land ownership was dealt with through land acquisition by the French state, and, as it lies 170 m below the surface in Switzerland, it was deemed to be below a useful depth, so land ownership was not an issue (Evans and Bryant, 2008). It uses the tunnel alignment constructed for the former Large Electron–Positron Collider (LEP). Conversion took place through the building of new caverns for the LHC equipment. In 2014 a feasibility study was announced for the Future Circular Collider, requiring a possible 80–100 km of tunnel alignment (Larson, 2014).

What makes this case interesting is that it illustrates how a massive underground network can be deliberately created beneath two nations that have different land ownership legislation. As a network, it appears on a map as a line.

1.3.6 Public underground networks

Underground networks that are publicly accessible are known by a variety of names such as the 'Tube', the 'Underground' and the 'Metro' or by abbreviations such as MRT (for mass rapid transport). The origin of the word 'metro' lies in the London Underground Metropolitan Line, the oldest mass rapid transport system in the world (Figure 1.5). The line opened in 1863 and led to a revolution in terms of public transport in London, and, indeed, the development of London itself. After London, other cities soon started developing their own versions, notably Istanbul (Turkey), Budapest (Romania), Glasgow (UK), Vienna (Austria), Boston (USA) and Paris (France). The Paris Metro opened in 1900; the other lines opened at the end of the 19th century (Wikipedia, 2017).

It is perhaps the advent of these underground transport systems that showed the way forward for successful use of the subsurface in a way that supports a city. Large mega-cities nowadays could not exist without these mass rapid transport systems. For New York City, the underground lines are often compared to the veins of the human body. Without these vital conduits, the city could not exist. But the success of these systems has in many ways also proven to be problematic. The growth of the London Underground has led to new lines being developed, each one deeper than the one before: for example, the new Elizabeth Line reaches a depth of approximately 40 m below the surface near the Barbican in the City of London (McDougall, 2014).

Due to its particular geology, one of the stations of the Kiev Metro lies at a depth of 105.5 m below the surface. Transporting people to and from the surface becomes a challenge at such depths – a statement needing no further explanation. At those depths, the subsurface temperature also plays a role: the platforms of the Pyongyang Metro (North Korea), also at a depth of over 100 m, are reported to be at a constant 18°C, irrespective of the season (Sawe, 2017).

1.3.7 Grab your space while you can

All these cases clearly illustrate the benefits of these objects and networks, although the advantages sometimes lie with individuals rather than with society at large. There are also pitfalls, as has been shown. Without any planning, these systems of objects and networks grow autonomously, leading to ever-deeper placements for future objects and networks, to avoid running into existing alignments. The same holds true for the placement of pipelines and cables below the surface. The traditional way of achieving this is by digging trenches and putting cables or pipelines inside these trenches. New development then takes place to either side of the already placed utilities so as not to hinder the existing one, resulting in ever-growing occupation and thereby congestion of the first shallow layers of the subsurface.

The cases examined in the previous sections all show that either the development itself leads to planning policy and regulations at the micro level or that, in time, planning policy and regulations are required to prevent chaos and congestion of the subsurface. This calls for policies and regulations that rise above the local interest and take regional and national interests into account at a more macro level in order to prevent future blocking of much needed development. Until this occurs, it literally is a

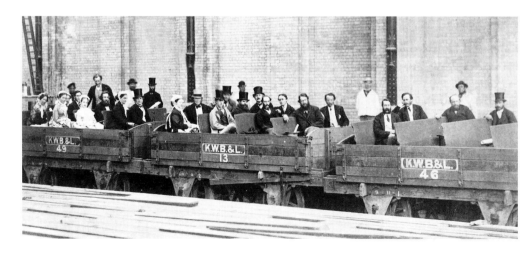

Figure 1-5 The Metropolitan Railway – contractors' train carrying notables on the first trial run of the entire route in May 1862 | Courtesy of Institution of Civil Engineers

case of staking your claim and grabbing the space while you can.

1.4. A new approach – spatial dialogue and beyond

1.4.1 The subsurface: from surface to core

However adventurous the exploration of the final urban frontier may seem, in geological terms we are barely scratching the surface. The Earth's crust varies in thickness, the oceanic crust being about 10 km thick, the continental crust varying from 30 to 70 km. This is only the crust – beneath it lies the mantle, and then the core of the Earth, both in excess of 3000 km thickness each. Figure 1.6 shows the use of the subsurface in a schematic way (Kastrup *et al.*, 2017). It clearly illustrates that although human activity in terms of oil and gas exploration can go as deep as 4 km, most other subsurface activities take place in the first 200 m, with urban utility networks often being placed in the top 1.5 m. Even when considering deep placement of sewers beneath Hong Kong at 90–160 m (Tai *et al.*, 2009), we can safely say that spatial occupation of the subsurface below 200 m has not taken place on any great scale. Exceptions to this general scheme are mining activities and underground laboratories, such as the one in Southwest China at 2400 m below the surface: the Jinping laboratory has been placed at this depth to protect its astrophysical research from cosmic rays (Li *et al.*, 2015).

It is in the light of this 'top-layer occupation' that we need to consider 'subsurface congestion' as is mentioned in Section 1.3.3, in the case of the City of Arnhem. The final urban frontier might prove to be illusive in the sense that it is a rather unknown, yet very occupied shallow layer of the subsurface and the total geology of our planet. When looking at the total geological timescale, the time that humans have been exploring and occupying the subsurface seems negligible, yet the impact is such that human activity could very well be altering the Earth's dynamics. It is in this sense that knowledge of the urban geology is not just about seeking out opportunities for human occupation, it is also about understanding the relationship between geology and human intervention and the impact this has on subsurface ecosystem services, as will be discussed in Chapter 2.

What we hope to illustrate with the Arnhem example is that, when it comes to planning the use of the subsurface, it is not entirely comparable with planning at the surface. Geology, all of a sudden, starts to play an important role, determining not only if any subsurface activities should take place but also whether this is desirable from an environmental point of view.

Up to now the term 'subsurface' has been used generically to mean everything we perceive to be below the surface. For the purposes of planning, this needs to be narrowed down. We have already established that there is a difference in terms of human activities between the 'top subsurface layer' and the 'deep subsurface'. The former occupies the first 200 m below the surface, the latter runs, for the sake of definition, for another 4000 m. Below that we enter geological layers that, as far as we can see now, can serve no purpose in sustaining the city we need. This is firstly brought about by practical

Figure 1-6 Schematic depicting
the diversity of subsurface use
Courtesy of Ulrike Kastrup

objections in terms of the distance between the surface and this boundary of the deep subsurface. Secondly, it would pose quite an engineering challenge given the great pressures at this depth and also the high temperatures. The thermal gradient below the surface is 25–30°C/km, which would mean that at 4 km depth we would expect temperatures in excess of 100°C. For the purposes of geothermal energy these temperatures are, however, very attractive, and Fridleifsson *et al.* (2008) have mentioned a project running down to 5 km: 'into a reservoir with supercritical hydrous fluids at 450–600°C … If this project succeeds, the power obtained from conventional geothermal fields can be increased by an order of magnitude.'

This shows that the lower boundary might be pushed further, as is the case with all kinds of human exploration. For the purposes of planning, we feel that the 'top subsurface layer' is sufficient as an object of investigation in relation to the urban fabric.

1.4.2 The subsurface resources model

Parriaux *et al.* (2004) first suggested a model of the subsurface as comprising four resources: space, water, energy and geo-materials. What makes this model interesting is that 'underground space' is but one of four resources that we can identify below the surface. The presence of water, the ability to obtain or store energy, and the ability to extract geo-materials are sometimes conveniently forgotten in the quest for space that cities undertake. This quest is real, as can be seen from a recent article in the *China Daily* (Wei, 2016):

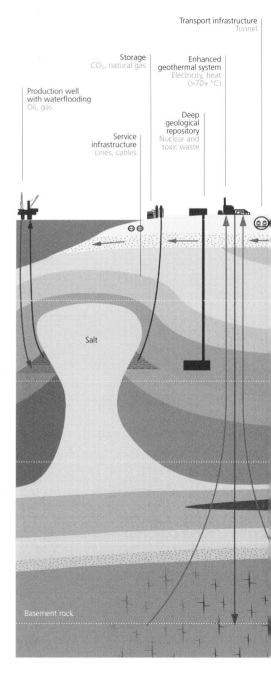

Transport infrastructure
Tunnel

Storage
CO$_2$, natural gas

Enhanced
geothermal system
Electricity, heat
(>70+ °C)

Production well
with waterflooding
Oil, gas

Deep
geological
repository
Nuclear and
toxic waste

Service
infrastructure
Lines, cables

Salt

Basement rock

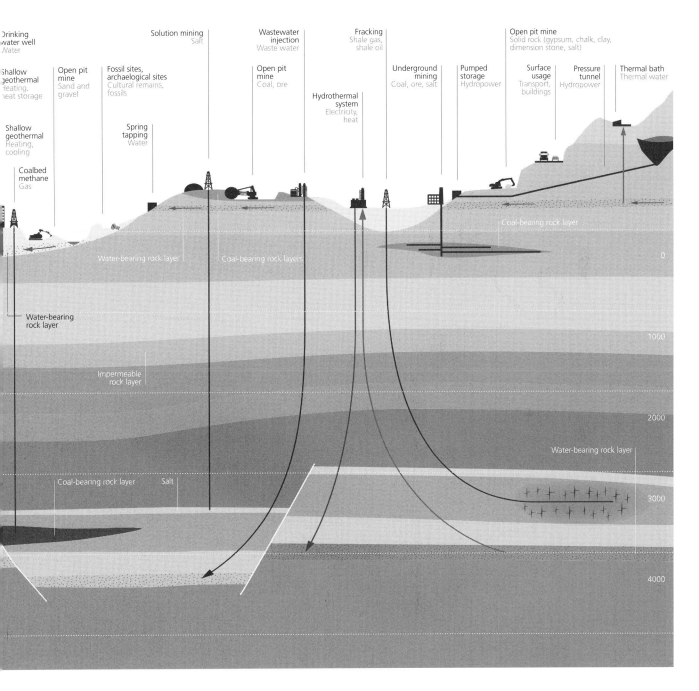

Drinking
water well
Water

Solution mining
Salt

Wastewater
injection
Waste water

Fracking
Shale gas,
shale oil

Open pit mine
Solid rock (gypsum, chalk, clay,
dimension stone, salt)

Shallow
geothermal
Heating,
heat storage

Open pit
mine
Sand and
gravel

Fossil sites,
archaeological sites
Cultural remains,
fossils

Open pit
mine
Coal, ore

Underground
mining
Coal, ore, salt

Pumped
storage
Hydropower

Surface
usage
Transport,
buildings

Pressure
tunnel
Hydropower

Thermal bath
Thermal water

Hydrothermal
system
Electricity,
heat

Shallow
geothermal
Heating,
cooling

Spring
tapping
Water

Coalbed
methane
Gas

Coal-bearing rock layer

Water-bearing rock layer

Coal-bearing rock layers

0

Water-bearing
rock layer

Impermeable
rock layer

1000

2000

Water-bearing rock layer

Coal-bearing rock layer

Salt

3000

4000

As land resources become increasingly scarce amid China's urban sprawl, local authorities have resorted to a new frontier for space: the world below our feet. A number of cities have decided to tap this underground space to reduce the mounting pressures on available land in high-density urban areas. In late December, Wuhan, the capital of Hubei province, announced that construction had started on one of the country's largest 'underground cities'. According to a blueprint released by the city government, the underground complex being built in the Optics Valley Central City will cost an estimated 8 billion yuan ($1.22 billion). The three-story project, scheduled to be completed within three years, will have an overall construction space of 516,000 square meters, equivalent to 72 soccer fields.

At the same time, Fridleifsson et al. (2008) have shown that the quest worldwide for renewable energy is taking place on a massive scale as well. They concluded that this is partially based on the limited environmental impact:

> One of the strongest arguments for putting more emphasis on the development of geothermal resources worldwide is the limited environmental impact compared to most other energy sources. The CO_2 emission related to direct applications is negligible and very small in electricity generation compared to using fossil fuel.

Parriaux et al. (2004), when asked how they see a possible clash between competing resources, stated that although they felt that it would be more common in a conflict between underground transport infrastructure and energy systems for policy-makers to choose to develop the former. We would argue that, given the quest for renewable energy, that decision would now not be made, and the first-come, first-serve principle would therefore apply through lack of policy and planning. Parriaux et al. (2004) commented that they hoped such a clash would lead to engineers getting together to design an underground infrastructure system that could serve as an energy system at the same time.

A new approach in planning underground space calls not only for policy and regulations – it also requires awareness that, without participatory planning processes involving all stakeholders, the solutions required to sustain the city we need will not be developed. The outcome of these processes will be a more multi-dimensional use of the subsurface brought about by cross-discipline collaboration.

1.4.3 The subsurface as an object of spatial planning

When we look at the subsurface from a spatial planning point of view, we can see two possible developments. One is the extension of parts of the urban fabric to below the surface. Buildings, either existing or new, have basements below them for various uses. Most common are spaces for parking cars, in effect using basements in their traditional role for storage. The other is creating networks that at some points are connected to the surface for access to the system below. The object of planning in this case is reduced to the question of how to regulate the development in order to prevent negative impact on existing buildings or systems. At most, planning can help in avoiding conflicts between resources, such as the contamination of drinking water aquifers through allowing underground space development at the same time. As was described in Section 1.2, this is a defensive way of planning brought about by the absence of policy and planning regulations and directed by the autonomous development of the subsurface.

A more pre-emptive approach would be to consider the subsurface from two perspectives. The first is to explore the subsurface in terms of gaining an understanding of what it consists of, and the interaction between subsurface ecosystem services and life at the surface. There is a strong interdependency between life at the surface and processes beneath the surface that can strikingly be formulated as follows: the subsurface supports surface life.

The second perspective is to look at the needs of our cities: what is required to make our cities resilient, inclusive, develop sustainably and become, above all, liveable. The only way that the use of the subsurface and the development of underground space within the subsurface is going to come about in a sustainable way is if we can discover how to meet the urban needs, and balance those with the opportunities the subsurface has to offer.

Both perspectives will offer us insights at the local urban level. However, the question is whether this would be sufficient, and whether input is also required from regional and national levels. In the Netherlands a spatial planning process is underway to develop the Subsurface Spatial Planning Vision, outlining the national policy on the subsurface (Government of the Netherlands, 2015). The main reason for this was the awareness that the subsurface below the country contains a wealth of resources, archives and ecosystem surfaces. There was also an acute awareness of autonomous human activities in the subsurface that proved not always to be beneficial. Mass contamination of both soils and water aquifers through the subsurface storage of industrial waste provided a painful historical lesson. At this time, it has become clear that, from a viewpoint of national interest, the government takes responsibility for activities in the 'deep subsurface', mainly relating to the extraction of natural resources. Regional governments are looking at the 'top subsurface layer' mostly in terms of cross-urban-boundary processes, such as underground water flows. Urban authorities are becoming increasingly aware that they need to address the planning of the subsurface, but up to now this has mainly been in a reactive manner, as outlined above.

Planning the subsurface is a matter of scale. Whether we are looking from a national, a supra-national or a more local perspective makes a vast difference in terms of what needs to be addressed. One thing stands out at the urban level, and that is the decision to either plan reactively or to take a more proactive stance. When following the latter, we can truly speak of planning the subsurface as part of creating the city we need. But doing so requires more than just the urban planners.

We need to look not only at urban planning but also at urban design and at architecture as disciplines that, among others, shape our cities and that are needed to shape the new urban tissue that the subsurface can offer cities. From this perspective, we need to discuss one vital element that is lacking in most worldwide development of underground spaces: connectivity.

1.4.4 Connectivity as the key to creating a new urban tissue

Without creating connections in the underground landscape the subsurface remains distinctly detached from the urban fabric, with only the entrance and exit points forming some kind of linkage. The objects in the underground landscape are at most basement extensions of existing surface buildings, the underground networks existing to serve a utility or transport purpose. Without connecting these various singular uses there is no urban tissue below the surface. Without corridors acting the way that streets do at the surface, underground development will remain isolated from the city and a long way from contributing to the liveable cities we need. It was Jane Jacobs (1961) who pointed out the importance of sidewalks and streets: 'Think of a city and what comes to mind? Its streets. If a city's streets look interesting, the city looks interesting; if they look dull, the city looks dull.'

One of the reasons why the development of underground space has stagnated over the years could lie in the inadequacy of its development to integrate into other developments, create public spaces and become a vibrant part of the urban fabric. In short, underground space is mostly dull and not a place you want to be in.

The only examples that seem to be capable of achieving this are the large underground cities we find in Canada and China, and at a lesser scale in South Korea and Japan. Although adverse climate is often quoted as a reason for the success of the Canadian underground cities, the real reason surely is the ability to integrate underground networks and objects in the underground landscape in such a way that a new urban tissue is created. This new tissue in many ways offers the same attractions as streets do at the surface, thereby attracting people and stimulating continuous development.

The core of the new approach therefore consists of a spatial dialogue between all stakeholders as part of a participatory planning process delivering a vision and strategy on how a new urban tissue can contribute to creating the city we need.

1.5. This chapter's core ideas

In this first chapter we have shown that urban underground space is only one of four resources that constitute the subsurface. The subsurface itself is limited in its size in terms of human activity. Most of the activities and developments are in the top subsurface layer that is at most 200 m deep. In terms of a new urban tissue, we need to think about development in the first 50 m at most. Below the top subsurface layer, we identify the deep subsurface, which runs to 4–5 km depth at most.

The rationale for looking at the use of the subsurface for the needs of a city stems not just from a lack of the resource space at the surface. If this is the case, a lot of development can be seen to have taken place in a haphazard way that has pushed local authorities into developing specific policies and planning regulations.

We feel that an urban underground future can only come about if a public participatory planning process is followed that balances the requirements of the city we need with the opportunities that the subsurface has to offer. Identifying those opportunities requires a process in itself, as the subsurface is not just geology but is also a historical archive (archaeological remains) and contains ecosystem services supporting life at the surface.

Geological cycles are part of a time frame that is incomparable with life at the surface, and yet some of our interventions are causing the Earth's dynamics to change. This fact necessitates a better understanding of human intervention in the subsurface.

Planning the urban subsurface requires not just the balancing of requirements and opportunities – it also asks urban planners, urban designers and architects to work together in shaping a new urban tissue beneath our cities. Key to this is creating connectivity below the surface comparable with city streets and public spaces.

Cross-discipline collaboration is required not just between those who have knowledge of shaping our cities and those with knowledge about the subsurface. Those having knowledge about creating the solutions need to work together as well to come up with multi-use solutions in the awareness that space is limited below the surface and that using it on a first-come, first-served basis is detrimental to sustainable development of the subsurface.

A new urban underground paradigm, in our opinion, is based on participation, collaboration, understanding, and innovative multi-use solutions. In this way, the final urban frontier could well prove to be an urban asset that contributes to creating the resilient, sustainable, inclusive and liveable cities we need.

References

1   Agence France-Presse (2017) Ieoh Ming
    Pei, the master architect behind Louvre
    pyramids, celebrates 100th birthday.
    Telegraph. http://www.telegraph.co.uk/
    news/2017/04/25/ieoh-ming-pei-master-
    architect-behind-louvre-pyramids-celebrates/
    (accessed 14/11/2017).

2   Baldy J-L, Lopez-Hernandez LA and Osborne
    J (2009) The construction of the LHC – civil
    engineering highlights. In *The Large Hadron
    Collider: A Marvel of Technology* (Evans
    L (ed.)). CERN and EPFL Press, Lausanne,
    Switzerland.

3   Ban K (2012) The future we want. *The
    New York Times*. http://www.nytimes.
    com/2012/05/24/opinion/the-future-we-
    want.html (accessed 14/11/2017).

4   Covent Garden Area Trust (2017) http://
    www.coventgardentrust.org.uk/resources/
    environmentalstudy/background/history/
    (accessed 14/11/2017).

5   Dowling T (2014) Deep concerns: the
    trouble with basement conversions.
    Guardian. http://www.theguardian.com/
    lifeandstyle/2014/aug/18/basement-
    conversions-disputes-digging-iceberg-
    homes (accessed 14/11/2017).

6   Dutch ATES (2017) http://dutch-ates.com
    (accessed 14/11/2017).

7   Evans L and Bryant P (2008) LHC
    machine. *Journal of Instrumentation* **3:**
    14 Aug. See http://iopscience.iop.org/
    article/10.1088/1748-0221/3/08/S08001/
    meta (accessed 14/11/2017).

8   Fridleifsson IB, Bertani R, Huenges E, Lund
    JW, Ragnarsson A and Rybach L (2008)
    The possible role and contribution of
    geothermal energy to the mitigation of
    climate change. In *Proceedings of the
    IPCC Scoping Meeting on Renewable
    Energy Sources* (Hohmeyer O and Trittin T
    (eds)). Intergovernmental Panel on Climate
    Change, Geneva, Switzerland, pp. 59–80.

9   Gemeente Arnhem (2012) Nieuwe
    Structuurvisie. https://www.arnhem.nl/
    Inwoners/wonen_en_milieu/Ruimtelijk_
    beleid_en_woonvisie/Nieuwe_Structuurvisie/
    Structuurvisie_deel_2.pdf (accessed
    14/11/2017). (In Dutch.)

10   Government of the Netherlands (2015)
    I&M 2016 Budget: innovative solutions
    for a sustainable and accessible country.
    https://www.government.nl/latest/
    news/2015/09/17/i-m-2016-budget-
    innovative-solutions-for-a-sustainable-and-
    accessible-country (accessed 14/11/2017).

11   Howard WW (1889) The rush to Oklahoma.
    Harper's Weekly **33:** 391–394.

12   Jacobs J (1961) *The Death and Life of Great
    American Cities*. Random House, New York,
    NY, USA.

13   Kastrup U, Gutbrodt B and Grün G (2017)
    *BodenSchätzeWerte: Unser Umgang mit
    Rohstoffen*. vdf, Zürich, Switzerland. (In
    German.)

14   Larson N (2014) CERN eyes new giant
    particle collider. Phys.org. https://phys.org/
    news/2014-02-cern-eyes-giant-particle-
    collider.html (accessed 14/11/2017).

15   Li J, Ji X, Haxton W and Wang JSY (2015)
    The second-phase development of the
    China JinPing Underground Laboratory.
    Physics Procedia **61:** 576–585.

16   McDougall H (2014) Crossrail completes
    tunnels in Docklands and southeast London.
    Crossrail. http://www.crossrail.co.uk/news/
    articles/crossrail-completes-tunnels-in-

docklands-and-southeast-london (accessed 14/11/2017).

17 Ostler C (2012) Iceberg homes: that's what today's billionaires are building – with underground discos, dog spas and even waterfalls … but it's driving the neighbours crazy. *The Daily Mail*. http://www.dailymail.co.uk/news/article-2243777/Iceberg-homes-Thats-todays-billionaires-building--underground-discos-dog-spas-waterfalls--driving-neighbours-crazy.html (accessed 14/11/2017).

18 Parriaux A, Tacher L and Joliquin P (2004) The hidden side of cities – towards three-dimensional land planning. *Energy and Buildings* **36(4):** 335–341.

19 Reynolds E and Reynolds P (2015) Planning for Underground Spaces 'NY-LON Underground'. In *Think Deep: Planning, Development and Use of Underground Space in Cities* (Admiraal H and Narang Suri S (eds)). ISOCARP/ITACUS, The Hague, the Netherlands.

20 Royal Borough of Kensington and Chelsea (2015) *Basements Planning Policy*. Royal Borough of Kensington and Chelsea, London, UK.

21 Sawe B (2017) Deepest metro stations in the world. Worldatlas. http://www.worldatlas.com/articles/deepest-metro-stations-in-the-world.html (accessed 14/11/2017).

22 Tai R, Chan A and Seit R (2009) Planning of deep sewage tunnels in Hong Kong. In *Proceedings of the ITA-AITES World Tunnel Congress*. Budapest, Hungary, pp. 22–28.

23 Utudjian E (1952) *L'urbanisme souterrain*. Presses Universitaires de France, Paris, France.

24 Wei X (2016) Digging deep to explore subterranean space. *China Daily*. http://usa.chinadaily.com.cn/china/2016-03/03/content_23719655.htm (accessed 14/11/2017).

25 Wikipedia (2017) History of rapid transit. Wikipedia. https://en.wikipedia.org/wiki/History_of_rapid_transit (accessed 14/11/2017).

26 World Urban Campaign (2014) The City We Need. http://www.worldurbancampaign.org/city-we-need (accessed 14/11/2017).

Chapter 2

Achieving harmony between humanity and nature – urban underground sustainability

2.1. Harmony between humanity and nature

The concept of sustainability is often explained by the definition given in the report *Our Common Future*, written by the World Commission on Environment and Development (1987) and chaired by Gro Harlem Brundtland. The concept itself is much older, and stems from the premise that our natural resources are limited. The English philosopher John Stuart Mill wrote, in his *Principles of Political Economy* (Mill, 1848),

> If the earth must lose that great portion of its pleasantness which it owes to things that the unlimited increase of wealth and population would extirpate from it, for the mere purpose of enabling it to support a larger, but not a better or a happier population, I sincerely hope, for the sake of posterity, that they will be content to be stationary, long before necessity compels them to it.

Mill postulated a society that is able to develop in a way that does not deplete the natural resources, through a 'stationary state' enabling future generations to enjoy the Earth as much, or better, than the present generation. Sustainable development is therefore not just concerned with preserving resources, it should also be concerned with, as Mill wrote, 'a better or happier population'. As the Brundtland Commission has stated: 'In its broadest sense, the strategy for sustainable development aims to promote harmony among human beings and between humanity and nature' (World Commission on Environment and Development, 1987).

There are many ways in which the subsurface can be characterised. The simplest would be to see the subsurface as the foundation of life. We use the subsurface to build our cities on. We use the subsurface to sow our crops and to harvest them. We extract materials from the subsurface to fuel our industries and to build our cities. We are exploiting the subsurface for our needs. The subsurface provides us with resources and with services. These resources are non-renewable – they can be depleted. The ecosystem's services are renewable – they can regenerate. This regeneration is, however, limited in the sense that, when the natural processes are disturbed, the ecosystem services lose their capacity to regenerate and will disappear.

Sustainable development calls for retaining resources for future generations: planning spaces for usage (exploitation) and regulations to prevent disturbing the processes that drive the ecosystem services (conservation). Sustainable underground development can only be achieved through balancing the exploitation of the subsurface with conservation of the subsurface. This requires the existence of models to analyse the use of the subsurface, as well as frameworks to decide on how to use it. In a way, this is no different from the way that surface development is subjected to urban planning and environmental scrutiny. What makes it complex in the case of underground space is obtaining the knowledge on how the subsurface is composed, what ecosystem services it delivers and what processes make these services possible.

In the following sections, we will explore this concept further and propose a frame-work for appraising sustainable underground development.

2.2. Human interventions below the surface

Looking back through history we can see that humanity has been labouring below the surface for a very long time. With the discovery of a Neolithic flint mine in Norfolk, UK, we can date back to as far as 3000 BCE the efforts of humans in cutting and digging mines to extract resources from the Earth (The Prehistoric Society, 2017). The material extracted was flint for making tools. Later, copper was mined for tools and ornaments.

Early civilisations used wood and peat for heating and cooking. For instance, the landscape of the Netherlands changed dramatically due to this, with forests being cut down and large lakes appearing where, once, peat was cut out of the soil.

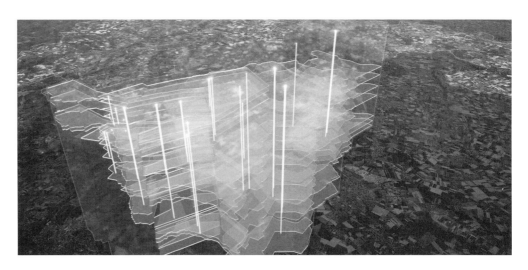

Figure 2-1 Mining heritage below the surface of Zuid-Limburg in the Netherlands. (Still from "Invisible Netherlands", ©VPRO, 2016)

The Industrial Revolution brought about an insatiable appetite for coal as the fuel for prosperity. Steam engines, locomotives and ships all required this black diamond for power. Beneath the surface of the Earth and spanning many kilometres are extensive shafts and corridors. In the rolling landscape of the southeast of the Netherlands, for example, shafts and galleries were cut to extract coal: 12 mines and 34 shafts, with the deepest reaching 1058 m below the surface (VPRO, 2016). In 1965, mining activities ceased, and the visible evidence of the once-active mines was removed from the surface, leaving an extensive network of galleries over eight or more levels stretching below the towns of Heerlen, Brunssum and Geleen. The plan to decommission the mines took 10 years and was named From Black to Green (ArchiNed, 2008). The only evidence that these mines existed remains deep below the surface, in the largest industrial complex in the country, invisible, preserved for posterity, and trapped in time in underground space (Figure 2.1).

As industrial activity in the subsurface grew due to an increase in the extraction of resources, beneath cities the subsurface rapidly turned into an urban service layer. Pipes and cables were placed below the surface, and industries used the subsurface to discharge the waste from their industrial processes. Waste storage using landfills became a common practice. Not until our level of environmental awareness was raised did we become critical of these extraction and storage practices. Human intervention below the surface slowly started affecting vital drinking water supplies. No longer was the subsurface able to purify this water, which meant that contaminants remained in the supplies and made drinking water unsuitable for human consumption.

As mining activity dwindled and mines were closed, the shafts and corridors were left behind, leading to the possibility of collapse and subsidence at ground level. Indeed, sink holes have been attributed to former mining activities. The French Geological Survey listed the Franchepré zone in the Lorraine iron basin as a 'high-risk' area, due to the constant threat of localised cavity collapse beneath a residential area, with an iron mine, active from the late 19th century until 1930, as the source of the threat (Bureau de Recherches Géologiques et Minières, 2013).

Industrial brownfields consist of contaminated soils that, without intervention, make human habitation impossible. Project developers are unwilling to develop these plots, and local councils are unable to pay for soil remediation. The industrial wastelands of the City of Glasgow were surveyed by the British Geological Survey as part of the development of the Geochemical Baseline Survey of the Environment (G-BASE) project. This project, together with the Clyde and Glasgow Urban Super Project (CUSP), aims at a 'greater understanding of the impacts of anthropogenic pollution and potential threats to ecosystems and human health' (Fordyce et al., 2013).

Coal and gas extraction in the Netherlands is increasingly dividing the population. As gas replaced coal as the nation's fuel, this not only led to social–economic misery in the south of the country through the closure of mines but also placed the north under threat – as it now faces human-induced earthquakes as a consequence of unlimited gas extraction. What has, for the large part, been of huge economic significance for the Netherlands has now turned into a potential nightmare of building remediation and legal claims, leading to compensation for both damage and loss of enjoyment. In a recent court case, the court decided that the earthquakes could not be seen as mere industrial nuisance but were also a direct intrusion into the personal lives of those concerned. As a consequence, damage caused through these activities should be compensated (Rechtbank Noord-Nederland, 2017).

What these examples illustrate is that anthropogenic intervention in the subsurface, even if it was successful at first and contributed greatly to societal and economic development, also impacts the lives of future generations. It is this single fact that has caused geologists, hydrologists, geochemists, ecologists and environmentalists to voice their concerns about large-scale underground space development. It has led to calls for conservation of the subsurface, and, in the most extreme cases, to prohibit further human intervention, at least until we know what the exact consequences are and what the possible long-term effects of exploiting the subsurface could be.

If anything has become clear in the last 20 years in respect of underground space development, it is that we still lack the knowledge and the models to fully understand the consequences of human intervention below the surface from an ecological point of view. This means that even though we can fully

demonstrate the merits of any underground space project, the possible effects of that project on the subsurface remain at best a guess. For decision-makers, this makes it a challenging and complex process to decide on underground space development, as no real answer can be given to the question: how will it affect ecosystem services in the long term?

An interesting case in this respect is the proposed tunnel for the A303 road (linking the south and west of England) in the vicinity of the ancient Stonehenge monument, part of a World Heritage Site that is currently divided in half by the existing highway. For environmentalists, this road near Stonehenge has been an eyesore that distracts from the great cultural heritage that the site represents. Diverting the road is not a practical option, so diverting it into a tunnel below the surface seemed, at first sight, a plausible solution. In reality, this proposal did not bring the appreciation that was expected. Rather, opposition grew against the plan, as the extent of the site below the surface was unknown and because related objects may remain undiscovered in the vicinity. Three heritage groups warned that 'the government's current proposals for the tunnel's western portal are a cause for concern and need significant improvement' (Morris, 2017). The concerns raised touch on one of the ecosystem services that the subsurface provides us with, namely cultural, through the preservation of our heritage.

Another major proposed tunnelling project, in the Netherlands, linking the A6 and A9 highways, was cancelled amidst public concern. The proposed tunnel alignment ran under the

Naardermeer, an area of outstanding natural beauty. The main issue with this project was that this lake could eventually disappear through leakage if anything went wrong during tunnelling or the construction of the shafts (Admiraal, 2006).

Both of these cases illustrate a high level of uncertainty of the effect of human interventions in the subsurface. These effects can be momentary when the intervention is done, or come to light at a later stage, oftentimes long after the initial intervention has taken place. They can disrupt the surface through soil subsidence or negatively affect the natural processes that ensure the ecosystem services we rely on to live.

Whether we're looking at building a new tunnel or decommissioning an existing one, both instances require a greater understanding of the subsurface and our dependency on it. We need to appreciate that any intervention below the surface immediately creates an interdependency between the development and its surroundings. This is not a new concept, and holds true for any intervention at the surface as well. What complicates matters in the case of the subsurface is that we are still struggling with our understanding of how this intricate relationship comes about. The big question is, of course, whether all this means that we should steer clear of the subsurface all together. In our opinion, the answer to that question is no. The potential benefits that underground space development can offer society are too great for that. Nevertheless, we do need a deeper understanding of the subsurface in order to take balanced decisions on its use. The lessons of the past are valuable in that we can learn

from them what not to do. Indiscriminate use of the subsurface in whatever way needs to be prevented. The past teaches us that underground space development can only be deemed to be sustainable if the project itself is sustainable and the project maintains or enhances subsurface sustainability.

2.3. Subsurface ecosystem services

In 2000, the then secretary-general of the United Nations, Kofi Annan, wrote a report to the UN General Assembly, *We the Peoples: The Role of the United Nations in the 21st Century* (Annan, 2000). In this report, he stated that

> The natural environment performs for us, free of charge, basic services without which our species could not survive. The ozone layer screens out ultraviolet rays from the sun that harm people, animals and plants. Ecosystems help purify the air we breathe and the water we drink. They convert wastes into resources and reduce atmospheric carbon levels that would otherwise contribute to global warming. Biodiversity provides a bountiful store of medicines and food products, and it maintains genetic variety that reduces vulnerability to pests and diseases. But we are degrading, and in some cases destroying, the ability of the environment to continue providing these life-sustaining services for us.

This can only lead to one conclusion according to Kofi Annan: 'We are failing to provide the

Achieving harmony between
humanity and nature –
urban underground
sustainability

freedom of future generations to sustain their lives on this planet.'

A major assessment – the Millennium Ecosystem Assessment – was called for in order to change this scenario. Its purpose was to gain a better understanding of ecosystems, their vulnerabilities and the way we could either manage or enhance their services (Annan, 2000).

The subsequent report on the Millennium Ecosystem Assessment contained a framework for defining ecosystem services that has since gained worldwide recognition. The basic framework is given in Table 2.1. It consists of four major categories of services: supporting, provisioning, regulating and cultural. Adaptations of the basic framework have been made recognising national variations and allowing for differentiation in habitats.

Price *et al.* (2016) gave an example of this when adapting the original framework based on the UK Millennium Ecosystem Assessment for urban areas and added a further category, citing Rawlins *et al.* (Table 2.2). This additional category, 'platform', recognises the ecosystem service providing support to surface buildings, but also allowing the earthing of structures. The addition of 'platform' is interesting in that it fills a gap within the original assessment, which did not take into account human interventions in the subsurface, and the consequent interdependency between these interventions and ecosystem services. As such, it underlines the need for sustainable underground space development to take into account this interdependency.

The Government of the Netherlands (2016) addresses this interdependency in its Subsurface Spatial Planning Vision, which is currently still under public consultation. Although the planning vision restricts itself to the deeper subsurface and use of national importance, it contains some interesting notions in terms of sustainable use of underground space. From a planning perspective, the document addresses two uses of the underground: providing goods and delivering services. As examples of the provision of goods, the extraction of

Table 2-1 Ecosystem services as proposed by the MA

Supporting	Provisioning	Regulating	Cultural
Nutrient cycling	Food	Climate regulation	Aesthetic
Soil formation	Fresh water	Flood regulation	Spiritual
Primary production	Wood and fibre	Disease regulation	Educational
	Fuel	Water purification	Recreational

Table 2-2 Urban ecosystem service as proposed by Price *et al.* (2016)

Supporting	Provisioning	Regulating	Cultural	Platform
Soil formation	Climate/temperature (air quality, soil quality)	Food (allotments)	Aesthetic	Support for development (above and below ground space, bearing capacity)
Nutrient cycling	Flood control	Water supply (drinking and industrial use)	Spiritual	Electrical earthing
Primary production	Disease control	Wood and fibre	Educational	
Habitat space	Water (attenuation of quality and quantity)	Energy carbon store/reg	Recreational and tourism	
	Noise		Archaeological	
			Sense of place	

non-renewable goods such as fossil fuels and minerals is given. These are of importance to provide energy and building materials. Services provided by the subsurface are the ecosystem services, such as infiltrated rainwater, which the subsurface purifies by turning it into potable water. The document states that these services remain renewable as long as the supporting processes are not interfered with. The primary difference from a planning perspective according to the spatial vision is that the usual planning practice of allocating space to a specific purpose can still be used in the case of goods below the surface as long as a three-dimensional approach is taken. In the matter of ecosystem services, this approach is not appropriate as there is need for a more regulatory method to set boundary conditions aimed at maintaining the services. These considerations, as laid down in the document, led to the following policy statement (Government of the Netherlands, 2016):

A general notion is that, given a sustainable and efficient use of the subsurface, for each new activity the adverse effects on the quality of soil and groundwater should as far as possible be limited and the existing land use should be disturbed as little as possible. The latter does of course not apply if it is decided to replace the current use by new ones. In that case, due attention to limiting possible negative influences on the quality of the environment above ground will also be given, now and in the future. The Government only reserves and protects areas for specific uses when necessary. In such an event, it is required that the usefulness and necessity for a certain use are determined, that the utilisation of the selected location meets the criteria for sustainable and efficient use, and that the reservation for that use is necessary to avoid other uses reducing the potential for that use. As a result, as much space as possible remains for future developments. In the case of new developments, the government chooses a proactive attitude. That is, in advance, the preconditions for new initiatives for the use of the subsoil are set, providing clarity for the market.

The contribution of ecosystem services to the wellbeing of humanity is generally recognised. The Millennium Ecosystem Assessment has shown that degradation of the ecosystem services must be avoided and reversed where possible. In urban areas, ecosystem services play a vital role in keeping our cities liveable. Bolund and Hunhammar (1999) analysed the ecosystem services in Stockholm, and stressed the importance of these services for quality of life in urban areas. They concluded that 'since land is so valuable in urban areas, a combination of different land uses on the same piece of land is probably needed in order to safeguard and improve the generation of ecosystem services'.

Bolund and Hunhammar pointed to the rationale for urban underground space use in urban areas: it is not just about balancing between conservation and exploitation of the subsurface but also about addressing the possibility of underground space use contributing to enhancing ecosystem services through an ecological approach.

Achieving harmony between
humanity and nature –
urban underground
sustainability

_____

2.4. An ecological approach

Brown (2014) described 21st-century infra-structures as stemming from an industrial past requiring a radical new approach in post-modern times. The way in which we plan, design, construct and operate our road, railway and urban utility systems has not altered much over time. Since the invention of the steam locomotive, rail lines have, to all intents and purposes, remained unchanged in appearance, albeit the specifications that they must meet have been revised as the speed with which carriages move along the rail lines has increased dramatically. City utilities are still placed below the surface along random alignments, just as they were at the beginning of the 20th century. Brown has argued for a radical rethink, calling for a new infrastructural ecology that is interconnected, multipurpose and consists of synergistic systems. As she put it herself:

> Today's transportation, waste disposal, water, sewage, and energy distribution systems are necessarily inter-dependent. Power plants require water cooling, water treatment and public transit require electricity, energy generation requires the transport of coal, and so on. And all of these systems rely on information technology (IT). Nevertheless, we continue to disaggregate them physically and jurisdictionally into distinct sectors, and we mentally separate utilities and the natural systems from which nearly all infrastructural services are derived. Infrastructural systems are man-made extensions of natural

flows of carbon, water, and energy, so appropriate modeling might be based on the symbiotic relationships of natural ecosystems. Based on this whole-system perspective, we might reinvent an ecologically informed, post-industrial generation of infrastructure.

The whole-system perspective in her opinion entails applying five principles to any new developments undertaken. Ecological infra-structures are multipurpose and apply mixed land use, reduce energy and greenhouse gas emissions, include green infrastructure, deliver social and/or economic benefits to surrounding communities, and contain climate adaptation measures (Brown, 2014).

An example of how these principles apply to an underground facility is the advent of underground data centres. As the use of the internet and cloud services grows worldwide, the need for ever-larger data centres is rising. Typically, these centres consist of power-hungry servers requiring cooling, as their processors produce excessive heat. Beneath the Orthodox Uspenski Cathedral in Helsinki, Finland, a former government bomb shelter was given a new lease of life. The Finnish IT company Academica installed a new 2 MW data server in the shelter. Water was taken in from the nearby harbour and used to cool the servers. Rather than returning the heated water to the sea, it is pumped into the city's district heating system, cooling around 500 homes with the heat the data servers produce (Vela, 2010). An extensive analysis of the growth of data centres and the way they reuse the heat produced is given by Velkova (2016). How well does this case hold up

Figure 2-2 Cross-section of the Transbay Transit Center in San Francisco | Project Architect: Pelli Clarke Pelli. Renderings courtesy of the Transbay Joint Powers Authority (TJPA)

against Brown's five principles? First of all, the criterion of multipurpose and mixed land use: as a previously created underground space is reused, it fulfils this criterion well. In terms of reducing energy and greenhouse emissions, it also scores. The intake of sea water to cool and the placement in an underground facility with a low ambient temperature reduce the need for energy to provide cooling. By supplying hot water to the district heating system, it benefits the local community directly. Lastly, the reuse of the cooling water also contributes to climate adaptation.

Taking the five principles to the next level is the example of the San Francisco Transbay Transit Center. This development is exemplary in the way the use of underground space is integrated into surface space use. It is a multi-modal transport hub, currently being constructed, as part of the redevelopment of the Transbay area (Figure 2.2).

The sustainability achievements are impressive (Figure 2.3). The development features a 2.2 ha rooftop park, which is publicly accessible and aimed at reducing the city's heat island effect, while containing efficient irrigation and drainage systems. Natural daylight is taken advantage of, thus reducing the need for electric lighting of the internal areas by using the 'light column' feature that also provides natural ventilation. The project required the demolition of the existing terminal,

Achieving harmony between humanity and nature – urban underground sustainability

Figure 2-3 Sustainability design of the Transbay Transit Center in San Francisco | Courtesy of Except Integrated Sustainability, Utrecht, the Netherlands, reproduced under CC BY 2.0

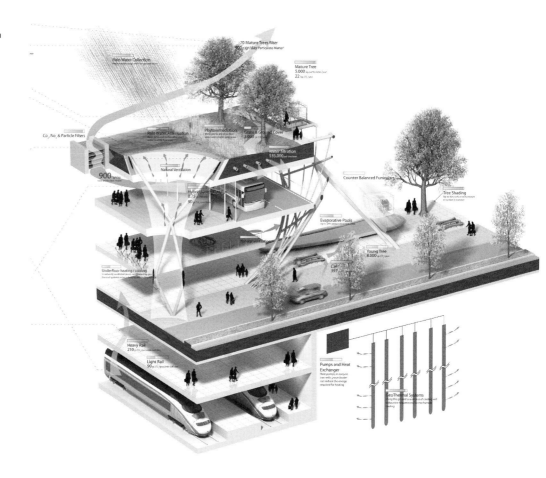

which created enough concrete waste to fill 28 Olympic-size swimming pools. All the waste will be recycled. The project also reduces storm water runoff through the use of grey water storage tanks (Transbay Program, 2017). The potable water use of the Transit Center will be reduced by half, saving nearly 6 million litres of potable water (Urban Fabrick, 2015).

Apart from complying fully with the five principles, this case study also shows how the development contributes to enhancing ecosystem services in the city. An example of an underground development that achieves this as well is the Croton Water Filtration Plant in the Bronx, New York City. The development consists of an underground facility that is topped by a green area consisting of a golf driving range (Brown, 2014). Interestingly, New York made its case for this facility through the valuation of ecosystem services: using nature's ability to filter and decontaminate water. The development also contributes aesthetic and recreational benefits by conserving green space by not covering it with the proposed facility, which is placed below the surface instead. Figure 2.4 shows the construction and the completed development.

The Croton project also underlines clearly what was stated earlier in terms of mixed land use safeguarding and improving ecosystem services. A similar example is the Dokhaven Waste Water Treatment Facility in Rotterdam, the Netherlands (Cornaro and Admiraal, 2012). This facility was placed inside a former inner-city dock and then covered with a green roof. A public green space was created, around which housing development took place. Needless to say, this would not have been possible if the facility had been developed at the surface. It is also a thought-provoking example of an urban regeneration scheme, redeveloping unutilised docks that would otherwise only serve as a reminder of former bustling, commercial port activities.

Figure 2-4 The green roof of the Croton Water Filtration Plant provides space for a golf driving range | © Alex MacLean and NYC Environmental Protection

Achieving harmony between humanity and nature – urban underground sustainability

Figure 2-5 The Madrid Rio project created 1.5 million m² of green public space for the city | Courtesy of Ayuntamiento de Madrid; aerial views courtesy of Burgos & Garrido, Porras La Casta, Rubio & A-Sala and West 8

Another exemplary case is the Madrid Rio project, which involved placing over 40 km of urban motorway built in the 1970s (as well as other urban facilities such as high-voltage electrical power lines) on the banks of the River Manzanares below the surface. Burgos & Garrido, Porras La Casta, Rubio & A-Sala and West 8 came up with a design that included the creation of 150 ha (1.5 million m²) of green public space with 15 000 trees being planted on the vacant space that was created after the motorway and a system of 25 storm water tanks were brought underground (Figure 2.5). It is a multipurpose project, a mixed-mode intervention on the territory, that overlays different uses at the same location (Madrid is an extraordinarily dense and, therefore, a very sustainable city): it includes an immense green infrastructure of considerable territorial dimensions; it incorporates social aspects, as it offers a large public space for the citizens; it reduces the heat island effect owing to its vegetation and permeability; it controls the vehicular emission of polluting gases, which are filtered in the tunnels and then released into the atmosphere; and it also improves the quality of the water of the river through filtration and retention of rainwater.

What all these cases have in common and illustrate is how we can appraise these projects in terms of sustainable development. Fulfilling the five principles and safeguarding or enhancing ecosystem services demonstrates the sustainability of a project. Alas, the question still remains of how to bring all this together in a model to determine sustainable urban underground development.

2.5. Towards a model for determining sustainable underground development

In the past, the rationale for using underground space was often driven by the argument that using this space was in itself sustainable. Constructing a tunnel would shorten the distance travelled and thereby reduce fuel consumption. In itself, this argument cannot be faulted; however, it only looks at one of the many aspects that need to be considered. The model we propose (Figure 2.6) attempts to bring together what has been discussed in previous sections and draws on work by Brown (2014), Price *et al.* (2016) and Admiraal and Cornaro (2014). The model not only aims at appraising whether a proposed underground space development can be deemed to be sustainable but, more importantly, it aims to provide urban planners, architects and urban designers with a framework for sustainable underground space development.

As we have seen, sustainable development is about developing now, in the present, drawing on the past and with due care for the future. In this sense, the various criteria of sustainable underground development must always be placed in these three dimensions of time. Although not always equally applicable, it frames each criterion within a context and helps to safeguard against short-term thinking. The presented principles can also be seen as a way to sort proposals, in that they serve as selective filters through which the proposals are funnelled. If sustainable development is the criterion on which proposals are appraised, then

Achieving harmony between humanity and nature – urban underground sustainability

_____

Figure 2-6 A model for appraising urban underground development

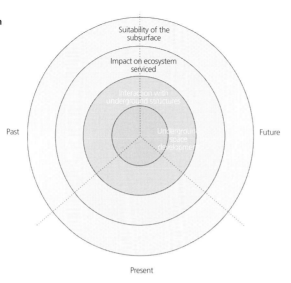

Suitability of the subsurface

Impact on ecosystem serviced

Interaction with underground structures

Underground space development

Past

Future

Present

failing to meet one criterion automatically rejects it as non-sustainable.

The first criterion is to determine the suitability of the subsurface for use in terms of anthropogenic intervention. Is the urban subsurface suitable for the proposed development? This needs to be determined in terms of geological and spatial planning suitability. Geological suitability depends on the analysis of the subsurface in terms of the possibility to physically construct the development. It also questions the suitability in terms of geochemistry. Does the soil contain contaminants that cannot be removed or does it need specific treatment before they can be extracted? Developing brownfield sites could result in the excavation of highly polluted or toxic soils that would be best left alone or require specific treatment at high cost. In terms of spatial planning, the guidance given by the

Subsurface Spatial Planning Vision (Government of the Netherlands, 2016) could be used. Will the development in any way adversely affect the quality of the soil and/or groundwater? Is it in any way detrimental to the environment above the surface? An example illustrating this is the concept of fracking. This requires facilities at the surface but also intervenes below the surface. The potential conflict with existing drinking water aquifers in terms of pollution was sufficient for a moratorium on fracking in the Netherlands. Areas containing drinking water aquifers are protected against outside intervention in the plan. The past–present–future appraisal would take into account the presence of the drinking water aquifer throughout those periods and uphold the protection in future situations.

The second step is to look at the way in which ecosystem services are impacted by the proposed development. At this point we only look at the ecosystem services below the surface. Any contribution that the development makes to ecosystem services above the surface will be appraised later. Here, we need to closely examine not just the services themselves but also the processes that support them. This can be extremely difficult to appraise. Our knowledge of the extent of these natural processes is sometimes limited, as the timescale at which these processes occur can differ vastly from the 50–100 years we might look at in terms of the life-time of an underground development. The previous example of human-induced earthquakes in the Netherlands further illustrates this. Preventive measures could have been taken had this been known at the time the decision to extract gas was made. In a worst-case scenario, it could have been deemed to be too dangerous to go ahead with the project.

When considering an underground development, care must be taken in terms of existing underground structures. These could be disused structures from the past, existing structures or possible planned structures in the future. When considering large-scale geothermal applications, a city also needs to consider the impact that this could have on future alignments for underground infrastructures. The fact that one development runs in the vertical plane and the other in the horizontal could lead to major conflicts or even prevent future development. This needs to be avoided from a sustainability point of view. The difficulty here is that it requires a vision of the future use of the urban underground space in light of current urban development. One solution in this respect could be to think in three dimensions and to layer the subsurface. The Subsurface Spatial Planning Vision distinguishes two major layers: the shallow subsurface consisting of the first 200 m and the deep subsurface continuing below that. Typically, urban utilities can be found in the shallow subsurface in the first layer, running to about 1.5 m. Further development is dependent on the geology, and the occurrence of groundwater can severely limit it, as we will discuss in Section 5.2. Urban planning methodologies that are considered by Shi *et al.* (2015), illustrate the principle of layering. In that sense, the allocation of uses to a certain underground space can be achieved in three dimensions through zoning in the horizontal plane and layering in the vertical plane.

Lastly, the underground space development itself needs to be appraised in terms of sustainability. Assuming that all previous filters in the funnel are passed, this is the final hurdle. We propose that the five principles given by Brown (2014) would be prime indicators for this criterion. They not only encapsulate a new way of thinking in terms of infrastructure development but can be applied to other urban developments as well.

Although the model aims at urban underground development, it does not necessarily need to be restricted to this, as is illustrated by the case of the Waferfab factory in Sargans, Switzerland. The factory, developed inside a cavern excavated inside the Gonzen mountain, was built for the production of semiconductor wafers, requiring a specific environment (Figure 2.7). The climate needs to be constantly controlled and the facility must be free from vibration. These aspects alone would have required complex foundations if the factory had been constructed at the surface. In terms of suitability of the subsurface, the mountain provided a solid rock mass that allowed for excavation using drill and blast techniques. The rock mass was stable enough not to adversely affect the mountain or its surrounding environment, including a 17th-century chapel. Given the surrounding environment, planning permission would not have been provided for construction of a factory at the surface even if land had been available. Construction inside the mountain did not disturb surface ecosystem services, but did provide economic benefits for the surrounding community in terms of jobs. As the facility is located inside the mountain, vibrations caused by surrounding activities such as vehicle

Achieving harmony between
humanity and nature –
urban underground
sustainability

Figure 2-7 The caverns created to
allow the Waferfab factory to be
placed inside the Gonzen mountain
in Sargans, Switzerland | With kind
permission of Amberg Engineering AG

use are avoided. The constant temperature inside the mountain also requires less cooling during summer as well as less heating during winter, thereby greatly reducing energy use. The excavated material was reused after treatment as aggregate for road projects (Ruegg *et al.*, 2013). Looking to the future, with the facility being placed inside a cavern, the space created can be reused if the present activities cease.

Appraising this development using the proposed model shows that it would be deemed sustainable, with the flexibility for future reuse of the created space in combination with reuse of the excavated material being major considerations.

We are aware of the fact that every model has its limitations. The model presented is a step towards providing a framework for sustainable underground space development. Its value lies in that it brings together geological, ecological, planning and environmental considerations, as well as a new approach to developing more ecological infrastructure. It also demonstrates that, to determine the sustainability of a development, it is not sufficient to just look at the capacity of the development itself. Advancing underground space development requires a holistic approach based on harmony between humanity and nature.

2.6. This chapter's core ideas

In this chapter, we started by looking at the need for harmony between humanity and nature – a need identified as being essential to the survival of humankind on this planet. It was shown that the concept of limited resources below the surface was identified as far back as the 19th century. Resources, or goods, are, as we have seen, only part of the balance we need to strike: considering that we now live in a geological epoch that some are proposing to call the anthropogenic, we need to consider human interventions below the surface and how they impact the ecosystem services provided by the subsurface.

Human intervention in the subsurface stretches from the Neolithic, when humans mined for flint to form tools and weapons, to the present-day extraction of minerals and carbon fuels. One of the lessons we have learned is that abandoned mines or large-scale extraction can, in certain situations, influence life on the surface. Soil subsidence, sink holes or human-induced earthquakes are all unforeseen effects of our interventions below the surface, sometimes impacting the ecosystem long after the last activity took place. All of this demonstrates that we need to have a deep knowledge of not only the suitability of the subsurface to carry out our planned developments but also of the long-term impact that these developments can have on the subsurface and, consequently, the surface. The geological and geochemical compositions caused by previous interventions determine the suitability in the present for subsurface and surface developments.

The Millennium Ecosystem Assessment made clear that life on Earth depends on the ecosystem services delivered by our planet. Ecosystem services are unique in that they are renewable, as opposed to the non-renewable resources or goods contained in underground space. The regeneration capacity of ecosystem services does, however, depend on underlying processes that could be disturbed or even disrupted by random human activity below the surface. This requires an appraisal of proposed developments in terms of their effects on the subsurface environment.

Infrastructure development has varied little over centuries from the basic concept of roads and railways. Post-modern infrastructures require a radical rethink for more than one reason: firstly, in order for them to develop in harmony with nature, and, secondly, a rethink could also provide new ways of financing these infrastructures as they gain multiple uses and enhance urban ecosystems. Sustainable urban underground development in this way could help cities to become more resilient, inclusive and liveable – contributing to quality of life but also delivering health benefits by reducing city heat island effects and pollution, and providing more green public spaces to recreate in.

Our model for determining sustainable urban underground development provides a holistic appraisal method for determining sustainability or for planning and designing for sustainability. Using the previously discussed approaches, it presents a four-step approach considering both the past, present and the future. As such, it aims at urban underground developments that preserve the past, enhance the present and respect the future.

Achieving harmony between
humanity and nature –
urban underground
sustainability

References

1 Admiraal JBM (2006) A bottom-up approach to the planning of underground space. *Tunnelling and Underground Space Technology* **21(3–4):** 464–465.

2 Annan KA (2000) *We the Peoples: The Role of the United Nations in the 21st Century*. United Nations, New York, NY, USA. See http://www.un.org/en/events/pastevents/ pdfs/We_The_Peoples.pdf (accessed 14/11/2017).

3 ArchiNed (2008) Van mijnstreek tot Parkstad. https://www.archined.nl/2008/01/ van-mijnstreek-tot-parkstad (accessed 14/11/2017). (In Dutch.)

4 Bolund P and Hunhammar S (1999) Ecosystem services in urban areas. *Ecological Economics* **29(2):** 293–301.

5 Brown H (2014) *Next Generation Infrastructure: Principles for Post-industrial Public Works*. Island Press, Washington, DC, USA.

6 Bureau de Recherches Géologiques et Minières (2013) Mine working: a major operation to prevent sinkhole risks. http:// www.brgm.eu/project/mine-working-major-operation-to-prevent-sinkhole-risks (accessed 14/11/2017).

7 Cornaro A and Admiraal H (2012) Changing world – major challenges: the need for underground space planning. In *48th ISOCARP Congress 2012, Perm, Russia*.

8 Fordyce FM, Nice SE, Lister TR and O Dochartaigh BE (2013) The chemical quality of urban soils in Glasgow, UK, with reference to anthropogenic impacts and current toxicologically-based soil guideline values: extended abstract. In *Proceedings of the SETAC Europe 23rd Annual Meeting, Glasgow*. Society for Environmental Toxicology and Chemistry, Glasgow, UK.

9 Government of the Netherlands (2016) Ontwerp Structuurvisie Ondergrond. https://www.rijksoverheid.nl/documenten/ rapporten/2016/11/11/ontwerp-structuurvisie-ondergrond (accessed 14/11/2017).

10 Mill JS (1848) *Principles of Political Economy with Some of their Applications to Social Philosophy*. Longmans, Green, London, UK. (1909 edition (Ashley WJ (trans.)).) See http://www.econlib.org/library/Mill/mlP.html (accessed 14/11/2017).

11 Morris S (2017) Stonehenge tunnel: heritage groups warn over ancient barrow. *Guardian*. https://www.theguardian.com/ uk-news/2017/feb/08/stonehenge-tunnel-heritage-groups-warn-over-ancient-barrow (accessed 14/11/2017).

12 Price SJ, Ford JR, Campbell SDG and Jefferson I (2016) Urban futures: the sustainable management of the ground beneath cities. *Engineering Geology Special Publications* **27(1):** 19–33, 10.1144/ EGSP27.2.

13 Rechtbank Noord-Nederland (2017) ECLI:NL:RBNNE:2017:715. https://uitspraken.rechtspraak.nl/ ziendocument?id=ECLI:NL:RBNNE:2017:715 (accessed 14/11/2017).

14 Ruegg C, Wannenmacher H and Schönlechner C (2013) Challenges during design of an underground chip factory (Waferfab). In *Proceedings of the ITA World Tunnelling and Underground Space Congress, Geneva, Switzerland*.

15 Shi W, Xiao Y, Zhao G and Liu W (2015) The utilization of underground space planning in Tianjin (China) Central City (2013–2020). In *Think Deep: Planning, Development and Use of Underground Space in Cities* (Admiraal H and Narang Suri S (eds)). ISOCARP/ITACUS, The Hague, the Netherlands, pp. 88–110.

16 The Prehistoric Society (2017) Grime's Graves Neolithic flint mines. http://www. prehistoricsociety.org/places/place/grimes_ graves_neolithic_flint_mines/ (accessed 14/11/2017).

17 Transbay Program (2017) Program sustainability. http://tjpa.org/project/ program-sustainability (accessed 14/11/2017).

18 Urban Fabrick (2015) Transbay Transit Center, Water Reuse System, San Francisco, California. http://urbanfabrick.com/ dev/wp-content/uploads/2015/04/UFK-PROJECTPROFILE-Transbay-Terminal-Water. pdf (accessed 14/11/2017).

19 Vela J (2010) Helsinki data centre to heat homes. *The Guardian*. https://www. theguardian.com/environment/2010/jul/20/ helsinki-data-centre-heat-homes (accessed 14/11/2017).

20 Velkova J (2016) Data that warms: waste heat, infrastructural convergence and the computation traffic commodity. *Big Data and Society* **3(2):** 1–10.

21 VPRO (2016) *Invisible Netherlands*. Episode: *Energy*. https://www.vpro.nl/ programmas/onzichtbaar-nederland/kijk/ afleveringen/2016/energie.html (accessed 14/11/2017). (Video.)

22 World Commission on Environment and Development (1987) *Our Common Future*. Oxford University Press, Oxford, UK.

Chapter 3

From yaodong to the third dimension – historical approaches to underground urbanism

3.1. The yaodong – natural subsurface habitats

Humans have been seeking shelter in caves from the early beginnings of human existence. Worldwide evidence in the form of cave paintings led to this conclusion, although some dispute this given the nomadic way of life of early civilisations. Large settlements in cave-like structures can be found in Turkey (Cappadocia, notably Derinkuyu), and also in Iran (Kish) and Tunisia (Magmata and Chenini). Seeking shelter from hostile environments, whether from the climate or hostile tribes, is, historically, the main reason for creating habitats inside hills or mountains or below the surface. In China, the concept of subterranean dwellings is known as yaodong (Figure 3.1). The yaodong are of interest because in many ways they can be seen to be the archetypical concept of human underground settlement. They are also of interest in that they have stood the test of time and are still widely in use today.

The yaodong and the dwellings in Tunisia all seem to have evolved from earlier pit-like structures that were partially sunken into the

Earth (Guo and Guo, 2001). The basic reasoning for settling below the surface or into hillsides can be found in environmental (climate) conditions and in the local geography and geology. The Loess Plateau, where these settlements are found in China, has a geology that makes it relatively easy to excavate material and create a structure that will retain its shape once material has been extracted. Although this may seem self-evident, it is important to note that as so many underground developments nowadays take place in less favourable geological circumstances, this will often give

Figure 3-1 Yaodong cave dwelling
Courtesy of Kevin Poh, reproduced under CC BY 2.0

From yaodong to the
third dimension –
historical approaches to
underground urbanism

rise to complex technical solutions to make such a feat possible. One lesson we can take from history is that underground development is intricately linked to geology.

The earliest yaodongs date back to the Qin Dynasty (c. 221 BC) according to Liu et al. (2002), and they are predominantly found in northern central China in an area consisting of six provinces that cover 400 000 km². The region boasts a population of over 40 million. Outside urban areas, 80% of the population live in yaodongs, amounting to millions of people still using this form of underground habitat.

Liu et al. (2002) saw the movement to retain the yaodong as important, as it is a prime example of regional architecture. They argued that it is essential from the point of view of 'critical regionalism' to merge in that sense the old and the new 'in contrast to the rampant and largely unreflective importation of Western architectural styles common to new construction in many of China's urban centers'. The yaodong

in that sense takes on a regional contemporary form of housing that has survived the test of time and can, to some extent, be easily adapted to the modern way of life, while retaining the basic concept bequeathed by previous generations.

With this basic concept, the yaodong, history has given us two basic forms for underground development:

- the yaodong that is created by excavating a large courtyard into the surface and then tunnelling sideways to create rooms

- the yaodong that is tunnelled directly into the hillside to create rooms inside the hill.

We can see these basic forms return in modern-day developments of underground space. Take for example the underground school that was built in Arnhem, the Netherlands. The Artez Faculty of Dance and Music is situated along the bank of the River Rhine in Arnhem in a building originally designed in 1963 by the renowned Dutch architect Gerrit Rietveld. The building

Figure 3-2 The edge of the Veluwe push moraine and the roof of the extension to the Faculty of Dance and Music | Courtesy of architect Bierman Henket, photography: Michel Kievits

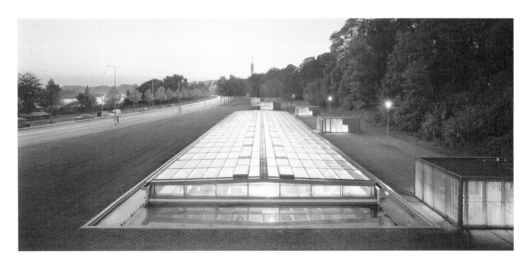

Figure 3-3 The inside of the underground faculty extension Courtesy of architect Bierman Henket, photography: Michel Kievits

itself lies directly in front of the furthest reaches of the Veluwe push moraine, created in the last Ice Age and deemed to be a protected sight – that is, no new buildings are allowed to take away from the view (Figure 3.2). This proved to be a challenge when the faculty required more space for its activities. On top of that challenge, no architect dared to come up with a design to compete with Rietveld's original. This seeming stalemate was broken when architect Hubert Jan Henket proposed an underground extension to the existing building, which was based on the concept of the yaodong.

An elongated atrium would be constructed, much like the yaodong courtyard, and sideways schoolrooms and meeting rooms constructed. The atrium was to be covered with a glass ceiling, allowing daylight to enter but also providing a stunning view of the push moraine. This line of sight proved to be vital as it creates a permanent link with the surface, thereby taking away any notion of being below the surface (Figure 3.3). Although initially there was opposition to the scheme from staff and students, the new extension is now seen as a brilliant achievement.

The second concept of creating space inside hills is nowadays used to find new space for industrial facilities in order to free up space for surface development. The Viikinmaki waste water treatment plant in Helsinki, Finland, was located inside a hill, to allow the development of a housing estate on the hill's surface without people realising that there is an industrial plant below their feet. The same holds true for the planned development of the Sha Tin Sewage Treatment Works in Hong Kong, which frees up 26 ha of prime real estate land (Drainage Services Department, 2017). On a lesser scale, housing can be integrated into the landscape by placing it inside hills, such as the Earth House Estate Lättenstrasse in Dietikon, Switzerland, designed by Vetsch Architektur (2017). These examples demonstrate the yaodong principle, but also broaden the concept by creating artificial hills that cover houses.

The British architect Lord Foster of Thames Bank once said (Von Meijenfeldt and Geluk, 2002),

> In my opinion, there are two extremes in architecture, namely the tent and the cave. Two spiritual spheres, which influence our senses in different ways. We shouldn't pretend they are the same. Whether on the scale of a house or a city, the greater the contrast in design between above and below ground and the more complex the spatial experience, the richer the traveling through it can be.

History shows us that the cave, be it in its natural form or shaped through human excavation, has indeed played and still plays an important role in providing shelter to the people of this planet. Furthermore, history can inspire us to continue shaping artificial caves to accommodate the functions that support our modern way of life, especially now that we have a much better understanding of geology and engineering. When doing so, we must, however, address the positive tension that can exist between spaces above and below.

3.2. The 19th century – revolutionary engineering and unrivalled optimism

Between 1848 and 1854 the 41 km-long Semmering Railway was built in some of the most difficult terrain that the Alps can offer. The railway was vital in providing a link between Vienna, the capital of the Austro-Hungarian Empire, and Trieste, its port on the Adriatic. The concept of this railway was seen as an impossible undertaking by many, as the alignment would include slopes and curves that no existing locomotives could cope with. It was Karl Ritter von Ghega who submitted an ambitious plan that was approved in June 1848, which included gradients and unheard of narrow curves that would require a totally new type of locomotive not yet built. The plan was based on his own surveying of possible alignments for which he had developed new surveying tools and methods. Despite enormous debates among both national and international experts on the merits of the project, work started in August 1848. In March 1850, an international competition was launched to design and build a new type of locomotive that would be able to cope with the project specifications. Although trial runs were made with proposed new locomotives in 1851, it required combining the best of three designs to come up with a special Semmering locomotive (BDA, 1995).

In the film *Under the Tuscan Sun* (2003) this feat is immortalised in a scene in which one of the main characters says,

> Signora, between Austria and Italy, there is a section of the Alps called the Semmering. It is an impossibly steep, very high part of the mountains. They built a train track over these Alps to connect Vienna and Venice. They built these tracks even before there was a train in existence that could make the trip. They built it because they knew some day, the train would come.

The Semmering Railway still operates today, after more than 150 years of operation, and became a UNESCO World Heritage Site in 1998.

It was this optimism of engineers as demonstrated by Von Ghega that is also mentioned and reflected on in Van der Woud's (2006) book on the development of communication and transport in Europe in the 19th century.

Van der Woud writes about the way in which new networks were formed with the advent of the railways. The first railway opened in 1830 and was just 50 km in length. The global network that came into existence after that had, by 1870, a total length of three times the Earth's circumference. Around 1890 this had grown to 15 times. From a philosophical point of view, Van der Woud observed that this meant that not only was humankind conquering time and space but that it was also undertaking a massive struggle with nature. Those first railway pioneers had to overcome deserts, high mountains, rivers, estuaries and – as we can see from the case of the Semmering Railway – the boundaries of technology itself.

With the opening of the Mont Cenis Tunnel in 1870, use of the horse-drawn stage coach to deliver mail and transport travellers became something belonging to the past. It was supplanted by mechanised horsepower, simultaneously giving rise to an enormous wave of optimism among engineers, proclaiming that it was just a matter of funding before even more ambitious projects would be constructed. After all, with the expansion of the railways through the mountains by tunnel, they had proved nature no longer posed a challenge and could be conquered through technology. Plans were drawn up (Van der Woud, 2006) for

- a tunnel below the Strait of Gibraltar
- an iron tunnel to be sunk in the Bosphorus near Istanbul
- a tunnel under the Sont to connect Denmark with Sweden.

This optimism was in sharp contrast to public perception at the time, as it had only been a couple of years since Marc Brunel and his son Isambard Kingdom Brunel had attempted to build a tunnel beneath the Thames.

On 20 May 1827, *The Sunday Times* published a letter from Brunel to the Directors of the Thames Tunnel Company. In this letter, Brunel wrote about the temporary stopping of work due to flooding of the tunnel:

From yaodong to the
third dimension –
historical approaches to
underground urbanism

The body of the Tunnel is at present filled with water, but I'm quite satisfied that the whole of the brickwork of the Tunnel is sound and uninjured, and that the injury is confined to a small spot over the top of the shield, in the frame of which the workmen, for their protection, carry on the excavation. It is extremely gratifying for me to report, that the workmen retired gradually without confusion, and Mr. Beamish, one of my assistant engineers, was the last to quit the shield, which has thus been proved to be an effectual safe-guard against any sudden disaster.

Brunel, after a further tunnel flooding in October 1827, had to resort to other means in order to convince the public of the soundness of his plans, and held a banquet inside the tunnel. By November 1827 the tunnel was cleared of water and ready to be entered (Rolt, 1957):

It was to celebrate this hard-won triumph over disaster that Brunel staged the most fantastic spectacle in the history of the tunnel. He resolved to entertain his friends to a banquet under the river. The side arches were hung with crimson draperies and a long table was brilliantly lit by gas candelabra when, on the night of Saturday 10 November, a company of fifty sat down to dine under the strains of the uniformed band of the Coldstream Guards … In organizing this remarkable entertainment, Brunel had not forgotten his corps d'elite, and in the adjoining arch one hundred and twenty miners sat down to the feast.

The question was, and still is: why has it taken so long for those projects envisioned in the 19th century, to come to fruition in the 20th and 21st centuries, as is the case with the Bosphorus Tunnel and the Øresund Link? One reason could be the so-called Jules Verne effect: the idea is fantastic; the timing is not quite right. In a way, engineers were maybe viewed as being too bold with their ideas, likened to Jules Verne – a contemporary of those pioneering engineers who imagined what up to that point had not been imagined. The plans drawn up by engineers were seen as visions of a future that, as was the case with Jules Verne's description of a voyage to the moon, were still not within reach, and therefore not something you would want to invest in. A second reason was that geopolitical considerations also played a part. The enormous network created by the railways and the underground railways made travel possible on a scale not seen before then. Anthony Trollope illustrated this in his 1857 novel *The Three Clerks*:

It is very difficult now-a-days to say where the suburbs of London come to an end, and where the country begins. The railways, instead of enabling Londoners to live in the country, have turned the country into a city. London will soon assume the shape of a great starfish. The old town, extending from Poplar to Hammersmith, will be the nucleus, and the various railway lines will be the projecting rays.

This concern voiced by Trollope was not unnoticed by the public. It was the main reason why the Channel Tunnel project, for which boring was started in 1876, was stopped in 1882. Mounting public pressure meant that making a permanent link with France became politically impossible. As adventurous and as bold the undertaking was, it only demonstrated the absolute height to which engineering science had progressed, as Van der Woud observed.

In 1897, the *Daily News* reflected on 60 years of progress, and noted:

> In the making of those railways and steamships what progress. Compare the slow and painful excavation of the tunnels sixty years ago by hand labour with the speedy execution done upon the soil to-day by tearing bits of the steam navvy, or contrast the toilsome heart-breaking, life-destroying work upon Brunel's Thames Tunnel with the magnificently rapid and safe passage made through the porous bed of the river the other day at Blackwall, and but the day before for the electric railway at London Bridge.

From the perspective of the engineer, we can conclude that technology and funding, in themselves, seemed insufficient to enable grand projects even if they offered more prosperity and a shorter travel time. Even far-reaching visions would need to be placed within the context of the times, and, as was shown before, public concerns about the possible negative outcomes could block the political will required to carry these projects through.

But the optimism of engineers prevailed, and underground railway networks and tunnels became vital conduits in a developing infrastructure spanning continents, allowing nations and cities to develop and grow. These new transport infrastructures became as vital to the economies of then as they are today, and as tunnelling technologies evolved and more daring projects were undertaken, an awareness took root of how these underground networks could be part of larger underground developments; it was the advent of underground urbanism.

3.3. The 20th century – underground urbanism

3.3.1 The cities of the future

At the end of the 19th century in Paris, France, the prefect of the Seine was Georges-Eugene Haussmann. Haussmann was responsible for reshaping Paris to how we know it today: the magnificent avenues and buildings of the City of Light. However, Haussmann's aspirations also took him underground. In his memoires, he wrote about his ideas on the use of the subsurface (Gandy, 1999):

> These underground galleries would be the organs of the metropolis and function like those of the human body without ever seeing the light of day. Pure and fresh water, along with light and heat, would circulate like the diverse fluids whose movement and replenishment sustain life itself. These liquids would work unseen and maintain public health without disrupting the

smooth running of the city and without spoiling its exterior beauty.

More than anyone else, it was Haussmann who contributed to developing the underground of Paris, and in doing so he gave rise to the concept of the underground as an urban service layer. In his mind, the underground served the purpose of taking away society's secretions in a way that no one would notice and without disturbing life at the surface: a service layer that supports life at the surface by, for example, providing gas for housing and lighting. Indeed, it was the ability to distribute gas that allowed Paris to gain its reputation as the 'City of Light'.

In 1914, a paper was published in the *Annals of the American Academy of Political and Social Science*, written by George S. Webster, Chief Engineer and Surveyor of the City of Philadelphia, USA. The title of the paper was 'Subterranean street planning', and Webster started by expressing his concern that, other than streets at the surface, little thought had been given to the planning and laying out of underground streets. Yet, these underground streets containing all kinds of services are vital to the existence of a city. The paper reaffirms Haussmann's vision that the primary function of urban underground space is that of an urban service layer. It also reaffirms that little or no thought is given to how to arrange, organise and manage such a service layer.

Webster painted an interesting picture of how he saw the future use of underground space. In his paper, he distinguishes between six different uses for the subterranean street, as shown in Box 3.1. What really makes his paper interesting is not so much the various uses but

more so the reasons he gives and the concerns he raises. The frequent breaking up of streets to lay pipes and cables or to repair them can be done if these were placed in subway galleries, barring that the permit to place the pipes or cables should include a period of 3–5 years after placement where no break-up is allowed for maintenance or repairs. More than 100 years on, this seems very reasonable advice – nonetheless, it is still waiting to be adopted by many cities in the world. The same holds true for managing the subterranean street by meticulously tracking the placement of pipes and cables and recording this placement. According to Webster, Philadelphia has been doing this since 1884; why are so many cities of our age still failing to do so?

Webster concluded that 'If healthy conditions are to be maintained and the comfort and convenience of the citizens conserved, it will be necessary to provide for carrying many

Box 3-1 Webster's vision on use of underground space

The Subterranean Street

■ Water pipes, sewers, gas pipes, electrical conduits, steam and hot water pipes, pneumatic tubes, refrigerating pipes, and an inconceivable number of other structures of a similar character which will be required in the future

■ Subway galleries for pipes and conduits

■ Vaults under sidewalks

■ Subways for passenger railway traffic

■ Tunnels crossing the subterranean streets

■ Subterranean freight service, to connect with railroad terminals, business houses and industrial establishments

more of those services which are essential to the comforts of life, in the subterranean streets.'

A conclusion that seems remarkably similar to the observation made by Haussmann a couple of years earlier.

In his paper, Webster quoted a contemporary of his, Eugène Hénard, who in 1910 published a paper titled 'The cities of the future' (Hénard, 1911). Hénard was as concerned as Webster about how cities were developing, especially with regard to services and how these were to be accommodated. His paper began by analysing a typical street with the presence of a sewer and other services in the form of cables and pipes. Webster then speculated on how, in the future, new services will be added that would continuously require the streets to be opened, disturbing the soil and necessitating replacement of the pavement each time. New services, in his mind, will consist of pneumatic tubes for the collection and dispersal of garbage and various other services, including coolants for refrigeration. To accommodate this, Hénard proposed a radical change to the layout of a city's streets. He felt that all problems arise from one fundamental error in human thinking, namely that 'the bottom of the road must be on a level with the ground in its original condition'. If we are prepared to no longer consider this as true, Hénard then stated that we can be open to other solutions, such as the two he proposed. For existing streets, he suggested elevating the street to such a level that the space below can be used as the urban service layer, and that new urban areas should have four underground levels that can accommodate the various services (Figure 3.4). Hénard foresaw platforms

that could be extended downwards as needed (Figure 3.5):

> By the expansion of such a plan we are led to conceive of a city in which all the streets with heavy traffic would have – according to the frequency of the traffic – three or four superimposed platforms. The first platform would be for pedestrians and carriages, the second for the tramways, the third for the various mains and pipes required for the removal of refuse, and the fourth for the transport of goods, &c. We should thus have a many-storied street, as we have a many storied house; and the general problem of traffic could be solved, however heavy it might be.

Hénard's paper ends with an ode to the new era of flight that, in his mind, will transform cities and the way people move around in them. Although Hénard's ideas might seem farfetched to us, the idea of manipulating the urban ground level and raising it is one of the cheapest and most effective methods of creating underground space. An example that showcases this idea is the city centre of the new town Almere in the Netherlands, which in 2005 was built using this concept. A lightly curved plateau provides space below the street level for parking cars, services and public transportation. The connection between the service level and the street level is served by escalators and lifts. The city centre master plan for Almere was developed by the Office for Metropolitan Architects (OMA). Rem Koolhaas, the principal architect at OMA, has explained the use of the curved street level plateau as essentially creating a clean slate on which to build magnificent buildings and provide citizens with space to admire and enjoy those buildings (Von Meijenfeldt and Geluk, 2002).

In a way, the plan for Almere is reminiscent of that created for Paris by Le Corbusier. In his

Plan Voisin, Le Corbusier included large office blocks, spaced out in such a way that large public spaces were created in between. Below each office block he proposed an underground station, thereby connecting the whole area by means of underground public transport. In his mind, this left the street level free for roaming, or, in his own words (Le Corbusier Foundation, 2017):

> You are under the shade of trees, vast lawns spread all round you. The air is clear and pure; there is hardly any noise. What, you cannot see where the buildings are? Look through the charmingly dispersed arabesques of branches out into the sky towards those widely-spaced crystal towers which soar higher than any pinnacle on earth. These translucent prisms that seem to float in the air without anchorage to the ground – flashing in summer sunshine, softly gleaming under grey winter skies, magically glittering at nightfall – are huge blocks of offices. Beneath each is an underground station (which gives the measure of the interval between them). Since this City has three or four times the density of our existing cities, the distances to be traversed in it (as also the resultant fatigue) are three or four times less. For only 5–10 per cent of the surface area of its business centre is built over. That is why you find yourselves walking among spacious parks remote from the busy hum of the autostrada.

At the beginning of the 20th century a firm belief emerged, a belief held to this day, that

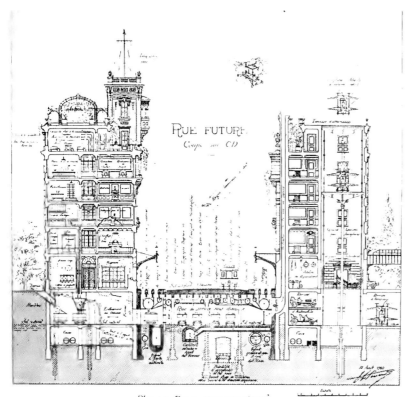

Figure 3-4 Hénard's duplicate street

the prime use of urban underground space is as the urban service layer, giving back to the surface the quality and liveability of the street by banning all those distracting uses to below the surface where they remain out of sight.

3.3.2 Underground urbanism

In 1933, Edouard Utudjian, a young French architect, founded the Groupe d'Etude et de Coordination de l'Urbanisme Souterrain (GECUS) – the Committee for the Study and Coordination

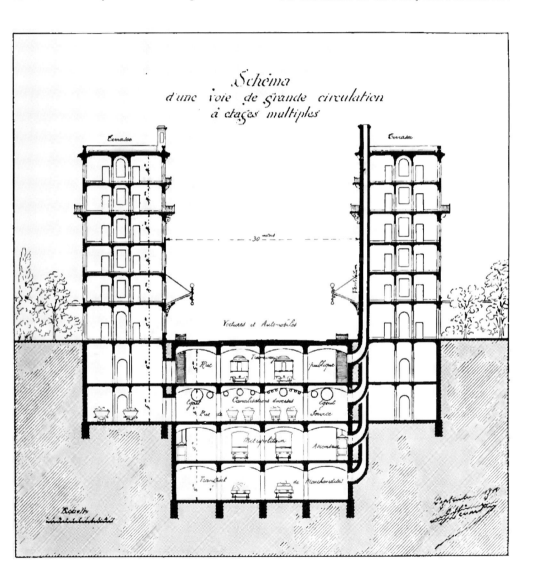

Figure 3-5 Hénard's superimposed platforms

**From yaodong to the
third dimension –
historical approaches to
underground urbanism**

of Urban Underground Development. For the first time in history, a committee dedicated to urban underground space was set up and the term 'underground urbanism' used. It marked a new beginning in the thinking on the role underground space plays in the development of cities. It marked a new beginning for the way underground space is thought about.

At the First International Congress for Urban Underground Development held in Paris in 1937 (at the same time as the World Exposition), Utudjian set out his ideas in his opening address to the conference. He began by explaining the reasons for looking at underground space (Heim de Balsac, 1985):

> The chaotic sight of our congested cities, along with the ever-increasing use of the underground for urban functions, have inspired us to look to the subsurface for remedies and improvements to the multiplicity of ills from which our great urban centers are suffering. In addition, we would like to introduce order and discipline to this immense field, in which a great number of the life-support arteries of the city are haphazardly buried and tangled.

In line with Webster, Hénard and Le Corbusier, Utudjian's thinking at this point in time was clearly focused on the subsurface as the urban service layer (Heim de Balsac, 1985):

> This is in no way an advocacy of underground living, or of burying man, who was destined to live in the sun and open air. Rather, underground urban development must contribute to

better utilization of urban space by hiding underground the various city systems that are a nuisance and an encumbrance when placed on the surface–placing them where, certainly, high-rise structures cannot be considered.

What marks out Utudjian (and GECUS) is that their thinking went further than just coming up with utopian visions of what could be. It was recognised from the beginning that underground urbanism would involve more than just planners and architects. It required knowledge of technology and it required the knowledge of geologists (Heim de Balsac, 1985):

> Above all, the underground urban developer's role will consist of overseeing a harmonious interdependence and coordinating the entire body of data in order that researchers and artists, scientists and technologists can freely endow this field with their richest and boldest creations. Here, where, more than anywhere else, professionals face a multiplicity of problems created at each step, there is a clear need for a strong liaison between the urban planner and the architect, the engineer, and the geologist.

It is this bold insight that sets Utudjian apart from other thinkers on underground urbanism. What he identified is the need for cross-discipline collaboration when it comes to urban underground development. In his own words: 'It is necessary that the urban planner thinks deep and that underground development of cities is done not through random necessities, but according to a definite commitment, legislation and a predetermined plan' (Utudjian, 1952).

GECUS shaped the thinking of underground urbanism. During the international congress mentioned earlier, an international group was set up, the International Permanent Committee of Underground Technologies and Planning (CTIPUS), which organised further congresses in Rotterdam (1948), Brussels (1959), Varsovie (1974) and Madrid (1964).

The far-reaching work done by GECUS is perhaps summed up best when considering the following quote from 1970 by Maurice Doublet, the then Prefect for the Paris Region (Heim de Balsac, 1985):

> The immense contribution of underground urban development is that it allows a separation of offices and businesses. Service and administrative offices can thus be placed underground, restoring the surface to its original state of equilibrium and 'Joie de vivre.' Underground urban development restores a hierarchy of urban functions by articulating the notion of what one will do with mankind. Thus, I truly believe that underground urban development leads to a philosophy of the city, which, in turn, rests upon a philosophy of man. By imagining cities in three dimensions, you have multiplied tenfold the perspectives offered to those having the responsibility for planning of the cities.

It is this third dimension that is the basis of urban underground planning and spatial design,

which we will explore in Chapter 4. It also shows how the work of GECUS evolved from looking at underground space as a spatial relief valve for services unwanted at the surface to a more integrated and appreciative approach to underground space as a potential new urban tissue for modern cities.

3.3.3 Contemporary thinking on urban underground space

The 1964 Madrid conference organised by CTIPUS was its last international congress. GECUS, however, organised many international symposia, study trips and meetings with international organisations well into the 1970s. In 1974, the International Tunnelling Association (ITA) was founded, and although the ITA's main focus was on tunnelling and tunnelling technology, it was recognised that underground space was an important field of study, and several working groups started looking into non-technical aspects of underground space use. During the 1980s and 1990s, it was mainly through the work of academics at various universities worldwide that a revival took place in organising conferences looking at the non-technical side of underground space use. In 1991, the Tokyo Declaration was signed, laying out the need for the urban use of underground spaces but also underlining the need for the further development of knowledge in this field. This declaration led to the inauguration of the Associated Research Centers for Urban Underground Space (ACUUS) in 1996 as a joint effort between research centres in the USA, the Netherlands and Japan.

At the beginning of the 21st century the ITA formally changed its name to the International Tunnelling and Underground Space Association. The ITA also set up four permanent committees to address strategic issues in the field of tunnelling and underground space. ITACUS, the ITA Committee on Underground Space, was charged with advocating and promoting the planning and use of underground space.

Both ACUUS and ITACUS are part of a long tradition and a rich legacy when it comes to underground space use and underground urbanism. More than 100 years after the first thinkers wrote down their thoughts on underground space use and underground urbanism, there is still a need for advocating and promoting the subterranean world below our cities as one of the largest, yet mostly forgotten and underestimated, urban assets.

3.4. This chapter's core ideas

Will the 21st century become the age of underground space? In this chapter, we looked at the history of underground space for trends pointing us towards a more planned and extensive use of the underground.

The idea to plan the use of the subsurface has been around for a long time. Planning, in that sense, can be seen as managing the use of the subsurface. It needs to be organised. Nevertheless, planning can be so much more, and indeed it evolved to an underground urbanism focused on the use of the subsurface as a spatial relief valve. By placing uses below the surface that are not required at the surface, vital surface space can be freed for better use. This remains a valid reason for using the subsurface,

but it will give rise to incidental underground development at most.

If the 21st century is to become the 'age of the underground', we need a cross-discipline integrated urban planning approach. 'Integrated' in this sense means that the surface and the subsurface need to be integrated into urban planning in such a way that a new urban tissue can be created below the surface: no more incidental underground networks or basements, but connections between networks and basements to complement the way we plan our surface at the surface.

What thinkers such as Utudjian have shown us is that use of underground spaces can be so much more than creating an underground urban service layer. But this does require cross-discipline collaboration: no single discipline can claim the underground space as its own. The remarkable words of Maurice Doublet illustrate the potential of urban underground space as being an integral part of the city: 'Thus, I truly believe that underground urban development leads to a philosophy of the city, which, in turn, rests upon a philosophy of man' (Heim de Balsac, 1985).

Through an underground urbanism we will enable urban underground space to become what it was always destined for: contributing to sustainable, resilient, liveable and inclusive cities.

References

1 BDA (Bundesdenkmalamt Österreich) (1995) World Heritage List: documentation for the nomination of the Semmering Railway cultural site. BDA, Vienna, Austria.

2 *Daily News* (1897) Sixty years of progress. *Daily News*, 21 June.

3 Drainage Services Department (2017) Relocation of the Sha Tin Sewage Treatment Works to caverns. STSTWinCaverns. http://www.ststwincaverns.hk (accessed 14/11/2017).

4 Gandy M (1999) The Paris Sewers and the rationalization of urban space. *Transactions of the Institute of British Geographers* **24(1)**: 23–44.

5 Guo Q and Guo Q (2001) The formation and early development of architecture in northern China. *Construction History* **17**: 3–16.

6 Heim de Balsac R (1985) The history of GECUS: a great adventure in contemporary urban development. *Underground Space* **9**: 280–287.

7 Hénard E (1911) The cities of the future. *Transactions of the Royal Institute of British Architects, Town Planning Conference, London, 1910*. The Royal Institute of British Architects, London, UK, pp. 345–367.

8 Le Corbusier Foundation (2017) Plan Voisin, Paris, France, 1925. http://www.fondationlecorbusier.fr/corbuweb/morpheus.aspx?sysId=13&IrisObjectId=6159&sysLanguage=en-en&itemPos=5&itemSort=en-en_sort=6&sysParentName=Home&sysParentId=11 (accessed 14/11/2017).

9 Liu J, Wang D and Liu Y (2002) An instance of critical regionalism: new Yaodong dwellings in north-central China. *Traditional Dwellings and Settlements Review* **13(2)**: 63–70.

10 Rolt RTC (1957) *Isambard Kingdom Brunel*. Longmans, Green, London, UK.

11 *The Sunday Times* (1827) Copy of the report made to the Directors by Mr. Brunel. *The Sunday Times*, 20 May: p. 4.

12 Utudjian E (1952) *L'urbanisme souterrain*. Presses Universitaires de France, Paris, France.

13 Van der Woud A (2006) *Een Nieuwe Wereld. Het ontstaan van het moderne Nederland*. Bakker, Amsterdam, the Netherlands. (In Dutch.)

14 Vetsch Architektur (2017) http://www.erdhaus.ch (accessed 14/11/2017).

15 Von Meijenfeldt E and Geluk M (2002) *Below Ground Level: Creating New Spaces for Contemporary Architecture*. Birkhäuser, Basel, Switzerland.

16 Webster GS (1914) Subterranean street planning. *Annals of the American Academy of Political and Social Science* **51**: 200–207.

Chapter 4

Spatial design – creating a new urban tissue

4.1. Beyond the urban service layer

Looking at history and even contemporary use of underground space, to the casual observer the use of underground space seems to be limited to that of the urban service layer. The thinking on the use of urban underground space as done by Webster, Hénard and Utudjian – discussed in Section 3.3 – seems to have concentrated at first and was indeed fixated on ridding the surface from urban blight and placing all those uses that do not require daylight into the subsurface.

In 2011 a plan by Foster + Partners was discussed on the website Co.Design. Interestingly, it showed a cross-section of the proposed plan with the caption 'traffic and pollution below'. Although the figure itself has since disappeared from the website, it illustrates that 'urban service layer' thinking is still present even in contemporary design.

When it comes to the future of underground space use, maintaining the 'urban service layer' concept will physically block the mixed-use and spatially integrated developments that will contribute to the future of our cities. In this sense, the concerns that Webster voiced at the beginning of the 20th century were not only

correct but still hold true today. The shallow subsurface up to depths of 1 m below grade has in many cities already become an urban service layer. It is the domain of cables and pipes: for the utilities that serve the city and without which the city would fail to exist. Below this layer, we find another service layer containing sewers and transport systems. Although transport systems tend to follow local geology, historically they are placed as close to the surface as possible. Being close to the surface inconveniences passengers the least and does not require complex solutions to move passengers from the surface to the platforms by using multiple escalators or lifts. The construction of the London Metropolitan Line using cut and cover construction methods quite clearly illustrates this (Figure 4.1).

Figure 4-1 Construction of the Metropolitan Railway close to King's Cross Station in 1861 | Courtesy of the Institution of Civil Engineers

Figure 4-2 How deep does
London go? | © Matt Brown /
Londonist Ltd

The development of new lines led to placements deeper and deeper below the surface. The deepest point on an underground line in London lies at 67 m below ground (Figure 4.2). The new Lee Tunnel, an urban waste water tunnel that is part of the Thames Tideway scheme, is between 60 and 70 m below ground. This shows the extension of the use but also of the depth that the urban service layer has taken on below modern cities. It also indicates that the focus on placing primarily public utilities below the surface has created a heavily congested layer that leaves little space for other uses. Furthermore, it illustrates ho w the urban service layer consists of multiple layers that all follow, more or less, horizontal alignments.

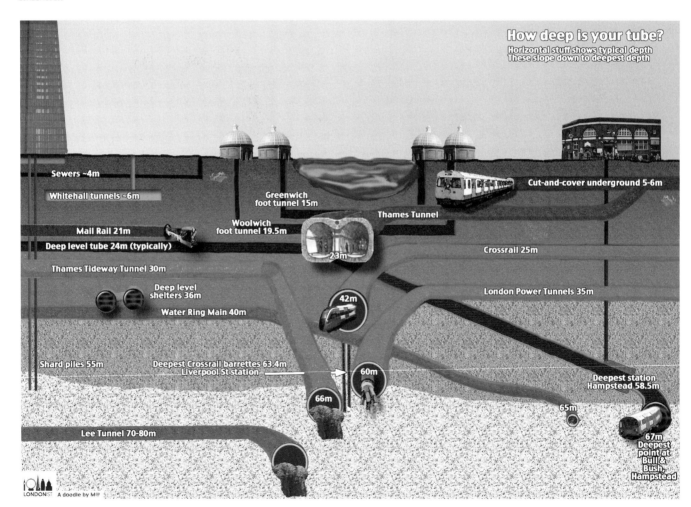

When considering using the subsurface for renewable energy in the form of geothermal energy or aquifer thermal extraction schemes, which require pipes running in the vertical plane for hundreds of metres, it becomes apparent that this would be impossible to achieve in areas that have a heavily developed urban service layer.

A second observation regarding the urban service layer is that it leads the focus of planners and decision-makers in the wrong direction. The extensive use of the subsurface in many cities as an urban service layer can easily result in the conclusion that this use is precisely what the subsurface is intended for. At worst, this has led to creating a heavily congested layer that came into existence largely through a haphazard development that would be intolerable at the surface. To paraphrase Utudjian: the layer consists of random necessities without a definite commitment, lacking appropriate legislation and most definitely without a predetermined plan. It has left many cities with an enormous legacy of cables and pipes and other structures, the existence of which is often not known as no register is available that provides information on location, use and ownership. In many cases, this legacy has a direct impact on the resilience of a city. Construction activities at the surface require intervention below grade, if only for building foundations. In the Netherlands, the underground utility network consists of 1.7 million km of cables and pipes. Annually, 40 000 instances of damage due to surface activities are reported. The risk associated with little or no information about the location and composition of the urban service layer is high. According to an underground location expert,

'every single day an underground gas pipe is being hit and damaged in Australia' (Minutoli, 2016). The consequences of running into a gas pipe could be catastrophic, and often results in emergency and rescue services declaring a major incident. Although many countries have systems in place to identify cables and pipes before starting construction works, most of these systems are self-regulated by the industry and non-compulsory. In the Netherlands, statutory legislation was introduced to formally regulate and replace the industry-regulated schemes. One of the reasons for doing so was the external safety considerations, but also the societal reliance on information and communication provided through underground networks. Further legislation compels an owner of underground infrastructure to remove cables and pipes when they are no longer in use. This only applies to cables and pipes, which makes it possible to imagine the other uses we have seen within the urban service layer, and what the implications are of not knowing the actual location of utilities, networks and underground tunnels. In reality, however, this is only part of the puzzle, and we will look at the implications more closely when discussing policy and planning (see Chapter 5).

This chapter will examine the spatial design and the ultimate objective of creating a new urban tissue below the surface. Underground urbanism, in our opinion, needs to be concerned with this aspect of the use of underground space. It should focus on the question: how can the use of underground space contribute to our cities and their liveability? Although it is clear that an urban service layer can serve (and

Figure 4-3 This spread: Beurstraverse in Rotterdam, the Netherlands | Courtesy of Aeroview, Tom de Rooij, and Architecten Cie

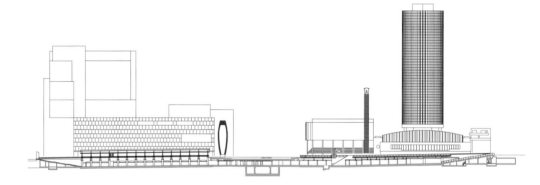

is already serving) the city, another question is: should we limit ourselves to this use – and is this using the subsurface in the best way?

Underground urbanism needs to evolve to the point where appreciating the subsurface becomes an integral part of surface development. To achieve this, we need to break down the physical and psychological barrier that both in practice and in our minds separates the surface and the subsurface as two incompatible domains. To see the road on which we walk as the limit to which the city extends is what Hénard called a fundamental error in our thinking. As cities moved skywards,

the concept of multi-layered development came into existence. The example given in Chapter 2 of the San Francisco Transbay Transit Center illustrates this. It has a public park placed at the highest level of the development that connects with the fifth floor of the adjacent Salesforce Tower. In the heart of the City of Rotterdam in the Netherlands is another interesting example of what happens when we lower a building's ground to the subsurface. The Beurstraverse is a project that was commissioned in 1991 to provide an underground pedestrian route linking the Lijnbaan and Hoogstraat shopping streets and the Beurs underground station (Figure 4.3).

The way it was designed by Pi de Bruin of de Architekten Cie and subsequently constructed created an open shopping street with additional retail spaces that reveals the underground station for all to see. With typical Rotterdam humour, which gives nicknames to all new developments in the city, the Beurs traverse became known as the Retail Trench. It turned out to be a trench of high spatial quality when it opened in 1996, attracting visitors and satisfying their recreational needs by including trees and water features that serve as an attraction for children to play, especially during hot summers. It has become a public open space in much the same way as the converted basement of Covent Garden creates a new atmosphere of enjoyment. The project led to the nearby Bijenkorf department store to connect its basement to the underground station and the pedestrian route, creating an entrance at the lower ground.

This latter case illustrates the transformation that can occur when the surface is not deemed to be an insurmountable barrier but as, at most, a temporary limit to the extent to which a city can grow. Underground urbanism should aim at integrating underground developments seamlessly into the urban fabric. It can lead to new spatial quality and to connecting the hidden underground transport networks to life at the surface and the flow of the city in a natural way.

Spatial design in this sense should concern itself with how to make this possible. It challenges our perceptions of the surface–subsurface interface and demonstrates that we can transcend this barrier to integrate underground urban tissues into the urban fabric.

4.2. From the yaodong via contemporary to future designs

In 2009 the Paris Transportation Authority (RATP) organised a competition for architects to design the metro station of the future. The three chosen entries best reflected RATP's ambitions, and were displayed between May and June 2010 at a public exhibition titled 'Les stations de métro en 2025 – Osmose' that took place in the Cité de l'Architecture et du Patrimoine, at the Trocadéro, Paris (RATP, 2010a). Farshid Moussavi, then still working with Foreign Office Architects in London, was responsible for one of the designs. Moussavi's plan consisted of opening up the underground platforms to the surface by creating intermediate platforms (Figure 4.4). In her own words (RATP, 2010b):

> If we could confront people as they go through their daily lives through this station with new sensations and therefore new ideas, I think that we have managed to take our stations from a servicing role to one that produces them. So what we have done is to take the intermediate platforms that you need in order to connect to the different lines or to connect to these spaces that we are lining around the station and we've oversized them, and we've also connected them with slopes on which we have ramps, on which we have steps, on which we have greenery; so at any one time you could be just moving through this space or you could just be lying down, you could also be sitting watching somebody perform, so you can constantly shift between

Figure 4-4 Design for a new open underground station for the Paris Metro I Courtesy of Farshid Moussavi Architecture and Richez Associés

being a spectator or a performer. Also, this building that wraps around this open space, it is designed or it can be designed to really become an infrastructure to use this space as a space of performance.

Moussavi sees the design as a form of urbanism that brings density and mixed use. In a way, she brings together those elements identified by Jane Jacobs in 1961 as part of what makes streets attractive and function – and with that the city – and merging them into one dense location surrounding the underground station, thereby integrating the underground space into the urban fabric. The design is also exemplary for expanding the yaodong concept into a modern concept that serves the city and those that live in it.

The Next City website commented on the Osmose competition, and made a valid point when concerning underground transportation and its stations (Freemark, 2010):

One paradox of subway systems is that while the whole point of putting the trains underground is to keep them from disrupting the city around them, it is vitally important to make their stations as obvious as possible, clearly in public view. Meanwhile, despite sitting in the heart of urban environments, subways are often inconvenient, too often lacking stores and gathering places that are essential to making them fully useful elements of the public sphere.

The relationship between the surface and subsurface has always been of interest to architects. Looking at the first designs of metro entrances, for example Hector Guimard's entrance for the Paris Métropolitain (Figure 4.5), these seem to have always marked the entrance to life below the surface through stairs or escalators. Even modern-day Metro entrances still use this concept, where the M or U logo serves as the primary indicator for the point of access to the underground. However, at the turn of the 21st century this idea began to change, as can be seen from the design of Kongens Nytorv Station on the Copenhagen Metro, which opened in 2002 (Figure 4.6). This design allowed for a more open transition, emphasising lines of sight with the surface. In a way, it followed the lead given by the design of British architect Lord Norman Foster for Canary Wharf Underground Station (Figure 4.7). His design integrated the surface and subsurface in a way that opened up the subsurface and at the same time connected it with the surface. Exiting the underground at Canary Wharf and standing on the escalators

Figure 4-5 Hector Guimard's original Art Nouveau entrance of the Paris Metro in Abbesses station | Courtesy of Steve Cadman, reproduced under CC BY-SA 2.0

Figure 4-6 Entrance to Kongens Nytorv Station on the Copenhagen Metro | Courtesy of Patrick Nouhailler, reproduced under CC BY-SA 3.0

Figure 4-7 Canary Wharf Underground station | Photo left by David Ilff. License CC-BY-SA-3.0

looking at the surrounding skyscrapers through the glass canopy brings an exhilarating feeling of enjoyment and amazement to the traveller.

Canary Wharf Underground Station consists of two identical entrances situated at the west and east sides of the station concourse. The two glass canopies mark the entrances to the station, and the area between the canopies consists of Jubilee Park, which provides a green public open space directly above the station.

We will take a closer look at Les Halles in Paris, to illustrate the concept of segregation of underground space from the urban tissue and its consequences. Like Covent Garden in London, Les Halles started life as just that: halls in Paris. Les Halles has been the site of a market since 1183, when two wooden buildings were built in the locality (Wakeman, 2007). From then onwards, a market has existed at Les Halles. At the same time, the area grew into a district of Paris that has been dubbed a heterotopia: 'Les Halles was a perpetual carnival. It was also the ultimate countersite of what Michel Foucault called "heterotopia", a place of otherness and

alternate ordering' (Wakeman, 2007). Les Halles continuously tried to keep up with the demands of the growing city surrounding it. Unfortunately, when gastronomy mixed with pleasure, the area became one of the seedier districts of the city (Wakeman, 2007):

> The history of Les Halles reads like a serial melodrama of architecture and urban design in the attempt to keep up with provisioning the city's growing population and clean out the sordid haven of ill repute. The site was a perpetual discourse on how a city should look and how its spaces should be organized, and it consistently drew the attention of the most influential architects of their day.

The 18th century saw a proliferation of architectural designs that tried to rectify the situation. In 1853, construction was started of Victor Baltard's Halles Centrales (Figure 4.8). The plan called for the demolition of much of the old buildings and expanded the market to

Figure 4-8 Victor Baltard's Halles
Centrales in Paris

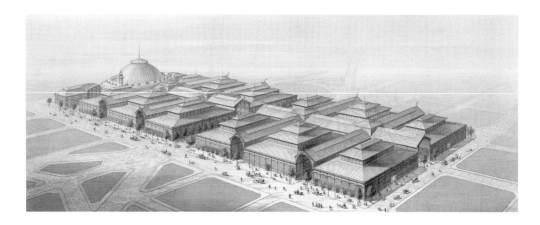

cope with the growth of the city. It was the time of Haussmann's reconstruction of Paris, and grand visions for the future of the city came into existence (Wakeman, 2007):

Les Halles was remade by a rational and hygienic architecture-urbanism that created ideal conditions for commercial trade and capitalist relations ... It became a visual and literary trope that represented Paris, its populist roots, its engaging sociability and eccentricity. Les Halles locates Parisian identity and communal citizenship.

However, this strong identification with what Paris is and what it stands for constrains development of the site. Another reason hampering development is that there has always been a struggle in the French political system between the ruling leaders and the local administration trying to leave their imprint on the city. Both Hénard and Le Corbusier came up with plans at the beginning of the 20th century that would have changed Les Halles

forever. The plans were utopian in their design, and looked at conceptualising new forms of urban modernity. Le Corbusier's Plan Voisin was, in that sense, one of the most utopian and provocative plans for Les Halles (Wakeman, 2007). In 1958 the Seine prefecture asked two architects to come up with 'grand ideas' for the complex. One of the architects, Robert Lopez, was a disciple of Le Corbusier. The plans very much drew on ideas of high-rise density to replace Baltard's halls. In an ensuing battle between the state and the Parisian city council, the latter pronounced that 'neither Washington, nor Wall Street' would be the future of Les Halles. 'Six teams of architects were then chosen to lay out detailed plans for what was alternatively called a "new city" or a "new capital". Their designs were revealed to the public in February 1968' (Wakeman, 2007).

The high-density development with high-rise towers produced a public outcry, indirectly leading to the future limiting of a building's height to 25 m in Paris (Heim de Balsac, 1985). It was then that Utudjian and his committee – Groupe d'Etude et de Coordination de l'Urbanisme Souterrain (GECUS) – presented their plans for a vast underground space development to the Paris city council. Because of the deadlock that had arisen, the GECUS proposal was quickly adopted by the council as an alternative that would fulfil the plans without destroying the city's identity – apart from demolishing Baltard's halls. The proposal centred on the following principles to carry it through (Heim de Balsac, 1985):

■ Changing from a surface density, judged as intolerable in this district, to an underground density;

Figure 4-9 The 'negative volume' created by the excavations for developing Les Halles

- Creating an exchange platform linking all the common underground transportation networks: subway, express subway (R.E.R.), buses, train stations, parking facilities, etc.;

- Thoroughly utilizing all resources to coherently fill the open excavation as required to allot the construction of an express subway station, but at the same time retaining the great 'negative volumes', or craters, so as to permit air and light to reach the outermost (underground) areas of the complex [Figure 4.9]; and

- Encouraging programs of a socio-cultural nature, and treating the free surface with paving stones and steps, and with numerous gardens or green urban areas.

Wakeman (2007) commented that

Although it was universally condemned from the moment of its inauguration in September 1979 as banal and unsightly, in the 1960s the subterranean Forum was on the cutting edge of spatial reengineering. The idea itself of a 'forum' or 'agora' was associated with urban centrality and with a mix of commercial, civic, and historic functions that would be the expression of the late twentieth-century city.

It was Utudjian's dream come true, although it was not the futuristic plans he foresaw for Les Halles that prevailed but his insistence on an underground urban complex (Heim de Balsac, 1985):

An underground urban complex is one that handles below the surface, in three-dimensional development, a network of connections for underground or surface transportation lines, circulating a large public through commercial, administrative, public, private, and amusement installations. This definition assumes that in order for the various functions to exist side by side, a considerable degree of conceptual coherence must prevail, along with the maximum amount of constructive logic.

Wakeman (2007) saw the development as 'an experiment in creating a unified urbanity that spread both horizontally and vertically'. In the years that would follow the opening of the Chatelets-Les-Halles underground station in December 1977, the underground space saw continuous development and redevelopment. It, however, failed to reach the unified urbanity it tried to achieve: 'The result was a site rich in the ironies born from political battle, diverse conflicting interests, and the compromises between modernism and historic preservation' (Heim de Balsac, 1985).

As Heim de Balsac (1985) pointed out:

For GECUS, the Les Halles underground complex has been simultaneously a great victory and a source of much bitterness. It is interesting to note that this project was performed without an architect and that it now lacks three-dimensional urban development – the feature that had the unique capability of creating a great spatial vessel that could have been one of the glories of urban development in Paris.

One of the main components missing in the development according to GECUS was the concept of the negative volume or 'crater' – 'that was retained in such modest dimensions that it loses all of its value' (Heim de Balsac, 1985).

Les Halles through all its faults proved to be a valuable lesson in segregating the surface and the subsurface. To create a unified urbanity that spreads both horizontally and vertically – as phrased by Wakeman – requires an integration of surface development and underground space development. By creating a negative volume as conceived by Utudjian *et al.*, this can be achieved, but it needs to be of sufficient proportions to fulfil its purpose of three-dimensional urban development. This fact was recognised by Dutch architect Rem Koolhaas, who was one of four designers selected to come up with new proposals to bring Les Halles into the 21st century. Koolhaas explained the concept behind his design as follows (Office for Metropolitan Architecture, 2003):

> The project consists therefore of a group of buildings that are in part structures that emerge from the underground and in part penetrations into the ground from the surface with the hope that this concept will once and for all do away with the schizophrenia that exists in Les Halles between the underground and the surface.

Unfortunately, his use of towers in an attempt to bring back the high-rise concept to the city that houses the Eiffel Tower was, as he said himself, not enough to convince the public, at yet another exhibition held in April 2004. 'Les Halles of Tomorrow' exhibited four plans, including one by French architect David Mangin. Mangin's design consisted of transforming Les Halles into a large open public space, bringing back a green landscape with a central boulevard. The site of the Forum Les Halles and the transportation hub would be opened up, to reveal the negative volume that Utudjian *et al.* insisted on, covered by a large canopy hovering 9 m above. The design of the canopy brought another international competition in 2007, won by architects Patrick Berger and Jacques Anziutti. The mayor of Paris inaugurated the new complex on 5 April 2016 (Figure 4.10).

Figure 4-10 The Canopée Les Halles opening up the underground space

The canopy has already been dubbed the 'yellow umbrella' and 'a custard-coloured flop' by a critical review in *The Guardian* newspaper (Wainwright, 2016). Whatever the critics may think of it, the real test is whether the latest Les Halles transformation has convincingly – once and for all – eliminated the schizophrenia between the surface and subsurface. Whether it has succeeded, time will tell. For now, it remains a valiant attempt, and one of the few examples we have of a unified urbanity integrating surface and subsurface development.

4.3. Privately owned public open underground spaces

Integrating the subsurface into surface development is one thing, creating a new urban tissue is a bigger step. When we think of creating a new urban tissue from a spatial design perspective, the task at first seems simple. But when we analyse the use of underground space we come across the earlier observation of the existence of public networks and private basements. One of the main challenges is the lack of public space beneath the surface. We illustrate this with a simple example. If we consider Canary Wharf Underground Station discussed in Section 4.2, we can create a simple schematic, as given in Figure 4.11.

As we can see from the diagram, all open space on the surface is part of the public domain. However, as soon as we leave the surface, all open space becomes the property of London Underground and immediately loses the characteristics of public open space. Although a public company owns the actual space, it has the appearance of private space. The fact that London Underground staff are in charge of the station clearly illustrates this. Policing is done not by the Metropolitan Police but by the British Transport Police – a police force funded by the train-operating companies Network Rail and the London Underground – the latter being part of Transport for London. Cameras that observe passengers inside the station are operated and monitored by London Underground staff from Transport for London's central control room. The main characteristic that turns the underground space into a private space is the plain fact of non-accessibility for the public during times that the underground line is not in operation. Outside operational hours there is no public access to the facility.

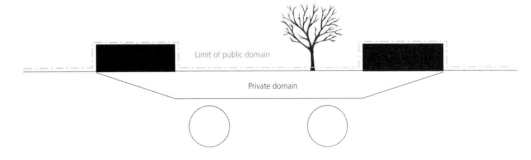

Limit of public domain

Private domain

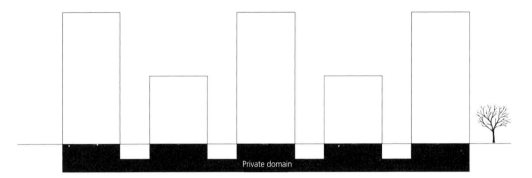

Private domain

Figure 4-12 Schematic of basements beneath buildings linked by corridors

The same holds true in the case of basements that extend privately owned buildings below the surface, whether they contain offices, stores, accommodation or a mix of these. Connecting the buildings by corridors does not automatically mean that these corridors are public spaces: they are private spaces by default, owned by the private developers that created them (Figure 4.12). Access to the corridors is limited to the opening hours of the basements they connect, so office hours or store opening hours determine when the public can access these spaces. A further question arises as to who is responsible for maintaining public order in these corridors. There is no active policing; it is left to the security guards that work for the companies owning the offices or stores. But do they have sufficient powers to maintain public order? Given the fact that these basements and corridors are deemed to be outside the public domain, who, then, is responsible in the event of a medical emergency? Although attending a medical emergency is a public responsibility, there is a duty of care that offices and stores have for the visitors to their facilities. Health and safety regulations could very well apply, meaning that in the event of an accident the first response needs to be made by those inside the building or store.

Pierre Bélanger (2007) first noted these observations in his paper on the Toronto PATH pedestrian system, one of Canada's biggest underground pedestrian networks (Montreal has an even larger pedestrian network). Bélanger (2007) observed that while these pedestrian networks seem to fulfil the dream of many urban planners in that all car traffic has been eradicated from these systems, in reality, given their private status, urban planners see these networks as outside their domain and consequently show no interest in them:

The reluctance of urban designers and academics to engage the dynamics of the underground is stunning. For almost 50 years, urban designers, landscape architects and planners have longed for car-free pedestrian environments that are safe, secure and accessible. From a planning perspective, the Toronto underground may be the ultimate form of attrition of the automobile on the urban landscape: there are no parking lots, no asphalt, and no congestion.

With its mass-transit accessibility, it is an ideal pedestrian network. This reluctance may in part be attributable to a prevailing attitude that privately-controlled under-ground shopping is undesirable, at best dismissible. As self-contained environments, they are perceived as lying outside the so-called public domain and that they kill off street life. As a more legitimate form of collective space, street-level activity located within municipal right-of-ways therefore receives much more advocacy.

When we look from the above perspective at the Beurstraverse in Rotterdam, we observe a subtle difference. Examining the schematic plan view in Figure 4.13, we observe that the public domain continues at the lower level in the constructed artificial trench. Even if a canopy covered the whole area, it would remain a public open space, as shopping hours or the operational hours of the underground do not determine accessibility. The actual underground corridor created is independent of the access to the shops and underground station served. Here, we see a crucial distinction from the other examples, where the system is, at least partially, formed by the basements or stations themselves, which makes public accessibility dependent on the opening hours of those private domains.

The Beurstraverse follows an important design principle formulated by William Whyte (1988):

> A good space beckons people in, and the progression from street to interior is critical in this respect. Ideally, the transition should be such that it's hard to tell where one ends and the other begins. You shouldn't have to make a considered decision to enter; it should be almost instinctive.

Although Whyte isn't one for 'sunk plazas' as he calls them, the Beurstraverse design is one that would certainly overcome some of his

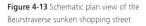

Figure 4-13 Schematic plan view of the Beurstraverse sunken shopping street

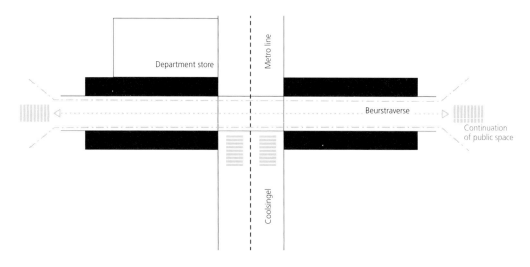

objections. One of his more astute observations is: 'It is difficult to design a space that will not attract people. What is remarkable is how often this has been accomplished' (Whyte, 1988). Apart from the fact that we need to extend the public domain into the private sphere to continue and maintain the flow of people, we also need to design underground spaces in such a way that they will attract people.

The question remains: how to solve the underground private domain conundrum? The solution could well lie with the concept of privately owned public open spaces (POPOSs). Whyte referred to this concept, which was introduced in New York City in 1961, in an annex to his book:

> In 1961 New York City enacted a zoning resolution that gave developers a floor-area bonus for providing plaza space. For each square foot of plaza space, the builder was allowed 10 feet of additional commercial floor area. The requirement of the plazas was that they be accessible to the public at all times. That, as it turned out, was about all they were.

Whyte then described how the 1975 amendments required making the plazas 'amenable' to the public, and detailed how to achieve this. The concept of POPOSs is now widely used in the USA, but also in cities such as Seoul in South Korea and Auckland in New Zealand. Not everyone is enthusiastic about the concept, as private owners sometimes seem to prefer keeping POPOSs hidden as much as possible. A survey done by students in Auckland on POPOSs in the city concluded that 'Most were found to be exclusive and often unusable due to restricted entry hours, with cold and unwelcoming furnishings, heavy surveillance, and inadequate signage to indicate they were public spaces' (Reeves, 2016).

This aspect of keeping these spaces out of the public eye was not lost on the San Francisco planning department. In 2012, new legislation was introduced dealing with the signage identifying POPOSs in the city, to make the public better aware of the spaces available in the city. POPOSs in San Francisco were, up to 1985, based on a voluntary scheme offering additional area much like the New York example. Since the introduction of the 1985 Downtown Plan, POPOSs are now a compulsory part of projects in the so-called C-3 Districts. Figure 4.14 shows

Figure 4-15 This spread: South
Kensington Subway

a POPOS in San Francisco on top of the Fairmont San Francisco hotel in Nob Hill. Access to this roof garden requires entering the hotel and navigating through it.

Creating a new urban tissue below the surface requires a different approach in that these spaces may well require restyling as privately owned public open underground spaces (POPOUSs). Doing so would at least solve the problem of accessibility outside office or shop opening hours. It would also give some control over the requirements these spaces must meet to ensure a flow of public to and from them. The need for urban corridors connecting underground spaces is paramount to creating a new urban tissue. Apart from a detailed spatial design, these corridors will also require additional considerations as we will discuss next.

4.4. Urban underground corridors

When exiting the London Underground at South Kensington Station, passengers who want to visit the Natural History Museum, the Victoria and Albert Museum or the Royal Albert Hall can use the South Kensington Subway instead of navigating through the traffic at the surface. The subway is a pedestrian tunnel that was built just below the surface, providing an urban corridor connecting the underground station with a basement entrance to the Victoria and Albert Museum and providing exits to the Natural History Museum gardens. It runs beneath Exhibition Road and emerges near the Science Museum. The pedestrian tunnel was constructed in 1885, and is 433 m long (Figure 4.15) (Historic England, 2017).

Although the subway is from the Victorian era, it survives today and provides a service allowing the public to flow from the London Underground directly to the museums. It remained a one-off development, in direct

contrast to the extensive pedestrian network beneath Toronto. As Bélanger (2007) observed, 'What is most compelling about the historical development of the Underground is its self-replicating behavior.' He then went on to identify the forces and dynamics behind this self-replication of the network. One overarching factor contributing to the development of the underground network of corridors is the climate in North America. Extremely hot summers

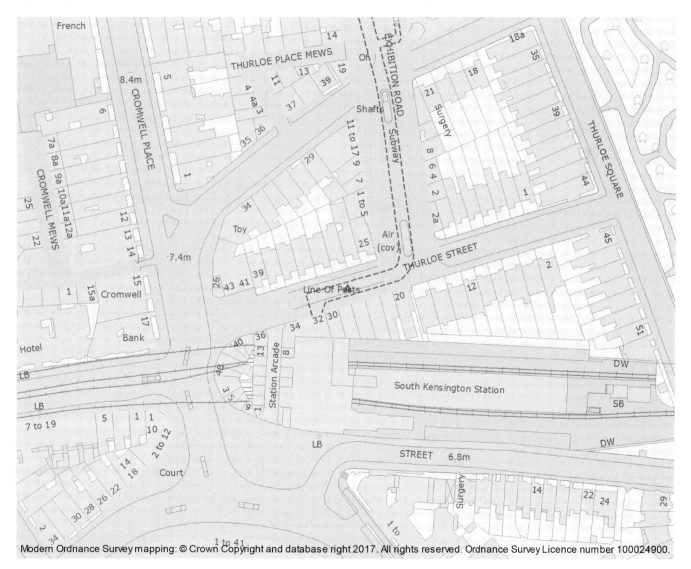

Figure 4-16 Düsseldorf Wehrhahnlinie Kirchplatz Underground Station
| Courtesy of Jörg Hempel – Aachen

and freezing winters make the subsurface a comfortable place to seek comfort. Bélanger also mentioned that smog is a contributing factor. The smog alert days in the city went from 1 day in 1993 to 41 days in 2005. Although 41 days proved to be a record high (Ontario Ministry of the Environment and Climate Change, 2017), smog remains a problem, and it is no doubt that the urban corridors provide an efficient refuge from the more disagreeable climate at the surface.

As much as the climate is a driving force behind this pedestrian network, the dynamics that Bélanger (2007) identified are also very relevant regarding the spatial design of urban corridors. He noted the following dynamics: spatial legibility, access and mobility, flow and usage, and spatial control and surveillance. We will explore these in more detail, using Bélanger's observations regarding the Toronto PATH pedestrian system and expanding where possible with other experiences:

> One of the most visible aspects of the network is its circuitous, often illegible space. The combination of tunnels, openings, shops, and courts that dot the network of the underground – when considered as a whole – is confusing and disorienting. The hyper-accumulation of signs, media, symbols, lights, materials, displays, and proportions – a natural effect of retail competition between 1200 different tenants – further compounds this condition, masking the more basic or essential components of the network.

Wayfinding is one of the most important aspects when it comes to allowing people to navigate through underground spaces and underground corridors. Devoid of any visual references to the surroundings, being aware of where you are becomes impossible without relying on signage. Finding your way around a large international airport on a first visit can be equally confusing. Without signage, this is an infeasible task, and even with signage it depends very much on the quality, clarity and logic of the signs. A different approach is through the actual design of the corridors. Rather than providing bland, sterile passages, the design could emphasise the surface through the design to allow the user of the network to form a mental picture, combining information of the surface with the location below the surface. This concept is advancing in the design of underground stations. Instead of making all stations look alike and relying on the identification of station names to let travellers work out where they are, the design identifies the location. The Moscow Metro is well known for this approach, with its elaborate designs. The Stockholm Metro has followed this concept, and employed artists to give stations different identities. For the design of the stations of the Düsseldorf Wehrhahnlinie, architects and artists teamed up. The Kirchplatz station was designed by Netzwerkarchitekten using art installations created by Enne Haehnle, giving the environment a unique appearance (Figure 4.16).

In 2008 the Amfora project was presented at an international congress in Amsterdam. The project was a private initiative by Dutch contractor Strukton Civiel and the Amsterdam-based ZJA Zwarts & Jansma Architects. Amfora was an attempt to reconcile two seemingly contradictory objectives in Amsterdam: removing all cars from the streets along the canals and increasing the inflow of traffic into the city, thereby reducing congestion on the Amsterdam ring road. A network of multi-level underground facilities directly beneath the city canals and the Amstel River was seen as the solution to this challenge. Although the proposed project has to date received little support from politicians and decision-makers, it does reveal the power of creating a new urban tissue below a city. The Amfora Amstel plan won the MIPIM Future Project Award for Big Urban Projects in 2010 (Figure 4.17). What is relevant in this context is that one of the aspects investigated for the plan was wayfinding. One proposed solution to overcome the problem of navigation was to project views of the surface directly above a location onto the walls – not only providing a means of navigation but also virtually connecting the subsurface with the surface. Projection not only allowed 'live' imagery but also provided information on time (day or night) and weather conditions (ZJA Zwarts & Jansma Architects, 2017).

When signage is the only option, this can easily lead to confusion given the enormous amount of visual stimuli in an underground retail environment. The hyper-accumulation of stimuli, as Bélanger (2007) called it, is not only misleading but also an information overload that causes people to avoid the system in the future. A study released by the Toronto Financial District BIA found that 'the current system is an "underused asset" because residents and tourists who use them often find getting around cumbersome and confusing' and that the current signage system was found to be 'confusing, inflexible, unpredictable, inconsistent and outdated' by users (Shum, 2016). A new system is now to be introduced by 2018.

The second dynamic identified by Bélanger concerns itself with 'access and mobility'. As we have already seen, accessibility is essential for developing an underground space that is part of the urban fabric. When the idea of an underground pedestrian system was conceived in Toronto, the main objective was to achieve the integration of the surface with the subsurface. Bélanger quoted from Edward Carpenter's book *Urban Design: Case Studies* to demonstrate this integration: 'By establishing open spaces adjacent to the pedestrian routes ... sunlight, sky, snow, trees, city-scape and street activity can and must be made accessible (visually and physically) to pedestrians.' However, when the city pulled out of the scheme in 1976, what remained was 'unchecked development in the underground that served only the single-mindedness of individual developers and property owners' (Bélanger, 2007). The one exception to this, according to the previously quoted Carpenter, is First Canadian Place. Carpenter observed that 'The variety of entrances, connections, paths, and light levels has made this city block a highly successful element in Toronto's underground pedestrian system' (Bélanger, 2007). An important consideration is to avoid discontinuity by being dependent on the office hours of the building above, and careful spatial design can contribute to preventing this.

As can be seen from Figure 4.18, First Canadian Place forms a node within the system.

Figure 4-17 Amfora Amstel – a planned large-scale underground facility beneath the Amstel River in Amsterdam | Courtesy of ZJA Zwarts & Jansma Architecten

The nodes are connected by axes, serving as urban corridors or people conduits. The nodes within the system give more freedom than the axes, as they are broad and expansive. The axes are long and linear, allowing for less freedom in the placement of services. It is the connection of the nodes with the surface and the accessibility to and from these nodes that determine the successful integration between the surface and subsurface.

Flow and usage are a further dynamic mentioned by Bélanger. He observes that regular peak hours of traffic flow exist within the Toronto PATH network. These are determined by the coming and going of office workers and the lunch breaks in between. During intervening periods, as well as on weekends, the system is mostly vacant. According to Whyte (1988), this phenomenon exists in many downtown plazas, but rather than despair he suggested ways to deal with this: the creation of more downtown housing, good restaurants and attractions to draw people into the plazas and keep them there are a few of his notions. For instance, the Pioneer Courthouse Square in Portland, Oregon, can be rented out for weddings. When it comes to the spatial design of underground systems, flow is important to consider. What Whyte helps us to understand is that, regarding usage, a direct link exists between urban planning and surface development. The vibrancy of underground spaces can only come about through accessibility and from providing the variety of uses that make plazas, and indeed streets, attractive places in which to exist.

The final dynamic influencing underground space according to Bélanger is what he called 'spatial control and surveillance'. With the example of the policing of London Underground stations and CCTV monitoring given earlier, we illustrated how a single underground facility becomes a private space partially open to the public. It needs no further comment to realise that this becomes even more complicated within multiple underground facilities linked together and all operated by different private companies. What Bélanger additionally observed, quoting

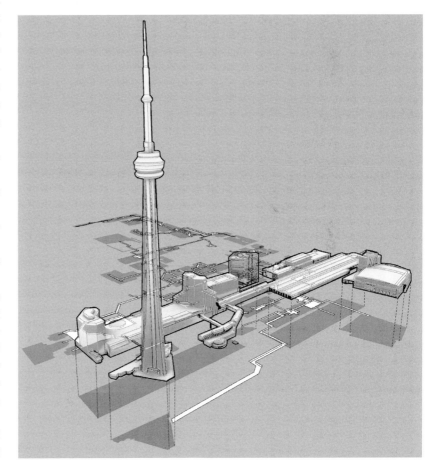

Figure 4-18 Three-dimensional representation of the CN Tower node of the PATH network | Courtesy of Pierre Bélanger, © 2007–2017 OPSYS/Pierre Bélanger

from Ken Jones's report *Retail Dynamics in the Toronto Underground System*, is the fact that private entities have the option to select who enters their properties. This selection of the public is commonly based on a subjective perception that may detract from the primary objective of the business; that is, the public deemed undesirable. Jones observed that this discrimination and possible unduly restrictive rules for conduct, even if only in perception, could be seen as a reason for not entering the pedestrian network. As previously discussed, albeit briefly, the aspect of safety and security can also become a complex one. Private companies have a duty of care regarding safety and security, but this also remains a public responsibility. Certainly, in underground spaces that have a significant accumulation of people at any one time, this could lead to public concerns that need to be managed primarily through private resources, almost certainly resulting in a mismatch.

From a spatial design point of view, the four dynamics discussed above help us in our understanding of how underground pedestrian networks work. They give us helpful pointers to how to design in such a way that we can meet the challenges posed by the identified dynamics. Just as the concept of POPOSs can help, the idea of an underground network provider could as well.

Bélanger (2007) formulated a strategy consisting of a minimum of three priority objectives, to set a direction that is clear yet flexible:

■ First, the mapping of the city's downtown core is urgently needed to provide a simple and precise way of navigating the downtown area with an emphasis on spatial references and street level connections.

■ Second, the synchronization of underground operating hours during the evenings and weekends must be addressed to respond to the needs of a growing downtown resident population.

■ Third, the development of a directive plan that integrates the future growth of retail amenities below ground with public spaces on the street level above ground.

The greatest lesson we can take from Bélanger is that planning and design form the basis for the development of a new underground urban tissue. Leaving the development unchecked and subject to the whims of private developers and owners can in the long term only lead to a less desirable result that would inevitably be detrimental to the same developers' and owners' objectives. Public and private goals become achievable by seeing the underground development as part of a larger planned surface development. In essence, this is the core of urban planning. In the next chapter, we will look at how policy building and urban planning can stimulate the use of underground space for the greater good, and thus create the cities we need.

4.5. This chapter's core ideas

This chapter started by examining how the use of the subsurface has evolved below many modern cities. It discussed the concept of the urban service layer, which in many ways appears to be the perceived use of the underground space. The shallow subsurface is very much the domain of cables and pipes – utilities that serve the city. Below that we find transportation uses in many layers that extend to a depth that remains manageable with regard to transporting people to railway platforms where they board trains. A new application of the subsurface is to provide renewable energy to the city through using water-carrying soils, aquifers or geothermal applications. Managing all these different applications is a major challenge in itself. Planning this use is an inevitable necessity to avoid future chaos, and unnecessarily limiting the development of the city. It is through developing an underground urbanism that a new urban tissue can evolve to the point where there is a seamless integration with surface development and activities.

The development of contemporary underground stations is paving the way forward: in the past, entrances to the underground were through well identified but narrow staircases. As a consequence, the underground remained hidden from the surface and, generally, segregated from the city. Designs such as Canary Wharf Underground Station and the Kongens Nytorv Station on the Copenhagen Metro follow a more open and broad entrance concept, which provides a more natural flow of passengers and opening of the subsurface to the surface. In doing so, this leads, at least visually, to a more connected approach, whereby underground space becomes more identifiable from the surface.

Utudjian and his fellow GECUS members created an underground urbanism by successfully proposing an underground solution for the Les Halles development in Paris. They defined an underground urban complex as (Heim de Balsac, 1985)

> one that handles below the surface, in three-dimensional development, a network of connections for underground or surface transportation lines, circulating a large public through com mercial, administrative, public, private, and amusement installations. This definition assumes that in order for the various functions to exist side by side, a considerable degree of conceptual coherence must prevail, along with the maximum amount of constructive logic.

By examining the concepts of public open space and private space, the conceptual coherence became a conundrum that exists as soon as privately created basements are connected to form an underground network. Private spaces in this sense can also consist of those operated by public companies, but without having the characteristics of public open spaces. They form areas that are limited in use in time, as they depend on the operational hours of the underground transport system or of stores. Further limitations exist, as these spaces are not open for use to everyone – such as access to the underground being open only to fare-paying passengers.

The concept of POPOSs could be followed as part of the solution to this conundrum. The four dynamics that Bélanger identified when studying the underground pedestrian network of Toronto contribute a more precise picture of the coherence we seek: spatial legibility, access and mobility, flow and usage, and spatial control and surveillance. These four dynamics are essential principles applicable to any underground spatial design. To achieve a new urban underground tissue and the integration between the surface and subsurface, policy building and urban planning need to acknowledge the existence of underground space and plan its use in conjunction with the development of the surface. What holds true for downtown plazas that empty after office workers head home in the evenings or that are deserted during the weekend also holds true for underground urban complexes. The vibrancy of underground spaces can only come about through sufficient accessibility and by providing the variety in uses that make plazas and indeed streets attractive places in which to exist.

References

1   Bélanger P (2007) Underground landscape: the urbanism and infrastructure of Toronto's downtown pedestrian network. _Tunnelling and Underground Space Technology_ **22:** 272–292.

2   Freemark Y (2010) When you get the chance to build a new subway station, take full advantage. Next City. https://nextcity.org/daily/entry/when-you-get-the-chance-to-build-a-new-subway-station-take-full-advantage (accessed 14/11/2017).

3   Heim de Balsac R (1985) The history of GECUS: a great adventure in contemporary urban development. _Underground Space_ **9(5–6):** 280–287.

4   Historic England (2017) South Kensington Subway. https://historicengland.org.uk/listing/the-list/list-entry/1392462 (accessed 14/11/2017).

5   Minutoli B (2016) Every single day an underground gas pipe is being hit and damaged in Australia. LinkedIn. https://www.linkedin.com/pulse/every-single-day-underground-gas-pipe-being-hit-ben-minutoli (accessed 14/11/2017).

6   Office for Metropolitan Architecture (2003) Les Halles. http://oma.eu/projects/les-halles (accessed 14/11/2017).

7   Ontario Ministry of the Environment and Climate Change (2017) Smog advisory statistics. http://airqualityontario.com/history/aqi_advisories_stats.php (accessed 14/11/2017).

8   RATP (Régie Autonome des Transports
    Parisiens) (2010a) *Osmose, quelles stations
    pour demain?* RATP, Paris, France.

9   RATP (2010b) *Demain … la station Osmose.*
    https://vimeo.com/11971353 (accessed
    14/11/2017). (Video.)

10 Reeves D (2016) Open up hidden
    public places in Auckland towers.
    The New Zealand Herald. http://m.
    nzherald.co.nz/nz/news/article.cfm?c_
    id=1&objectid=11702774 (accessed
    14/11/2017).

11 Shum D (2016) New downtown Toronto
    PATH wayfinding signage eyed for 2018.
    Global News. https://globalnews.ca/
    news/2731703/new-downtown-toronto-
    path-wayfinding-signage-eyed-for-2018/
    (accessed 14/11/2017).

12 Wainwright O (2016) A custard-coloured
    flop: the €1bn revamp of Les Halles in Paris.
    The Guardian. https://www.theguardian.
    com/artanddesign/2016/apr/06/les-halles-
    paris-architecture-custard-coloured-flop
    (accessed 14/11/2017).

13 Wakeman R (2007) Fascinating Les Halles.
    French Politics, Culture and Society **25(2):**
    46–72.

14 Whyte WH (1988) *City: Rediscovering the
    Center*. University of Pennsylvania Press,
    Philadelphia, PA, USA.

15 ZJA Zwarts & Jansma Architects (2017)
    Amfora Amstel, Amsterdam. http://www.
    zja.nl/en/page/2819/amfora-amstel-
    amsterdam (accessed 14/11/2017).

Chapter 5

Policy building and urban planning

5.1. Policy building

5.1.1 A greater awareness

Including underground space in spatial policy plans or other strategic plans is not something we see happening in the world on a large scale. The cause is not so much the disinterest of policy-makers, decision-makers or planners but more a lack of awareness and understanding. Demonstrating that underground space can play a role when it comes to developing policies in a wide range of fields could be one way of overcoming this.

The International Tunnelling Association Committee on Underground Space and the Associated Research Centers for Urban Underground Space (ITACUS and ACUUS – see Section 3.3.3) introduced the concept of underground space through a variety of activities that took place in Medellin, Colombia, during the United Nations (UN) World Urban Forum in 2014.

What transpired from the sessions was that policy-makers are not helped by merely quoting the merits of underground space. They need to know how the use of underground space can assist them in pursuing their policy goals. By demonstrating the role that the subsurface

Figure 5-1 The contribution of underground space to the UN's Sustainable Development Goals (SDGs) | ©United Nations. Reprinted with kind permission.

plays, and by providing examples, the awareness, understanding and appreciation of the role of underground space for cities will improve.

The need for including underground space into urban planning has been previously explored. We concluded that 'The underground space is a very strategic part of the urban fabric and can provide valuable additional space for real estate and public spaces for cities' (Admiraal and Cornaro, 2016). We also stated that

The United Nations has recently agreed on the new Sustainable Development Goals (United Nations, 2015). Of the 17 goals, the use of the subsurface can contribute to seven of these goals [Figure 5.1] … As such it requires no discussion that an urban underground future should be part of the development of cities.

In the following sections, we are going to expand on what we wrote in 2016, and add examples that demonstrate how underground space can contribute. In this way, we hope to create a greater awareness, understanding and appreciation of underground space.

5.1.2 Zero hunger

The UN (2017) described SDG 2 as 'End hunger, achieve food security and improved nutrition and promote sustainable agriculture', where one of the targets is

> By 2030, ensure sustainable food production systems and implement resilient agricultural practices that increase productivity and production, that help maintain ecosystems, that strengthen capacity for adaptation to climate change, extreme weather,

drought, flooding and other disasters and that progressively improve land and soil quality.

We believe that the subsurface has a significant role to play in reaching this goal and this target. In the common understanding of the subsurface, it is self-evident that soil is required to achieve these aims and that, as such, it is vital to protect agricultural land for this purpose. The question is if all the arable land available is sufficient for future food production. Do we want to maintain the present system of large crops in certain parts of the world and then having them transported to other regions? Are traditional production methods sufficiently resilient to cope with climate change in terms of extreme weather, drought, flooding and other disasters? The damage done to crops in Hainan, China, by hurricane Sarika in 2016 illustrates this point clearly (Figure 5.2).

Underground space can and does already offer an alternative. An example exists beneath the streets of London, where a former air raid shelter has successfully been adapted to grow herbs and vegetables for restaurants in the area: Growing Underground (Rodionova, 2017). This example not only makes it clear that we can reuse abandoned underground infrastructure but that we can grow crops and create supply within an area of demand. Urban farming is a fast-growing trend. We believe that urban underground farming should not be discounted and has a future in providing food safety and security.

According to the website Urban Gardens (Plaskoff Horton, 2015), quoting the Japanese Ministry of Economy, Trade and Industry, 'Japan currently has about 211 computer-operated

Figure 5-2 Crop damage after hurricane Sarika

plant factories – hydroponic and aeroponic farms growing food in closed environments without the utilization of sunlight.' The efficiency of these farms is impressive, they

> produce 100 times more per square foot than traditional methods using 40% less power, 99% less water usage, and 80% less food waste than traditional agriculture. As self-sustaining urban-based food systems, they also produce fewer food miles and a lower carbon footprint.

Although not all of these farms are underground, they confirm the possibility of food grown under artificial conditions and that this method provides enormous efficiency. In Japan, one farm exists in the basement of an office building, right in the heart of Tokyo in what used to be a bank vault. It consists of a hydroponic vegetable field and a rice paddy. The crops are protected from the environment and have the added benefit of not requiring pesticides.

Growing Underground has expanded into a serious business supplying London and the wider area with organic produce guaranteed pesticide free (Figure 5.3). What is interesting is that the whole venture is supported by well-known British chefs, making it more than just a unique experiment but also a disruptive production method pointing to a new way of providing food security, nutrition and sustainable agriculture that is replicable in highly densified urban areas.

5.1.3 Clean water and sanitation

'Ensure access to water and sanitation for all' is SDG 6 of the UN (2017). This goal has several targets that underground space use can help to reach:

> By 2030, achieve universal and equitable access to safe and affordable drinking water for all

> By 2030, achieve access to adequate and equitable sanitation and hygiene for all and end open defecation, paying special attention to the needs of women and girls and those in vulnerable situations

By 2030, improve water quality by reducing pollution, eliminating dumping and minimizing release of hazardous chemicals and materials, halving the proportion of untreated wastewater

Figure 5-3 Urban underground farming in London, UK | © Growing Underground

and substantially increasing recycling and safe reuse globally

> By 2030, substantially increase water-use efficiency across all sectors and ensure sustainable withdrawals and supply of freshwater to address water scarcity and substantially reduce the number of people suffering from water scarcity.

Water is one of the resources that are essential to our planet. Storing water in underground aquifers through rainfall infiltration is part of the natural cycle. Built-up areas have, however, led to rainwater flowing off in sewers, thereby preventing this infiltration. Capturing rainwater and reusing it as grey water is one way of reducing the use of drinking water. How does underground space use help in this case? Firstly, by freeing up hardened spaces in urban areas by placing infrastructure below the surface and bringing back green areas. Secondly, underground space contains drinking water transport pipelines and distribution pipes. Thirdly, through the natural aquifers that are present in the subsurface. It requires no argument that all of these uses need to be balanced and planned and in some cases protected through regulation. In new developed urban areas, it is becoming common practice to separate drinking water, sewage and run-off water. This separation leads to less pressure on treatment plants but also allows for grey water reuse.

5.1.4 Affordable and clean energy

SDG 7 of the UN (2017) is 'Ensure access to affordable, reliable, sustainable and modern energy for all'. Various targets need to be reached to achieve this goal. The following are related to the use of underground space:

> By 2030, ensure universal access to affordable, reliable and modern energy services
> By 2030, increase substantially the share of renewable energy in the global energy mix
> By 2030, double the global rate of improvement in energy efficiency.

Both geothermal energy and aquifer thermal energy storage systems play a significant role in energy transition. An interesting case is the Minewater project in Heerlen, in the Netherlands. Beneath Heerlen lies the largest industrial complex in the Netherlands, and consists of former mine shafts and galleries (see Section 2.2). By drilling wells into this underground maze, utilising the temperature difference that exists in the water-filled levels becomes possible. Water from the deepest galleries has an average temperature of 28°C, whereas water from galleries close to the surface has an average temperature of 16°C. Although the hot water would be insufficient to heat homes directly, the temperature difference between it and the typically cold drinking water that is used reduces the energy required to heat homes. Using renewable sources to do this makes the whole system very sustainable. The relatively cold water is used to cool homes, thereby saving on the energy that would otherwise be consumed by air-conditioning systems. An added benefit is that 'mine water' as such is not fit for human consumption. Exploiting this water leads to a reduction in demand for the more widely used potable water. The project is now working together with a project in Sweden to develop a district energy controller (Figure 5.4) (Mijnwater, 2017):

> In the Heerlen district, flooded mine galleries act as renewable energy sources and provide a total 500,000 m² floor area connected to a low-temperature district heating and cooling network. The purpose of the STORM project is to develop a controller for the hybrid energy system, in which underground storage systems can be integrated, in order to aim towards an energetically self-sufficient district.

The Minewater project demonstrates how underground storage systems when incorporated into an energy mix aiming at only using renewable sources can cut the need for fossil-based energy, and reduce the overall carbon dioxide emissions for heating and cooling by 65% (Verhoeven *et al.*, 2014).

5.1.5 Decent work and economic growth

SDG 8 of the UN is 'Promote inclusive and sustainable economic growth, employment and decent work for all' (UN, 2017). Although this SDG focuses primarily on developing nations, the need to maintain high levels of economic production applies to all cities in equal measure to eradicating poverty and preventing mass unemployment. One of the targets associated with this goal to which the use of underground space can contribute is to 'Achieve higher levels

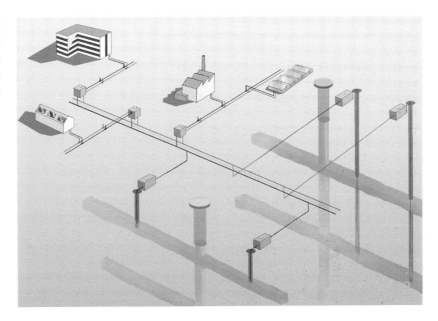

Figure 5-4 The Minewater concept | Courtesy of Minewater

of economic productivity through diversification, technological upgrading and innovation, including through a focus on high-value added and labour-intensive sectors'.

One example of this is the proposed development of an 'underground science city' in Singapore. Construction of Science City will take place beneath the existing Science Parks 1, 2 and 3 and the Kent Ridge Park. A study has shown the feasibility of this project that would allow 4200 scientists, researchers and other professionals to work below Singapore on a 20 ha site. The site would contain R&D facilities but also a data centre (Chang *et al.*, 2013).

In the UK, London has an insatiable appetite for warehouses, with demand for storage space growing every year. Planning permission was given in 2017 by Hounslow Council to extract gravel from below dormant agricultural

Figure 5-5 Rectory Farm – artist impressions showing the new park on top and the warehouse space below | Courtesy of Formal Investments and Vogt Landscape Architects

land – part of the Green Belt but conveniently located in the vicinity of Heathrow Airport. The plan foresees the extraction of gravel and at the same time the creation of a massive underground storage facility not unlike the SubTropolis facility located in a former minenear Kansas City, USA. The proposal for the Rectory Farm (2017) project (Figure 5.5) states that

> Rectory Farm is the site of the proposed new park for the people of Hounslow. This is an ambitious project

that will deliver a 110 acre park and leisure facilities for use by everyone in the community, between 1,870–2,540 direct jobs and many other benefits … The large new public park will provide much needed recreational space linking local communities and will include full size grass and all-weather football pitches, hockey and cricket pitches, plus a variety of other facilities alongside fields and tree-lined paths for walking, running and cycling. Historically the 110 acres of green belt land was agricultural but has not been farmed since 1996 due to years of antisocial behaviour, fly tipping, trespass, vandalism and concerns over food safety. Currently inaccessible to the public, the site will be transformed into an open and freely accessible park.

5.1.6 Industry, innovation and infrastructure

We live in a changing world that requires industries to rethink their entire business strategies. The pressure to become more sustainable by disconnecting from fossil-based resources is mounting. The chemical industry is looking at new sources for their processes, and at the same time looking at how by- or waste products can be reused or used by others. These developments, much in line with the principles of the circular economy, in themselves raise the question of connectivity. The UN defines SDG 9 as 'Build resilient infrastructure, promote sustainable industrialization and foster innovation'. The targets associated with this goal to which underground space can contribute are (UN, 2017)

Develop quality, reliable, sustainable and resilient infrastructure, including regional and transborder infrastructure, to support economic development and human well-being, with a focus on affordable and equitable access for all

Promote inclusive and sustainable industrialization and, by 2030, significantly raise industry's share of employment and gross domestic product, in line with national circumstances, and double its share in least developed countries

By 2030, upgrade infrastructure and retrofit industries to make them sustainable, with increased resource-use efficiency and greater adoption of clean and environmentally sound technologies and industrial processes, with all countries taking action in accordance with their respective capabilities

Significantly increase access to information and communications technology and strive to provide universal and affordable access to the Internet in least developed countries by 2020.

These targets all centre on 'connectivity' as the ability to connect people, cities and industries. The chemical transition consists of new innovative developments such as 'industrial symbioses' and 'power-to-X'. The industrial symbiosis concept looks at connecting industries so that one company's waste can become another company's raw material. Power-to-X aims to use wind power and solar power to produce synthetic gas as a renewable source for the chemical industry and the intermediate storage of energy. Both of these developments require connectivity through transport pipelines.

Connectivity at the urban and regional levels has been successfully achieved through constructing underground mass rapid transit systems. Concepts such as Hyperloop are being developed with the potential to disrupt our traditional thinking on transportation and changing the nature of the question 'Where do we live and where do we work?' We believe that underground space has a significant role to play in connectivity but will require the construction of underground infrastructure corridors. These corridors in the shape of tunnels should contain all the connectivity solutions for both 'smart

cities' and 'smart industries'. These corridors will provide multi-use facilities that can carry anything from pipelines, logistical distribution systems and district heating systems to glass fibre for high-speed internet connectivity as well as high-speed people-moving systems. In creating these corridors, we are building 'ecological infrastructures' as proposed by Brown (2014): 'Based on this whole-system perspective, we might reinvent an ecologically informed, post-industrial generation of infrastructure', and discussed previously in Section 2.2. It requires, as Brown says, a 'whole-system perspective'. Although not commonplace, we think that developments such as 'industrial symbiosis' can only come about from a whole-system perspective and therefore are able to open

Figure 5-6 The principle of industrial symbiosis as achieved in Kalundborg, Denmark I Courtesy of www. symbiosecenter.dk

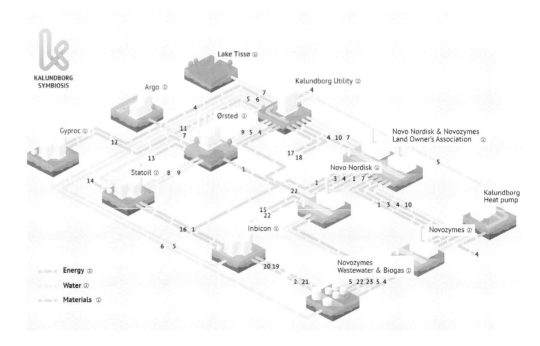

the way for integrating this concept in future infrastructure development (Figure 5.6).

5.1.7 Sustainable cities and communities

In October 2016 the Habitat III conference took place in Quito, Ecuador. As part of the road to Habitat III, the World Urban Campaign initiated the General Assembly of Partners. The outcome of this global consultation was the report *The Cities We Need: Towards a New Urban Paradigm* (World Urban Campaign, 2016). This document, which served as a basis for further input into the Habitat III process, recognises underground spaces as being a vital part of the new urban paradigm. The report states that

> The city we need has planned underground infrastructure for city utilities, underground transportation and underground public spaces that are well connected with each other. This infrastructure needs to be well managed and recorded and information made accessible to avoid potential conflicts of use and disruption of services.

Although this recommendation was not adopted in the outcome document of Habitat III, it illustrates that underground space is becoming recognised as a concept that can contribute to the future cities we need but requires planning and management to be sustainable and resilient.

The UN targets set for SDG 11 that underground space may help to achieve are (UN, 2017)

> By 2030, provide access to safe, affordable, accessible and sustainable transport systems for all, improving road safety, notably by expanding public transport, with special attention to the needs of those in vulnerable situations, women, children, persons with disabilities and older persons

> By 2030, enhance inclusive and sustainable urbanization and capacity for participatory, integrated and sustainable human settlement planning and management in all countries

> Strengthen efforts to protect and safeguard the world's cultural and natural heritage

> By 2030, significantly reduce the number of deaths and the number of people affected and substantially decrease the direct economic losses relative to global gross domestic product caused by disasters, including water-related disasters, with a focus on protecting the poor and people in vulnerable situations

> By 2030, reduce the adverse per capita environmental impact of cities, including by paying special attention to air quality and municipal and other waste management

> By 2030, provide universal access to safe, inclusive and accessible, green and public spaces, in particular for women and children, older persons and persons with disabilities

> Support positive economic, social and environmental links between urban,

peri-urban and rural areas by strengthening national and regional development planning.

Planning underground spaces can only take place if this process is part of a participatory, integrated and sustainable planning and management (see Sections 5.2 and 5.3). In a sense, the opportunities that underground space offers to urban areas might not only lie in physical objects but also in the fact that the attractiveness of underground space can serve as a driver to explore new planning methodologies.

In line with the above, a whole-system perspective applies equally to creating the cities of the future. It is from such a perspective that solutions can be derived such as the Stormwater Management and Road Tunnel (SMART) in Kuala Lumpur, Malaysia – a mixed solution that prevents flooding of vast areas of the city, while providing an infrastructure solution at the same time (Figure 5.7). The investment was recovered rapidly by levying a toll for the road tunnel (The World Bank, 2010; UNISDR, 2012).

5.1.8 Climate action

SDG 13 of the UN is 'Take urgent action to combat climate change and its impacts'. Apart from the massive migration we see from rural areas to urban areas, the impact of climate change is the single most important factor influencing our decisions on the cities of the future. Although at present all our efforts are focused on carbon dioxide reduction in an attempt to mitigate the effects of climate change, planners need to think ahead regarding climate adaptation. Cities need to take measures now to cope with high-intensity rainfall events, and use underground space to achieve this (Bobylev, 2013). The targets associated with this goal and to which underground space can contribute are (UN, 2017)

Strengthen resilience and adaptive capacity to climate-related hazards and natural disasters in all countries

Integrate climate change measures into national policies, strategies and planning

Improve education, awareness-raising and human and institutional capacity on climate change mitigation, adaptation, impact reduction and early warning.

Figure 5-7 Operation of SMART in Kuala Lumpur, Malaysia

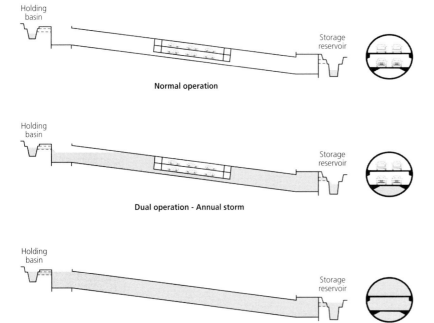

Normal operation

Dual operation - Annual storm

Storm operation - Major storm

Where the principle of the SMART tunnel relies on capturing water and redirecting its flow through the city, other cities are looking at how to capture and temporarily store the excess water in those cases where city sewers or ponds, canals and lakes are threatening to overflow (Prasad *et al.*, 2009). In Tokyo, Japan, an enormous human-made cavern was constructed specifically for this purpose as part of the Metropolitan Area Outer Underground Discharge Channel (Figure 5.8) (Kashik, 2012):

Built between 1992 and 2006, at the cost of $3 billion, this huge underground water management system comprises of 6.4 km of tunnels up to 50 meters underground connecting 5 giant silos, 65 meters tall and 32 meters wide, to one massive tank – the Temple … This giant metal reservoir measures 25.4 meters by 177 meters by 78 meters and is supported by 59 gargantuan pillars. Flood water from the city's waterways are collected through the tunnels and into the silos.

On a slightly different scale, the City of Rotterdam has constructed a large water storage basin beneath an underground car park. By combining both projects into one, an overall project cost reduction of several millions of euros was possible (Doesburg, 2012).

These examples are only one aspect of how underground space use can help in adapting to climate change. Carbon capture storage is another concept actively being pursued. It

involves inserting carbon dioxide into geological formations that have previously been used to extract minerals, salt, gas or oil. Although public debate on the merits and dangers of permanent storage is still ongoing, temporary storage seems achievable by converting the captured carbon dioxide into synthetic gas as part of, for example, the 'power-to-X' concept.

5.1.9 Breakthrough

As we saw in Section 2.2, Brown (2014) made a case for a cross-policy approach. She felt that many of the issues we have today with our infrastructure stem from the segregation that exists between policy silos: 'Nevertheless, we continue to disaggregate them physically and jurisdictionally into distinct sectors, and we mentally separate utilities and the natural systems from which nearly all infrastructural services are derived.'

What the previous sections show is how underground space, through a multitude of solutions, can contribute to achieving at least seven of the UN's SDGs to be reached by the end of 2030. What we have also seen is that this is no mean achievement and sometimes requires cross-discipline and cross-policy collaboration to achieve. The example of the SMART tunnel in Kuala Lumpur shows how cooperation between the city's transport division and water management division made a unique and inspiring solution possible. The same happened in Rotterdam when the water division and city parking management were brought together. How do these meetings of mind take place? Do they happen by chance or are they orchestrated? And if orchestrated, who is the conductor ensuring that harmony exists?

We feel this is where urban planning comes into play. In the following sections we will discuss this further and show what methodologies exist to create a new dialogue as part of the new urban paradigm and agenda. It requires a breakthrough from conventional thinking; we need cross-discipline, cross-sector collaborations to ensure cities take full advantage of the opportunities that lie below the surface.

5.2. Planning methodology for the underground

Mexico City has a unique square right in the heart of the city. The Zocalo is an enormous square with an area measuring 57 600 m² (240 m × 240 m). The cathedral, the national palace and significant government buildings, housing the world-renowned Diego Rivera murals, illustrating Mexico's rich history, surround the square. A flagpole dominates the centre of the plaza, where each day an impressively sized national flag is ceremoniously raised. Mexico City respects its heritage and translates this into restrictive regulations in terms of the permitted height of new buildings. At the same time, the pressure on its surface space is increasing. As part of an architecture competition, two architects from BNKR Arquitectura found a solution to the challenge of creating new space and at the same time respecting history. They developed a concept they aptly named the 'earthscraper' (Figure 5.9). BNKR Arquitectura (2011) describes its concept as follows:

The Earthscraper is the Skyscraper's antagonist in a historic urban landscape where the latter is condemned and the preservation of the built environment is the paramount ambition. It preserves the iconic presence of the city square and the existing hierarchy of the buildings that surround it. It is an inverted pyramid with a central void to allow all habitable spaces to enjoy natural lighting and ventilation. To conserve the numerous activities that take place on the city square year round (concerts, political manifestations, open-air exhibitions, cultural gatherings, military parades …), the massive hole will be covered with a glass floor that allows the life of the Earthscraper to blend with everything happening on top.

What the earthscraper so pointedly illustrates is the difference between constructing beneath and above the surface. Where the skyscraper is a universally accepted and applied concept, building the earthscraper requires specific conditions. High-rise buildings depend on the subsurface for their foundation. When it comes to buildings below the surface, a certain complexity arises. Firstly, the subsurface itself plays a role, as it exerts forces on the building. This can be soil pressure, or pressure caused by groundwater – which plays an important role too. The local geology becomes the most important determinant in deciding on the construction of an earthscraper. The groundwater table determines how deep we can reach. Where in some locations the water table can be 25 m or more below the surface, in other areas, such as deltaic regions, the water table can be as little as 1 m below the surface. Looking back at Section 4.1, the use of underground space in London utilises the local geology, the London Clay. In

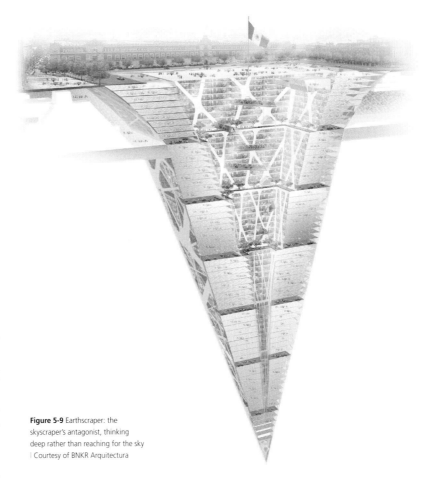

Figure 5-9 Earthscraper: the skyscraper's antagonist, thinking deep rather than reaching for the sky | Courtesy of BNKR Arquitectura

deltaic regions, such as the Netherlands, the presence of groundwater limits the depth of construction.

Secondly, we need to ask ourselves what the effect will be of an intervention on the regenerative ecosystem services that the subsoil delivers (see Section 2.3). Apart from this concern, we also need to address the environmental impact of the volume of material that will be generated by the project. A project on the scale of an earthscraper could potentially result in 5–10 million tonnes of sand. This is about 10% of the annual amount of sand needed to maintain the coastline of the Netherlands and to realign the surface due to soil subsidence. For the construction of the Gotthard Base Tunnel in Switzerland – with a length of 57 km the longest rail tunnel in the world – 28.7 million tonnes of material were extracted. Of this, 90% was turned into building material through recycling. The redevelopment of the old docks in the City of Helsinki in Finland also used material extracted from the construction of the city's metro line.

Geology plays an important role when it comes to planning the underground space. It can limit the depth of development through the presence of groundwater, as we have mentioned, or, as is the case in Central America, the presence of magma chambers makes underground construction almost impossible – although geothermal applications can harness the enormous heat they produce. The presence of stable bedrock formations provides the ideal geology for creating large underground spaces. These human-made caverns are flexible in their applications, with Singapore, Hong Kong and the Nordic countries noted for their use. The caverns are vast and typically used for the storage of fuel or other resources, waste-water treatment facilities, sports arenas and military airfields. The presence of this favourable geology can provide opportunities for using underground space. The London Underground, as we saw earlier, makes use of the properties of the London Clay, mainly its non-permeability, preventing ingress of water. Through years of use, however, the heat released by the underground tunnels has been affecting the soil, causing it to dry out. Over time this could cause the favourable London Clay to become less favourable, as it changes its properties through human intervention. On top of that, the sheer volume of underground networks including water pipes are rapidly filling up the layer, thereby decreasing the possibilities of future use of that layer.

Spatial planning of underground space requires us to address planning in a different way from how we approach planning above ground. As mentioned, the type and quality of the geology beneath a city are important determinants. When a city is built on hard granite, for example the City of Helsinki, the order in which underground development takes place within a layer does not limit future development. Figure 5.10 schematically shows underground space creation in Helsinki, where

Figure 5-10 Schematic section showing underground space use below Helsinki

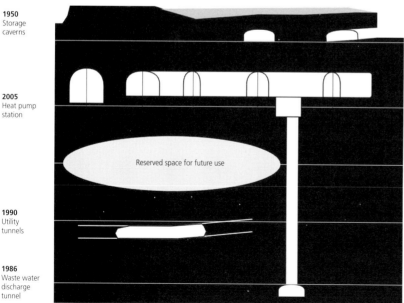

1950
Storage
caverns

2005
Heat pump
station

Reserved space for future use

1990
Utility
tunnels

1986
Waste water
discharge
tunnel

there is no direct relation between the order of placement and the time at which each development took place. In softer soils, an order of development like this would be unthinkable. It would be inconceivable to develop the underground space in such a way – construction activities would influence each other significantly and at the same time the surface itself. Additionally, sometimes access to underground infrastructures is required. Pipelines are placed in pipeline corridors next to each other, stacked in the horizontal plane. In this way, access for repair or maintenance remains possible. This practice, however, requires quite a lot of space, with building nearby or under not allowed. Spatial planning, especially in softer soils, calls for the planning of uses not only within layers but also in time. At this juncture, underground space planning requires more than a 3D approach: by adding the component of time, it becomes four-dimensional.

The question we need to ask ourselves from a planning perspective is whether the development of the subsurface can continue autonomously; that is, on a first-come, first-served basis, or whether a form of planning and management should guide it, even if only from the standpoint of a functional and future-oriented use. The latter requires a three-dimensional (3D) approach. In contrast with the surface where height is a limiting and structuring factor, we need to understand depth within the context of the linear and network patterns that characterise the human use of underground space. There is no other way to do this than to view underground space as consisting of physical layers.

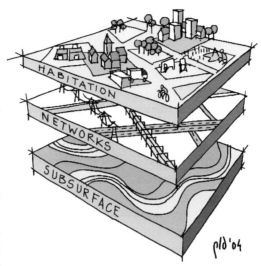

Figure 5-11 The layered approach as a model of spatial analysis | Courtesy of Peter Duvallier

In June 2001 the then National Planning Department of the Netherlands Government published *Spatial Explorations 2000: The Importance of a Good Subsurface* (RPD, 2000). What was remarkable about the publication was the choice of topic: the subsurface. With ongoing social debate on the use of the surface and subsurface, especially in the context of large infrastructure projects and the new ability to use tunnel-boring machines in the typical soft soils of the Netherlands, the time had come for the nation's planners to start to think deep. The observations brought two important insights: the recognition of the subsurface as part of spatial planning and the layered approach as a method of analysis.

The layered approach divides space into three imaginary layers: habitation, networks and subsurface (Figure 5.11). Each of these three layers typifies a form of spatial use characterised in time by change cycles. The most stable layer in this approach is the subsurface. This layer contains the subsurface system, the water system and the biotic system. Transformations in this layer take place in periods of greater than a century. The network layer contains infrastructures above the surface, at the surface and below the surface, and includes air routes and digital connections. Changes in this layer typically occur between 40 and 60 years, which is the time required to create a new infrastructure system. Human occupation patterns form the third layer. It is the layer of human activities such as living, working and recreation. The change cycle time of this layer is typically that of one generation – between 10 and 30 years.

The value of the layered approach lies in the identification of the different rates at which the layers develop. This method shows its potential where these layers meet, according to *Spatial Explorations 2000*. The interface between the various layers is important, as we have seen previously that human intervention in the subsurface consists of the penetration of the subsurface layer from the occupation and network layers. This penetration inevitably means that, from the perspective of spatial planning, differences in development speed will come into play.

Spatial Explorations 2000 considers analysing underground space to require three different points of view, each perspective having unique characteristics, which further complicates multi-dimensional planning. The subsurface as a spatial reservoir is the first and most common perspective. This view can be characterised using geometrical dimensions: length, width, depth and height. A different perspective sees the subsurface as a complex ecosystem, consisting of the soil system, the groundwater system and biotic systems. Previously, we discussed the way that these systems work together through natural cycles. *Spatial Explorations 2000* points out that it is this perspective that has grabbed the attention of conservationists and environmental activists. These two views typify the tension that exists between exploitation of the spatial reservoir and conservation of the underground ecosystem. It is not about conservation *per se*, but rather stems from concerns that arise from a lack of awareness of the natural processes and the way these interact. The latter complicates making an objective appraisal of human interventions below the surface. The discussion surrounding underground carbon capture storage illustrates this. The third perspective is the subsurface as the base layer of the layered approach. The three dimensions that characterise this view are then the subsurface, networks and habitation. *Spatial Explorations 2000*, in this case, notes that a potential use of the subsurface layer requires taking into account the difference in change cycle times of the other layers. Doing so requires setting boundary conditions based on both human uses and normative values. In other words, when planning underground space we need to employ both zoning and layering to allow its use, and we need regulations to preserve in those cases where this is required. These findings are consistent with what we concluded when looking at the sustainable development of the subsurface.

The layered approach as proposed in *Spatial Explorations 2000* led two researchers to see whether it would be possible to adapt this method – initially intended to be an instrument of analysis – for use as a tool for urban planning. Hooimeijer and Maring published their paper 'Designing with the underground' in 2013, and highlighted three compelling reasons for the need to plan underground space. Firstly, they mention the role that the subsurface plays in adapting to climate change. The subsurface has a vital role when it comes to capturing rainwater due to extreme precipitation events. It also forms the base layer for green spaces in the city that provide urban cooling. Secondly, in the energy transition from fossil-fuel-based energy to renewables, the subsurface also comes into play. Hooimeijer and Maring specifically pointed to geothermal energy applications and aquifer thermal energy storage systems. Thirdly, they identified the relatively high cost of creating physical structures below the surface – all the more reason to be smart and efficient and plan for it, in their view. As a further argument, they pointed to the critical role of the subsurface when it comes to spatial quality and urban resilience. Their method is based on the fact that, in practice, the layered approach has become a design tool. The existing three-layer model is expanded into a model consisting of the following layers: people, metabolism, buildings, public space, infrastructure and subsurface. The 'people' layer forms the social component, whereas the 'metabolism' layer addresses all the processes that are necessary to maintain urban liveability and its attractiveness to its citizens. The importance of this latter layer is further underlined by Hajer and Dassen (2014). They see a future of cities as 'smart cities', where the urban metabolism plays a significant role in this context:

> We have to reconnect the biophysical and social domains in new ways. Our first task is to create a broader awareness of what is required to make a city function. The urban metabolism is hidden. If we could unveil the urban metabolism, it would become clear what contemporary urban life consists of, and we would get an idea of what disconnect requires.

By 'disconnect', Hajer and Dassen are referring to the challenge of freeing society from the concept of fossil-based fuels as a wealth creator. In the context of underground planning, it is important to realise that unveiling the urban metabolism is just as important as revealing the subsurface metabolism. Both are hidden and not visible to the urban planner, yet essential when it comes to planning the smart cities of the future.

The strength of Hooimeijer and Maring's approach lies in the dialogue it creates between, as they call them, domain owners. The layers of the model make it possible to identify ownership at the discipline level, where the subsurface is divided among disciplines rather than uses. In this way, Hooimeijer and Maring defined the following domains: water, soil, civil structures and energy. Within these domains, a further distinction is made using the depth dimension: the deep subsurface (over 500 m), the water layer and the shallow subsurface. The approach is called System Exploration Environment and Subsurface (SEES). What makes SEES attractive is that it calls for a dialogue between domain representatives to identify opportunities and

Figure 5-12 The SEES canvas
| Courtesy of Linda Maring/
Deltares

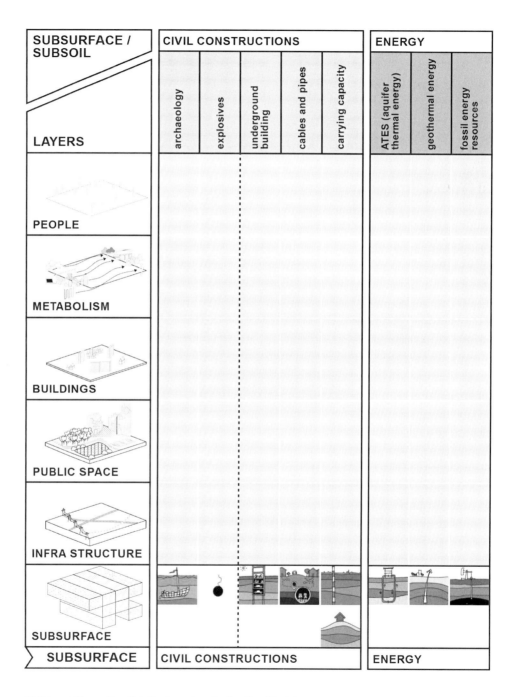

Colour plates

Figure 1-3 Page 9
Figure 2-2 Page 31

 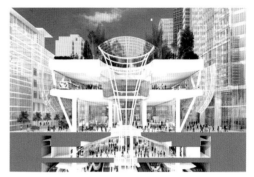

Figure 1-4 Page 10

Underground Spaces Unveiled Planning and creating the cities of the future

Figure 2-1 Page 24
Figure 1-6 Page 14–15

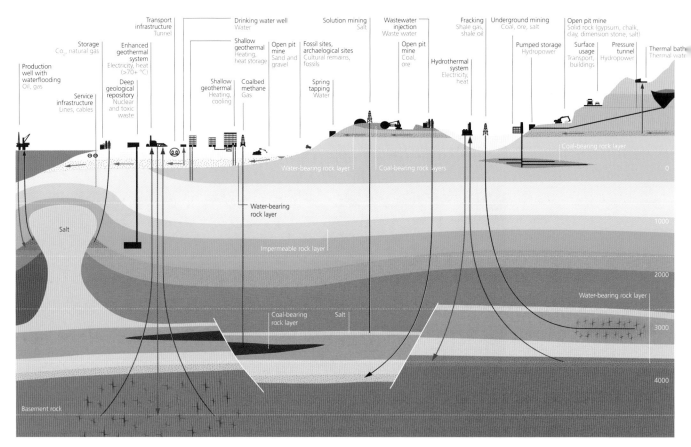

Figure 2-5 Page 34
Figure 2-3 Page 32

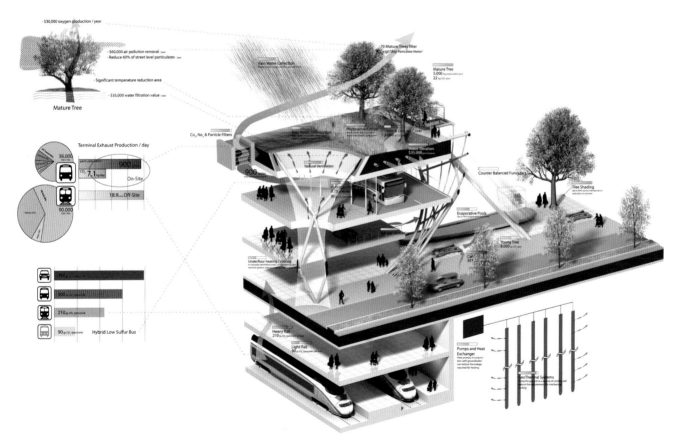

Colour plates

Figure 3-2 Page 44
Figure 3.3 Page 45

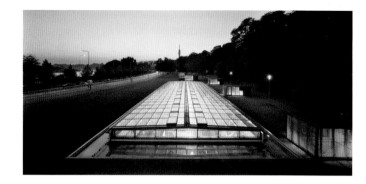

Underground Spaces Unveiled Planning and creating the cities of the future

Figure 4-3 (top right and top left) Page 62
Figure 7-1b Page 131

Figure 4-10 Page 69

Figure 5-3 Page 87
Figure 4-17 Page 78

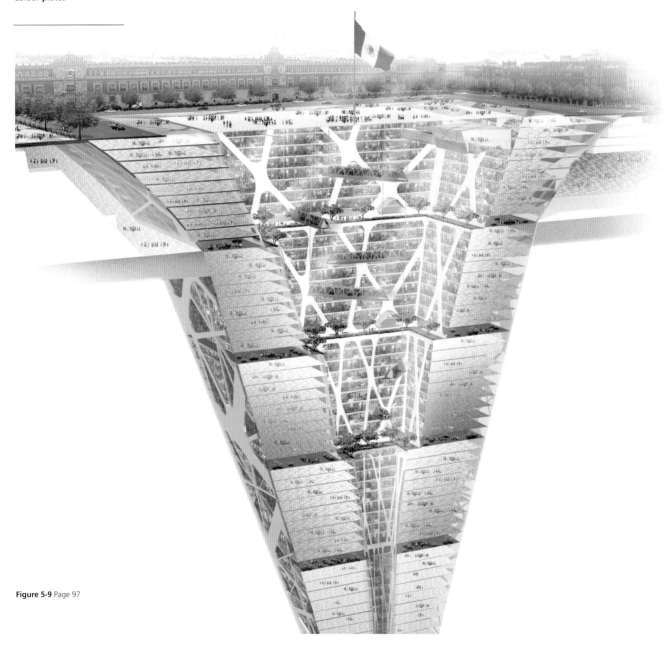

Figure 5-9 Page 97

Figure 4-18 Page 79

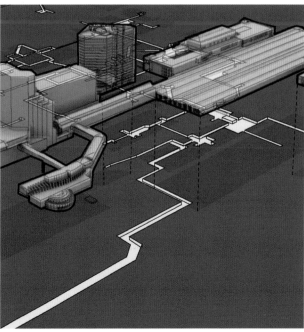

Figure 5-5 Page 90

Figure 4-16 Page 76

Underground Spaces Unveiled Planning and creating the cities of the future

Figure 7-3 Page 133
Figure 7-4 Page 135

Figure 7-5 Page 136

Colour plates

Figure 7-2 Page 132
Figure 7-6 Page 138

Underground Spaces Unveiled Planning and creating the cities of the future

Figure 7-13 Page 145
Figure 7-12 Page 145

Figure 8-2 Page 158

Figure 9-2 Page 175

Underground Spaces Unveiled Planning and creating the cities of the future

Figure 9-1 Page 174

Figure 9-6 Page 181

Figure 9-7 Page 181

Underground Spaces Unveiled Planning and creating the cities of the future

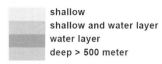

			shallow
			shallow and water layer
			water layer
			deep > 500 meter

WATER			SUBSURFACE						SUBSURFACE / SUBSOIL
water filtering capacity	water storage capacity	drinking water resources	clean soil	subsoil life / crop capacity	geomorphological quality & diversity landscape ecology	ecology	sand/clay/gravel resources	subsurface storage	**LAYERS**
									PEOPLE social structure (neighbourhood typology) social behaviour labour productivity labour capital
									METABOLISM energy / food water waste air (building) material products
									BUILDINGS offices housing utility culture
									PUBLIC SPACE living environment culture nature agriculture
									INFRA STRUCTURE mobility network
									SUBSURFACE subsurface subsoil water energy civil constructions
WATER			SUBSURFACE						SUBSURFACE

challenges. It asks participants actively to identify synergies to achieve a more efficient use of the subsurface. It is this participatory planning that can lead to the combinations that Brown (2014) referred to as 'ecological' solutions. The work sessions use a canvas (Figure 5.12) that consists of a matrix combining both layers, domains and the depth dimension.

The development of the *Vision of the Subsurface* by the Municipality of Zwolle in the Netherlands demonstrates the synergy that is possible by including underground space into urban planning (Weytingh and Roovers, 2007). In the foreword to the policy document, the city executive specifically mentions the positive results achieved unexpectedly by introducing the subsurface as a new spatial dimension. The report notes the following achievements:

> CO_2 reduction by 17%; reduction of soil decontamination cost by 75%; generating new resources for the development of rural areas; sustainable water table management; flood prevention yet at the same time the ability to counter drought; clean groundwater and drinking water reserves for future generations; attractive supply of energy, cooling and water for industries, reducing the annual energy cost by 150 million euros over a 25 year period.

A remarkable reduction of the carbon dioxide footprint for a new housing development was achieved by disconnecting the development from natural gas as the primary energy source and using a system of aquifer thermal energy storage for heating and cooling houses. By using contaminated groundwater as the transfer medium, decontamination takes place as the water passes through the system. Thereby a synergy is achieved that not only leads to zero carbon dioxide emissions for heating and cooling but within 10 years leads to clean groundwater.

The objective of urban planning is a future of smart cities – cities disconnected from fossil-based fuels and that use an open system of participative planning. It is this combination that for the first time will enable planning of the subsurface and at the same time make it necessary. Combining the biophysical domain and the social domain is not possible without unveiling the urban metabolism, including its base layer: the underground.

5.3. Underground urban planning cases

Given the importance of integrating the subsurface into urban planning, the question is whether there are good examples of planning practice that aims to achieve this. One of the pioneering cities in this respect is the City of Glasgow. Other cities have produced maps showing underground use and future development. However, they lack a methodical approach that allows both urban planners and geologists to work together. The City of Glasgow differs in this sense. The British Geological Survey is working closely with the city planning department and even has an expert embedded within it. Glasgow is thus a good example of institutionalising the cross-discipline approach so necessary when integrating the subsurface into urban planning.

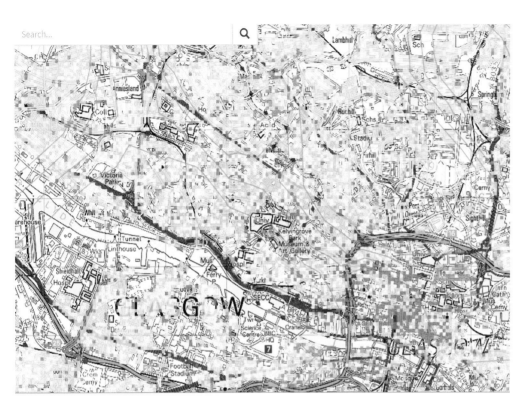

Figure 5-13 Screenshot of the Scotland Heat Map website showing heat resources beneath Glasgow

5.3.1 Case study: Glasgow, UK

The City Development Plan is the new statutory Local Development Plan for Glasgow. Based on the requirements as set out by The Town and Country Planning (Scotland) Act 1997, the City Development Plan contains a reference to the integrated approach, including the subsurface. The plan was adopted by the city's council on 29 March 2017. On the subsurface, it states that (Glasgow City Council, 2017a)

The Council supports an integrated approach to the planning and development of the infrastructure which can often be necessary to facilitate new development. This includes sub-surface infrastructure such as utility services, district heating, energy and broadband infrastructure and transport, Sustainable Drainage Systems SUDS and water management infrastructure.

The Council intends to bring forward a strategy to support such an approach. Updated Supplementary Guidance may be necessary to address any land use planning implications arising from such a strategy. This work will help highlight potential infrastructure opportunities and constraints across the City.

Policy building and urban planning

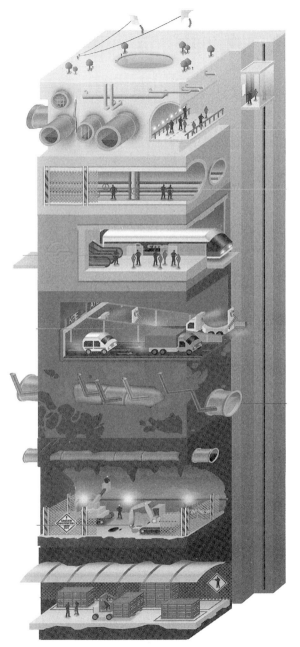

The supplemental guidance to the plan gives criteria for assessing applications for district heating, heating networks and heat pumps (Glasgow City Council, 2017b). The document cites the Scotland Heat Map (Figure 5.13). This interactive map is available online, and gives an overview of heat sources in the subsurface. It is this kind of availability of data that helps not only planners but also other professionals and the general public in identifying renewable alternatives for heating (Scottish Government, 2017).

5.3.2 Case study: Singapore

In Singapore, the drive to incorporate underground space into policy and planning started with an appeal by the prime minister, based simply on the fact that the surface space was rapidly running out. Land reclamation could solve part of the problem, but underground space could also provide a new development direction (Government of Singapore, 2009). Zhou and Zhao (2016) have presented an interesting overview of how policy and planning evolved thereafter. It started with setting up a taskforce to develop an underground masterplan for Singapore in 2007. Delivering this masterplan turned out to be a larger challenge than anticipated. According to Zhou and Zhao, several complications caused this, including the lack of 3D data on the subsurface and a mechanism to identify underground space applications and a vertical zoning framework. In the meantime, the concept of using underground space was given strategic importance by the Singapore Economic Strategies Committee in 2010. What the first attempts achieved was that all government agencies acknowledged the potential of underground space and started identifying knowledge and information gaps that required filling in. In 2012, the bi-monthly publication of the Urban Redevelopment Authority, *Skyline*, discussed the need for vertical zoning (Figure 5.14). In 2015 the Government of Singapore introduced new legislation, which prompted the State Lands Bill and the Land Acquisition Bill to be amended. The changes were motivated as follows (Singapore Ministry of Law, 2015):

> The proposed amendments are necessary to facilitate the Government's long-term planning for the use and development of underground space in the future. More extensive use of underground space in land-scarce Singapore will benefit all Singaporeans as surface land may be used for other purposes, such as parks and greenery, homes and offices.

The corresponding legislative aspects are further discussed in Chapter 8.

One of the more defining changes was reported on by Zhou (2017): he referred to a paradigm shift that makes the use of underground space the default for future major utility and infrastructure developments and compels government agencies to justify cases not using underground space. Although a comprehensive planning methodology has yet to be adopted by Singapore, the determination being shown by this city state is extraordinary.

5.3.3 Case study: the Netherlands

Two studies in the Netherlands (COB, 2003; SKB, 2012) reached the same conclusion, in that the current planning instruments used in the country allow for the introduction of the third dimension (inclusion of underground space in urban planning). Both studies also concluded that this practice was not widespread, and often depended on whether a city wants to use the instrument to protect or to allow the use of specific subsurface properties. In the case of the City of Arnhem, we have already seen that zoning was introduced to regulate the use of underground water volumes for aquifer thermal energy storage systems (see Section 1.3.3). A pilot project in the City of Maastricht showed the difficulties in identifying the spatial claims even when actively asking city departments about their demands (SKB, 2012). The National Master Plan for the Underground identifies the national demands on the subsurface. Eventually, through regional plans, these claims will need to be taken over in local zoning plans, either as regulations or reservations for future use. An important conclusion of the SKB study was that including the underground in spatial plans requires thinking about volumes rather than areas. Volumes, however, need a 3D approach. Given the current practice of mapping in two dimensions and the cost of making 3D plans, the SKB concluded that it will take some time to achieve the desired outcome. Despite this, the City of Maastricht has included the underground in its Strategic Development Plan 2030 (City of Maastricht, 2012). Within this strategic plan, it identifies the following uses of the subsurface as being essential for future planning: soil, groundwater, archaeology, energy, cables and pipelines, and glass fibre networks. The plan calls for integrating the subsurface into surface planning where the intrinsic value of the underground is a starting point for assessing possible future uses.

5.3.4 Summary of the case studies

In addition to the above cases, there are examples where the process of planning is not driven by urban planners (or started without them), or even, as was the case with PATH Toronto where urban planners pulled back, resulting in unchecked development of the underground (see Section 4.4).

In the Netherlands, the COB developed a methodology based on identifying opportunities and obstacles in the underground (Admiraal, 2006). However, the Underground Space Potential Map never caught on with planners. The reason for this could lie in that, as an instrument of analysis, it was presented at a time when urban planners were still struggling with the concept and had no clear policy directions. In Helsinki, Finland, an underground masterplan was developed, and became incorporated into the legal framework of the city. It is unclear, however, how this process took place from a methodological perspective and if replication elsewhere is possible. The process seems to be driven by geologists, and the resulting map has a conserving nature rather than being part of a larger vision on how the city will develop in the future and what role the subsurface can play in this (Ikävalko *et al.*, 2016).

These cases show that although the potential of underground spaces in urban areas is increasingly recognised, a universal planning methodology is not available. The reason for this can be found in the rich variety of legislation systems and corresponding urban planning practices worldwide. The largest obstacle remains the non-awareness of the role of the subsurface in the future of urban areas. Once this role is understood, as was shown in the cases of Glasgow and Singapore, the development of new methodologies is stimulated, or the subsurface is incorporated into the current practice, as is the case in the Netherlands. However, the single most important lesson is that urban planning is a profession in its own right. Although other disciplines can be enthusiastic about planning the underground, in theory it is the right and privilege of the urban planner to actually do so. In practice, we often see those working daily in the subsurface initiating or driving the planning process. So far, urban planners have not been trained to integrate the subsurface with surface planning. In the end, this is bound to lead to non-satisfactory results, which is why we strongly support an interdisciplinary approach, and one in which urban planners should be heavily involved, if not taking the lead.

5.4. The need for data

The planning of underground space is inter-dependent with geology and soil composition. From this, it follows that, without data on these aspects, planning becomes a difficult undertaking – at most just registering physical object present in the subsurface or plans for constructing these. As the subsurface is also a cultural heritage archive, archaeology can also play a key role. The general opinion is that this data needs to be acquired, stored digitally and made available by combining it in 3D models to support urban planning.

5.4.1 Acquisition of data

The British Geological Survey and Glasgow City Council are working together to get both public and private sector partners to collaborate in the Accessing Subsurface Knowledge (ASK) Network. The aim of the network is that of accessing subsurface knowledge, and the means to do this is by bringing together all present and future data in urban 3D models.

One of the primary reasons quoted for developing the ASK Network was 'Knowledge of the subsurface is key to delivering successful construction and regeneration projects. Poor understanding of ground conditions is widely recognised as the largest single cause of project delay as well as overspending' (Barron *et al.*, 2015). Although this might not directly seem related to urban planning, the collected data can help in creating the models that urban planners may find useful.

Geologists are, however, struggling with developing these models. No regulatory mechanism requires private parties to provide the data that they have acquired. Often, this data comes at high costs. Secondly, there is no standard format for delivering the data. Tegtmeier *et al.* (2014) identified the lack of harmonisation of information as one of the major aspects that is causing problems in creating 3D models. National geological surveys

also recognise that the data cells they use for geological information are often too coarse for specific needs in urban areas. However, refining the cells to the detailed level required dramatically increases the amount of data that needs to be stored and processed.

5.4.2 What about urban planners' needs?

Apart from data acquisition, presenting the data in 3D models for urban planners to use in their daily practice requires specific expertise from the planner that will be using it. The prevailing issue, however, is pinning down what information the urban planner requires. The current acquisition of information appears to be driven by the needs of geologists and civil engineers. This data is then compiled and presented in 3D models to urban planners, who are left to try to make sense of all the information.

5.4.3 The Deep City Project

At École Polytechnique Fédérale de Lausanne, the Deep City Project is seeking to combine all information within a decision framework based on an approach to the subsurface based on the 'sources to needs' paradigm. In effect, the methodology takes in all available data and transforms this into maps illustrating the city-wide opportunities for subsurface use related to surface use (Doyle, 2016). The method allows for an approach integrating surface and subsurface planning. Although it is still in the development phase, this approach shows promising potential in that it uses available data and considers the needs of the urban planner. Doyle concluded 'that the Deep City method is not only applicable to cities without complex models of their geology, but also to cities in both developed and developing countries'.

5.5. Urban systems integration

Hajer and Dassen (2014) proposed reconnecting the biophysical domain and the social domain in new ways. Core to this idea is unveiling the urban metabolism to identify what urban life consists of. In the light of the previous discussion, this is no small task. From the perspective of the subsurface, we can see that both disciplines and policy silos claim their stake. In many ways, the emerging awareness that the subsurface has a significant role to play in the development of our cities can result – if we are not careful – in a 'Wild West' type of territorial claim. This is what we want to avoid by planning the underground in the first place.

Can urban planning play the role of conductor in trying to orchestrate harmony in the symphonic chaos that is becoming apparent? We think that this is still possible, but a new discipline is required that assists the planner in doing so. As the urban metabolism is unveiled, including the potential of the underground, the urban systems need to be understood and, where possible, integrated. This requires an urban system integrator as part of the spatial dialogue to achieve this. By understanding the multitude of processes and systems that shape our urban existence, this integrator can identify opportunities for merging systems. In doing so, the urban system integrator can assist the urban planner in reaching the outcomes that will lead to the cities we want and the cities we need.

5.6. This chapter's core ideas

In a few cases, the pressure on surface space becomes such that the only way left to proceed is to seek the third dimension beneath the surface. Singapore and Hong Kong, among other localities, have discovered this and are actively pursuing a policy driven by political support. In other cases, the awareness of what the underground spaces below the city have to offer is lacking or dormant. Demonstrating the opportunities of the subsurface helps create necessary awareness. We have shown that, regarding policy development, underground space can contribute to at least seven of the SDGs set by the UN to be reached by 2030.

In doing so, we have also shown the attractiveness of underground space, ranging from reuse of abandoned structures to grow food below the city to contributing to the amelioration of climate change and using groundwater for heating and cooling homes. These examples illustrate not only the diversity of using the subsurface but also that it takes a cross-discipline and cross-policy spatial dialogue to lead to efficient and sustainable use.

The urban planner is key to orchestrating the spatial dialogue and taking the results forward in the urban planning process. Whether this requires sophisticated 3D modelling with a high volume of subsurface data remains to be seen. Research is showing us that the challenge can be tackled in other ways, by using and analysing the available information, and producing maps that detail the opportunities that exist below the urban surface.

Unveiling the invisible urban metabolism is needed to fully comprehend urban life and its needs, and urban system integration incorporating the subsurface can help in achieving this.

References

1   Admiraal H and Cornaro A (2016) Why underground space should be included in urban planning policy – and how this will enhance an urban underground future. *Tunnelling and Underground Space Technology* **55:** 214–220.

2   Admiraal JBM (2006) A bottom-up approach to the planning of underground space. In *Proceedings of the ITA World Tunnelling Congress, Seoul, South Korea*.

3   Barron HF, Bonsor HC, Campbell SDG *et al*. (2015) The ASK Network: developing a virtuous cycle of subsurface data and knowledge exchange. In *Geotechnical Engineering for Infrastructure and Development: XVI European Conference on Soil Mechanics and Geotechnical Engineering*. Institution of Civil Engineers, London, UK.

4   BNKR Arquitectura (2011) *Stop: Keep Moving: An Oxymoronic Approach to Architecture*. Arquine, Mexico City, Mexico.

5   Bobylev N (2013) Urban physical infrastructure adaptation to climate change. In *Global Change, Energy Issues and Regulation Policies, Integrated Science and Technology Program 2* (Saulnier JB and Varella MD (eds)). Springer, Berlin, Germany, Ch. 4.

6   Brown H (2014) *Next Generation Infrastructure: Principles for Post-industrial Public Works*. Island Press, Washington, DC, USA.

7   Chang A, Ng KW, Schmid HC *et al*. (2013) Feasibility study of Underground Science City, Singapore, Paper 2. Planning, architectural, engineering, fire safety and sustainability. In *Advances in Underground Space Development* (Zhou Y, Cai J and Sterling R (eds)). Research Publishing, Singapore.

8   City of Maastricht (2012) Structuurvisie Maastricht 2030 – Deel II. https://www.gemeentemaastricht.nl/fileadmin/files/GeMa/Doc/00_Algemeen/Structuurvisie_Maastricht_2030_Deel_II_29_mei_2012.pdf (accessed 14/11/2017). (In Dutch.)

9   COB (Centrum voor Ondergronds Bouwen) (2003) *Ondergrondse Ordening, Naar een meerdimensionale benadering van bestaande praktijken*. COB, Gouda, the Netherlands. (In Dutch.)

10 Doesburg A (2012) Car parks and playgrounds to help make Rotterdam 'climate proof'. *The Guardian*. https://www.theguardian.com/environment/2012/may/11/water-rotterdam-climate-proof (accessed 14/11/2017).

11 Doyle M (2016) *Potentialities of the Urban Volume: Mapping Underground Resource Potential and Deciphering Spatial Economies and Configurations of Multi-level Urban Spaces*. École Polytechnique Fédérale de Lausanne, Lausanne, Switzerland.

12 Glasgow City Council (2017a) Glasgow City Development Plan. https://www.glasgow.gov.uk/index.aspx?articleid=16186 (accessed 14/11/2017).

13 Glasgow City Council (2017b) City Development Plan. SG5: Resource Management. Supplementary Guidance. https://www.glasgow.gov.uk/index.aspx?articleid=20790 (accessed 14/11/2017).

14 Government of Singapore (2009) Transcript of Prime Minister Lee Hsien Loong's speech at the NTU students' union Ministerial Forum on 15 September 2009. Prime Minister's Office. http://www.pmo.gov.sg/newsroom/transcript-prime-minister-lee-hsien-loong%E2%80%99s-speech-ntu-students%E2%80%99-union-ministerial-forum (accessed 14/11/2017).

15 Hajer M and Dassen T (2014) *Slimme Steden: de opgave voor de 21e-eeuwse stedenbouw in beeld*. Nai010, Rotterdam, the Netherlands. (In Dutch.)

16 Hooimeijer FL and Maring L (2013) Ontwerpen met de ondergrond. *S+RO* **6:** 52–55. See https://repository.tudelft.nl/islandora/object/uuid:e6f9cbe9-8cc5-4a2e-b706-d32224db2191/datastream/OBJ/download (accessed 14/11/2017). (In Dutch.)

17 Ikävalko O, Satola I and Hoivanen R (2016) *Helsinki: TU1206 COST Sub-Urban WG1 Report*. COST, Brussels, Belgium. See https://sub-urban.squarespace.com/s/TU1206-WG1-007-Helsinki-City-Case-Study.pdf (accessed 14/11/2017).

18 Kashik (2012) G-Cans: Tokyo's massive underground storm drain. Amusing Planet. http://www.amusingplanet.com/2013/03/g-cans-tokyos-massive-underground-storm.html (accessed 14/11/2017).

19 Mijnwater (2017) STORM district energy controller. http://www.mijnwater.com/mijnwater-nu/storm/ (accessed 14/11/2017). (In Dutch.)

20 Plaskoff Horton R (2015) Indoor & underground urban farms growing in size and number. Urban Gardens. http://www.urbangardensweb.com/2015/10/18/indoor-underground-urban-farms-growing-in-size-and-number/ (accessed 14/11/2017).

21 Prasad N, Ranghieri F, Shah F, Trohanis Z, Kessler E and Sinha R (2009) *Climate Resilient Cities: A Primer on Reducing Vulnerabilities to Disasters*. The World Bank, Washington, DC, USA.

22 Rectory Farm (2017) Proposal. http://rectory-farm.com/proposal/ (accessed 14/11/2017).

23 Rodionova Z (2017) Inside London's first underground farm. *The Independent*. http://www.independent.co.uk/Business/indyventure/growing-underground-london-farm-food-waste-first-food-miles-a7562151.html (accessed 14/11/2017).

24 RPD (Rijksplanologische Dienst) (2000) *Ruimtelijke Verkenningen 2000. Het belang van een goede ondergrond*. Ministerie van Volkshuisvesting, Ruimtelijke Ordening en Milieu, RPD, The Hague, the Netherlands. (In Dutch.)

25 Scottish Government (2017) Scotland heat map. http://heatmap.scotland.gov.uk (accessed 14/11/2017).

26 Singapore Ministry of Law (2015) https://www.mlaw.gov.sg/content/minlaw/en/news/press-releases/legislative-changes-planning-development-underground-space.html (accessed 14/11/2017).

27 SKB (Stichting Kennisontwikkeling en Kennisoverdracht Bodem) (2012) *De ondergrond in het bestemmingsplan. SKB-project 4141R. Eindrapport*. CSO Consultancy, Maastricht, the Netherlands.

28 Tegtmeier W, Zlatanova S, Van Oosterom PJM and Hack HRGK (2014) 3D_GEM: geo-technical extension towards an integrated 3D information model for infrastructural development. *Computer and Geosciences* **64:** 126–135.

29 The World Bank (2010) *Natural Hazards, UnNatural Disasters: The Economics of Effective Prevention*. The World Bank, Washington, DC, USA.

30 UN (2017) Sustainable development goals: 17 goals to transform our world. http://www.un.org/sustainabledevelopment/sustainable-development-goals/ (accessed 14/11/2017).

31 UNISDR (UN Office for Disaster Risk Reduction) (2012) *How To Make Cities More Resilient: A Handbook for Local Government Leaders*. UNISDR, Geneva, Switzerland. See https://www.unisdr.org/we/inform/publications/54256 (accessed 14/11/2017).

32 Verhoeven R, Willems E, Harcouët-Menou V *et al.* (2014) Minewater 2.0 project in Heerlen the Netherlands: transformation of a geothermal mine water pilot project into a full scale hybrid sustainable energy infrastructure for heating and cooling. *Energy Procedia* **46:** 59–67.

33 Weytingh KR and Roovers CPAC (2007) *Visie op de ondergrond. Hoe de ondergrond kan bijdragen aan duurzame ontwikkeling*. Gemeente Zwolle, Afdeling Ruimte & Strategie, Zwolle, the Netherlands. (In Dutch.)

34 World Urban Campaign (2016) *The City We Need: Towards A New Urban Paradigm*. UN-Habitat, Nairobi, Kenya. See http://www.worldurbancampaign.org/sites/default/files/documents/tcwn2en.pdf (accessed 14/11/2017).

35 Zhou Y (2017) Advances and challenges in underground space use in Singapore. In *SRMEG Networking Night, Singapore*.

36 Zhou Y and Zhao J (2016) Advances and challenges in underground space use in Singapore. *Geotechnical Engineering* **47(3):** 85–95.

Chapter 6

Future cities – resilient cities

6.1. Resilience as a concept

All over the world there are places like New Orleans that need new approaches to cope with the reality that the future climate will be different from today's, and probably less stable. We will need a greater resilience at all scales – local, regional and global – to cope with the changes in the climate that are already occurring as we write this book.

Here, Bloomberg and Pope (2017) were writing about New Orleans and Hurricane Katrina that hit the city in 2005, and used it as an example of the need for more urban resilience.

We would like to echo that sentiment. As we write this book, we are aware of the challenges that natural and human-made hazards are bringing to cities. The definition of resilience itself is not one people argue about: it is the ability and capacity of urban areas to bounce back socially and economically after being hit by a freak event. Resilience as a concept is linked to the fact that more and more people on this planet are living in denser areas. At any given moment, more people than ever before are being threatened by local events, whether a storm, freak rainfall or an enduring heatwave. In the 100 Resilient Cities Campaign, the Rockefeller Foundation went even further in identifying challenges that cities face and need to become resilient to. The threat of cyber-attacks becomes more plausible each day, and could severely disrupt city life. In this case, the Rockefeller Foundation (2017) chose a broad approach to resilience, not just defining it as a response to natural hazards:

We live in a world of increasing dynamism and volatility, where technology and greater interconnectedness have accelerated change and altered the way people live. Resilience is the capacity of individuals, communities and systems to survive, adapt, and grow in the face of stress and shocks, and even transform when conditions require it. Building resilience is about making people, communities and systems better prepared to withstand catastrophic events — both natural and manmade — and able to bounce back more quickly and emerge stronger from these shocks and stresses.

Urban resilience is also at the core of the objectives managed by the UN Office for Disaster

Risk Reduction (UNISDR), which is mandated with this task based on the Sendai Framework. The UNISDR works together with cities and non-governmental organisations in the Making Cities Resilient – My City is Getting Ready! campaign. In a recently published handbook for local government leaders, one of the essentials for urban resilience was identified as 'pursue resilient urban development and design' (UNISDR, 2012). The rationale for this essential is described there as

> Pursuing resilient urban development based on risk-informed urban plans is essential to reducing current disaster risks and the prevention of future ones. Participatory urban planning processes and focus on vulnerable groups will not only decrease risk and facilitate the implementation of urban plans, but will also help in attaining equitable and sustainable development of urban communities.

We feel that in this light the subsurface plays two roles that need to be addressed when it comes to urban resilience: the first is that of a possible stressor in the sense that, beneath the surface, there could be acting processes that will threaten the city (or parts of the city) over time. A deeper knowledge of local geology will help to identify these processes and create the possibility of counteracting them, or at least helping with preparations in the event that they should act on the city. We will look at these more specifically in Section 6.2.

The second role that the subsurface can play is that of an asset. The use of underground space could help alleviate some of the stresses acting on the city and play a role in urban resilience in the aftermath of an event. This role will be explored in a bit more depth later on.

What urban resilience, as a concept, is bringing to the table is the understanding that not only are people living and working in dense urban areas, which makes them vulnerable to more and more events that are hard to control, but also how preparing for these events or trying to counteract the worst effects is something that can be done. An example of this could be as simple as updating local building codes to reflect changing wind conditions that act on surface buildings. Coping with the urban heat island effect might require a much broader strategy, which will affect urban planning and how land is used within the city boundaries.

It is at this point that we need to start to appreciate the urban complexity we discussed earlier and the fact that urban underground space is part of that complexity. Although in certain situations it could contribute to the threats facing a city, more often we will see that it can be part of the solutions a city can look at in terms of counteracting or as an element of disaster relief management.

Brown (2014) has directed us towards a post-industrial paradigm for infrastructure that could help us to find solutions for making cities resilient:

> Whereas the legacy of industrial-era infrastructure is one of independent, single-purpose assets and 'non-reimbursed', or one-way flows, post-industrial solutions are modeled on the multifunctional, closed-loop exchanges characteristic of

natural eco-systems … systems should be multipurpose, interconnected, and, ideally, synergistic.

When it comes to creating the cities of the future, cities that are resilient for their citizens, we need to look at solutions based on what Brown called the 'first principle of the post-industrial paradigm'. We need to look at multipurpose, interconnected and synergistic systems. Doing that by looking at integrating surface and subsurface development, based on the need for urban resilience, could prove to be a valuable contribution to the conundrum our cities are facing.

6.2. The threatening subsurface

The biggest and most well-known threat of how the subsurface can be a liability for cities over time is, of course, earthquakes. These are natural phenomena but, as we explored in Section 2.2, human intervention can cause artificial earthquakes, as is the case with gas extraction. The collapse of old mine galleries or shafts can also cause subsidence at the surface through sinkholes. Underground works on new metro lines can cause damage, as was the case at a busy junction in Fukuoka, Japan. The sinkhole caused a lot of disruption but was repaired within 1 week (Katz, 2016). This would have been a far more severe incident if the sinkhole had caused buildings to collapse.

The biggest challenge we face when it comes to the subsurface as a liability is that data is often not available to assess whether a threat exists or not. Processes below the surface have a different time scale from life at the surface.

It can take many years for brownfield pollution to reach groundwater; however, once it does, the possibility of contamination and the effect of that on drinking water supplies could be enormous. As cities become more dependent on the ecosystem services that the subsurface delivers, the greater the insight that is required to protect those services.

Integrating the subsurface into urban planning, as we have argued for, will solve some of these concerns; however, it is human interventions from the past that were never documented that can raise concerns. Historical evidence of human activity below the surface of the city must be taken seriously and investigated thoroughly to determine whether this could be threatening in the future.

Resilient cities can bounce back from the stresses they face. Preventing those stresses from occurring or being prepared for them requires an extensive understanding of urban geology, interventions by humans and the existing physical constructions. A potential threat analysis can only be made once this has been charted and collated into a model of the urban subsurface.

Urban resilience is another argument as to why cities need to be considering their underground space, and use that knowledge in urban planning. As we saw from the unexpected and very disruptive earthquakes induced by human activity in the Netherlands, interventions can have unforeseen effects in the long term. When looking at the use of the subsurface for energy purposes, this also needs to be considered. While acknowledging the enormous potential of the subsurface for geothermal applications and aquifer thermal energy storage schemes, we also need to be confident that what we view now as green power sources will not result in future hidden brownfields. As the subsurface requires a balance between exploration and preservation, as pointed out before, this balance could prove to be vital in terms of urban resilience in certain cases.

6.3. Challenges for urban areas

The definition of urban resilience is somewhat dependent on what school of thought is followed. In Section 6.1, we saw that the Rockefeller Foundation has the broadest vision when it comes to resilient cities. In terms of resilience, it distinguishes between chronic stresses and acute shocks. Chronic stresses are, in its vision, 'slow moving disasters that weaken the fabric of a city', and acute shocks are 'sudden, sharp events that threaten a city' (100 Resilient Cities, 2017).

Bloomberg and Pope (2017) identified the following threats to cities: rain, heat, disease and drought. The warning has sounded: what may have been considered freak events up to now are turning into the new normal. We would add wind actions to this short list: wind being another event that plays havoc within urban areas.

In 2011, *Newsweek* reported that 'the reality of global climate change is upon us' (Begley, 2011). The story impressed in that it tried to convince readers that freak weather events are, in actuality, part of an emerging pattern due to climate change: 'Even those who deny the existence of global climate change are having trouble dismissing the evidence of the last year. In the U.S. alone, nearly 1,000 tornadoes have ripped across the heartland, killing more than 500 people and inflicting $9 billion in damage.'

Figure 6.1 shows the number of climate-related disasters in the period 1980–2011 on a global scale. We can observe a clear increase in the number of disasters year on year. This increase was also confirmed by the insurance company Munich RE (2017), which reported that by the end of June 2017 its database had recorded '350 loss-relevant natural catastrophes, less than the previous year's figures (390) but more than the ten-year average (310)'. The same report also highlighted the unpredictability of changing weather patterns, so much so that, in 2017, hail and thunderstorms caused significant damages in the USA: 'A series of hailstorms and tornadoes in the USA dominated the natural catastrophe statistics in the first half of 2017.

Figure 6-1 The number of climate-related disasters (1980–2011) | © 2018 United Nations, reprinted with the permission of the United Nations.

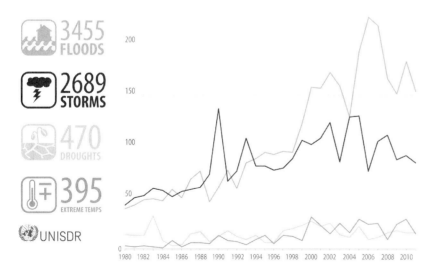

A total of six severe, large-scale thunderstorms were recorded, each causing billions of dollars of losses.'

What all this illustrates is that natural hazards are increasing in occurrence and are impacting society. They have the potential for severe loss of life, disrupting city life and inflicting major costs.

Let's take a closer look at these natural hazards. Rainfall is one that is having significant effects at present. Rather than talking about rain, we need to look at precipitation in general, which includes hail. Cities that have been built over recent decades have a singular aspect in common: the abundance of hardened surfaces. Whether concrete, asphalt pavements or paving stones, surfaces have been hardened, as this serves the primary purpose of city life: mobility. Without streets and parking lots, city life would grind to a halt. As our daily lives became ever busier, there is less time for chores such as gardening, and paving our gardens became part of the drive towards efficiency. What nobody realised was the impact that this would have in terms of diminishing the natural infiltration of rainwater. Firstly, it meant run-off of rainwater into our sewer systems and overstretching the capacity of our water treatment plants. Secondly, the lack of natural infiltration may lead to groundwater tables lowering and soils drying out. As with most hazards, we can observe that there is a short-term direct impact, and a more long-term impact following it. It is the latter we most often overlook, as these are often slow processes taken for granted until the real damage begins to show. In that sense, the initial impact could be seen as an acute shock, causing a chronic stress in the long term. As precipitation increases, and more specifically as the intensity of each event increases, the potential of sewers overflowing and urban areas being flooded becomes a reality.

Drought is the direct opposite of increased precipitation. The lack of water is threatening our cities as well. The consequences of drought include lack of drinking water, failing crops, wildfires, and flash floods once rainfall does occur. Drought is associated with heat, and, as global temperatures rise, this is also affecting our cities. The hardened surfaces and the abundance of concrete in urban areas mean that our cities have the capacity to soak up heat and retain it. Soaking up and retaining heat causes urban areas to be hotter than surrounding rural areas on average, and to remain hotter – that is, to cool less rapidly. This effect is known as the urban heat island, and has been directly related to causing health problems and loss of life during prolonged heat waves.

Storms are causing major problems, both as a single event and in combination with other events. It is these combinations of events that are compounding the challenges that cities are facing. Drought followed by a storm causes dust storms, and, when rain falls, flash floods can follow.

What this all adds up to is that we need to rethink how we shape our cities. Already we are discovering that relatively simple solutions can go a long way in coping with these challenges. There are, however, more far-reaching consequences as well. Building codes need to be updated to take into account changing weather patterns. Cities that have never had

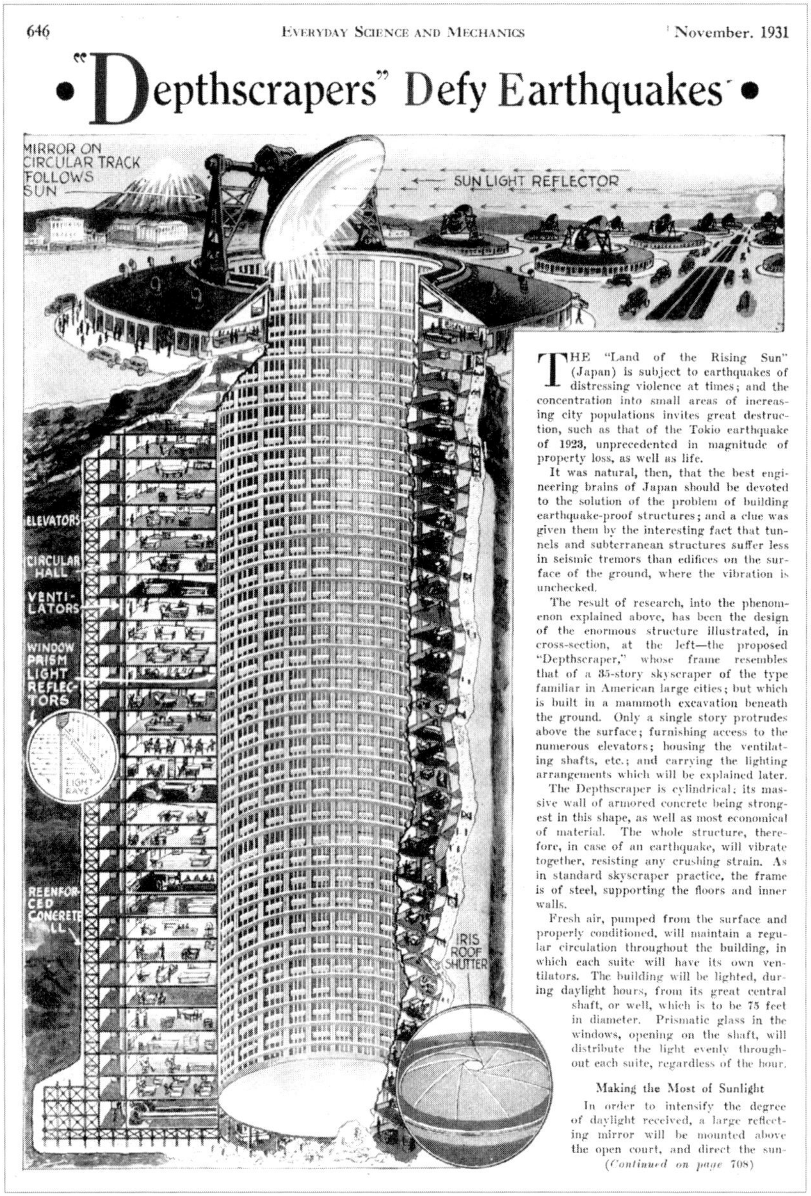

Figure 6-2 The 'Depthscraper' – a page from *Everyday Science and Mechanics*, November 1931

646   EVERYDAY SCIENCE AND MECHANICS   November. 1931

"Depthscrapers" Defy Earthquakes

MIRROR ON CIRCULAR TRACK FOLLOWS SUN

SUN LIGHT REFLECTOR

ELEVATORS

CIRCULAR HALL

VENTILATORS

WINDOW PRISM LIGHT REFLECTORS

LIGHT RAYS

REENFORCED CONCRETE WALL

IRIS ROOF SHUTTER

THE "Land of the Rising Sun" (Japan) is subject to earthquakes of distressing violence at times; and the concentration into small areas of increasing city populations invites great destruction, such as that of the Tokio earthquake of 1923, unprecedented in magnitude of property loss, as well as life.

It was natural, then, that the best engineering brains of Japan should be devoted to the solution of the problem of building earthquake-proof structures; and a clue was given them by the interesting fact that tunnels and subterranean structures suffer less in seismic tremors than edifices on the surface of the ground, where the vibration is unchecked.

The result of research, into the phenomenon explained above, has been the design of the enormous structure illustrated, in cross-section, at the left—the proposed "Depthscraper," whose frame resembles that of a 35-story skyscraper of the type familiar in American large cities; but which is built in a mammoth excavation beneath the ground. Only a single story protrudes above the surface; furnishing access to the numerous elevators; housing the ventilating shafts, etc.; and carrying the lighting arrangements which will be explained later.

The Depthscraper is cylindrical; its massive wall of armored concrete being strongest in this shape, as well as most economical of material. The whole structure, therefore, in case of an earthquake, will vibrate together, resisting any crushing strain. As in standard skyscraper practice, the frame is of steel, supporting the floors and inner walls.

Fresh air, pumped from the surface and properly conditioned, will maintain a regular circulation throughout the building, in which each suite will have its own ventilators. The building will be lighted, during daylight hours, from its great central shaft, or well, which is to be 75 feet in diameter. Prismatic glass in the windows, opening on the shaft, will distribute the light evenly throughout each suite, regardless of the hour.

Making the Most of Sunlight

In order to intensify the degree of daylight received, a large reflecting mirror will be mounted above the open court, and direct the sun—

(Continued on page 708)

to cope with rainfall and have no urban water management schemes now, all of a sudden, have to face up to the fact they need to deal with a lot of water over short periods during the year.

We will look at solutions, and particularly at how underground space can help to meet some of these major challenges that the cities of the future have to face. In our opinion, the use of underground space can play a significant role in alleviating the pressures caused by acute shocks and chronic stresses to the urban system.

6.4. Meeting the challenges using underground space

In 1923, Tokyo was hit by a large earthquake, which caused enormous loss of life and damage to the city. According to the magazine *Everyday Science and Mechanics* (1931):

> It was natural, then, that the best engineering brains of Japan should be devoted to the solution of the problem of building earthquake-proof structures; and a clue was given them by the interesting fact that tunnels and subterranean structures suffer less in seismic tremors than edifices on the surface of the ground, where the vibration is unchecked.

The proposal that came out of this research was to build a colossal 'depthscraper' (Figure 6.2), which in some ways bears a striking resemblance to the earthscraper (see Section 5.2) and the way that daylight is brought into the Lowline (see Section 7.2).

Although the depthscraper has stayed a concept just like the earthscraper, the core finding that underground space structures are much less susceptible to earthquakes than surface structures remains valid. This point is further supported by the conclusions of the US National Research Council (2013) with regard to the 1989 Loma Prieta earthquake in the San Francisco Bay Area:

> Underground transportation systems can remain operational during, or quickly resume operation following, natural hazardous events such as earthquakes, tornadoes, lightning, and thick fog or dust conditions. According to a review of several studies documenting earthquake damage, large diameter underground tunnels have historically suffered less damage than surface structures.

Specifically, regarding the Bay Area Rapid Transport System (BART), the report states that 'This system improved disaster resilience for this urban area following the Loma Prieta earthquake in 1989 by allowing the continued functioning of the economies of these communities.'

In comparison with the San Francisco–Oakland Bay Bridge, which was closed for repairs for a month after the earthquake hit, BART services resumed within half a day after the event (US National Research Council, 2013).

These examples not only show us that underground structures have a certain resilience when it comes to earthquakes, they also point towards the possibility of underground transport infrastructure being used as part of the disaster relief effort after an earthquake.

Where surface infrastructure is often severely damaged and impossible to use due to debris, the underground transport infrastructure could prove to be a lifeline for reaching devastated areas. The BART case clearly demonstrates the economic significance of operational public transport soon after an event has occurred.

When Hurricane Sandy hit New York City in 2012, it flooded vast areas of the city, including the subway system; this could be seen as a sign that such systems are not very resilient when it comes to flooding. However, what many people are not aware of is that ingress of water did not cause flooding of the New York subway system through street level ventilation vents or street level access to the system. According to Diaz (2012), the New York City subway at the time 'relied on 700 fragile pumps' to keep the system from flooding on an average day. When these pumps were taken out by Sandy, the system became flooded through groundwater ingress – the flood waters only adding to the speed with which flooding took place.

In Thailand, Bangkok is used to rainfall and flooding. As a direct result, the Bangkok mass rapid transit system (MRT) was designed with this in mind. Entrances to the MRT are all raised above street level to prevent flood water from entering the system, much as is standard practice in Japan. It has proven to be an effective measure in preventing these systems from flooding.

Mega-cities such as Tokyo and Kuala Lumpur have to find new ways to cope with flooding due to rainfall. The Stormwater Management and Road Tunnel (SMART) in Kuala Lumpur (see Section 5.1.7) and the vast cavern build in Tokyo (see Section 5.1.8) both deal with excessive flood water in different ways. Where SMART acts as an underground river allowing the flood water to run off and bypass the city, the cavern in Tokyo serves as an intermediate storage facility and is later pumped empty after the event has passed. This storage is reminiscent of the underground car park and retention basin facility found in Rotterdam, the Netherlands (see Section 5.1.8).

A further strategy that can be deployed as part of urban water management is to increase blue and green areas. Ponds and lakes can work as catchment facilities, and green areas allow natural infiltration. Sunken plazas used for recreational activities can also be used as temporary overflow facilities. These examples show the need for open spaces in urban areas, and how these can be created by transferring surface uses to the subsurface. The example of Madrid Rio illustrates this, in the way it allowed new green public space to be created (see Section 2.4).

The climate in cities can play havoc with city life. According to Whyte (1988), climate provides the context through which we can understand the reasons for creating underground plazas such as those in Montreal and Minneapolis (see Section 7.2). Research is now suggesting that, with the average temperature rising and extreme heat events occurring more regularly, the urban heat island effect is starting to affect life in our cities. The US Environmental Protection Agency has stated that 'Air temperatures in cities, particularly after sunset, can be as much as 22°F (12°C) warmer than the air in neighboring, less developed regions' (US EPA, 2017). This leads to all kinds of effects such as increased energy

demand for cooling and increased smog in cities. The urban heat island effect 'can affect human health by contributing to general discomfort, respiratory difficulties, heat cramps and exhaustion, non-fatal heat stroke, and heat-related mortality' (US EPA, 2017). Overall, the effect on human health is quite significant, as the US EPA (2017) found:

Excessive heat events, or abrupt and dramatic temperature increases, are particularly dangerous and can result in above-average rates of mortality. The Centers for Disease Control and Prevention estimates that from 1979–2003, excessive heat exposure contributed to more than 8,000 premature deaths in the United States. This figure exceeds the number of mortalities resulting from hurricanes, lightning, tornadoes, floods, and earthquakes combined.

A study by Rajagopalan et al. (2014) reported on the impact the layout of the urban fabric could have on preventing wind flow from reducing the urban heat island effect. They found, for the city of Muara, Malaysia, that 'the chaotic development in Muara caused reduced ventilation in urban canyons. Combination of tall buildings and narrow streets entrap heat and reduce the air flow, resulting in high temperatures.'

When it comes to the urban heat island effect, there are two main mitigation strategies. The first is to green the city by creating more parks, planting trees or covering buildings with green roofs. The second strategy is to carefully consider how fresh winds from, for example, the sea at night or from high mountains can flow into the city uninterruptedly, and thus help to cool it.

Both strategies require surface space to be reserved – surface space that cannot be built on for other uses. The use of underground space to compensate for this or purposely freeing up surface space could be part of these strategies. It goes without saying that, in cities suffering from extreme heat, following the example of Montreal and creating an underground city would contribute enormously to maintaining liveability.

Droughts can severely affect human life through loss of crops and shortage of drinking water. The lack of drinking water is by far the more global problem, with some estimating that, for as many as 1 billion people, clean drinking water is scarce (The Water Project, 2017).

In 2015, *The Guardian* newspaper reported on the global water shortage, and highlighted the problems in São Paulo (McKie, 2015):

> Last week in the Brazilian city of São Paulo, home to 20 million people, and once known as the City of Drizzle, drought got so bad that residents began drilling through basement floors and car parks to try to reach groundwater. City officials warned last week that rationing of supplies was likely soon. Citizens might have access to water for only two days a week, they added.

The story quotes Jean Chrétien, the former Canadian prime minister and co-chair of the InterAction Council, as saying, 'The future political impact of water scarcity may be devastating. Using water the way we have in the past simply will not sustain humanity in future.'

In Section 5.1.3 we discussed the importance of the subsurface for drinking water. Radical new strategies will be required to access groundwater as a new supply of drinking water. This new supply can only be sustainable if the hydrological cycle remains intact. The natural infiltration of rainwater and the filtering capacity of the subsurface provide drinking water, which puts an additional strain on urban planners to consider this and to carefully look at water aquifers that could be present below cities to provide a strategic reserve of drinking water for the future.

This leads to the question of whether drinking water will in the future become so scarce that it becomes a commodity – much as we now extract crude oil from the subsurface and ship it around the world to refineries. Indeed, Tully (2000) foresaw this when he wrote 'Water promises to be to the 21st century what oil was to the 20th century: the precious commodity that determines the wealth of nations.'

Drought, due to shifting climate patterns, is causing concern across the globe, and, in a world already struggling to deliver drinking water to all, this is making the challenge of access to drinking water greater. The total amount of fresh water on our planet is more than sufficient. The difficulty is that 99% of that water is trapped as groundwater below the surface and not readily accessible (McKie, 2015).

Future cities will need to consider this, and move away from surface water reservoirs as the primary supply of drinking water. Looking below the surface could well prove to be a valid option in the long term.

Hurricanes and cyclones are on the increase and turning into the new normal rather than being freak events. The 2017 hurricanes Irma and Maria left a trail of devastation over the Caribbean and Southern Florida, and the news reports are testaments to the impact of this kind of natural disaster (Ahmed, 2017):

> The woman carried a small suitcase, enough for her and her child to try to start over. The arduous passage to evacuate her broken island was nearly done – through the chaos of a port filled with capsized boats, the traffic-choked drive lined with buildings and homes torn from their foundations, and the desperation of the masses at the airport, hoping to flee the wreckage as armed soldiers kept order. But as the evacuees finally prepared to board their flight, the airline announced that they could not take their suitcases with them. The woman, a civil servant, fell apart. 'I can't take it anymore,' she screamed, crumpling onto the tarmac and pounding it with both hands. Her home destroyed, her child forced to seek even the most basic things elsewhere, her country reckoning with the staggering task of rebuilding and, in the much more immediate term, simply surviving. A soldier rushed to comfort the woman while her daughter broke into tears, fighting with the attendant to keep her mother's bag,

a final indignity in a world stripped of its moorings.

The destruction and human misery caused by nature's forces unleashed are a poignant reminder for the need to consider resilience to these disasters as much as to preparedness and recovery. For us, the question is whether underground space can help in making cities, towns and communities more resilient against these forces.

In Chapter 3 we discussed the yaodongs in China – houses sunk into the Earth. The reason why humans started to excavate these dwellings lies in the fact that the plateau where they are found is turned into an inhospitable environment by wind. Wind-proofing these communities was achieved by constructing earth-covered houses, with the covering providing shelter from the prevailing wind direction. Although earth-covered houses have advantages over typical surface dwellings and are very sustainable, the main benefit in this case would be the shelter they can provide from hurricanes. In cities with a developed use of underground space, it goes without saying that shelter from the weather, including hurricanes, can be provided by underground transport systems and shopping malls.

We feel this is an area of underground space use that requires more research in the coming years. Just as Whyte (1988) was unsure about the concept of underground plazas, we do not see underground space as prime real estate for living in the future. At the same time, we need to be realistic in that we are living in a change of eras rather than in a time of change. New paradigms need to be found for creating cities that are resilient, provide their citizens with safety and shelter, and can bounce back after hazards strike: this may require us to look with more than glancing interest at the subsurface. A yet to be published 'Words into Action' report by the UNISDR as part of the development of the Sendai Framework (Narang Suri et al., 2018) states the following:

> The above notwithstanding, urban development and infrastructure projects can build disaster resilience in the following ways … Design large scale underground spaces (e.g. car parking, tunnels, etc.) so they can serve a variety of DRR functions (e.g. as temporary water retention basins, as refuges) while also providing efficient access for servicing dense urban building blocks with water, energy and waste removal services.

This is one example of how the thinking on disaster risk reduction and urban planning is not only developing but incorporating the use of underground space, including providing refuge for storm events.

It's historical fact that humanity started with two basic concepts for habitation: the cave and the tent. Throughout history, humans have been building tents on the surface, and continue to do so. We may well find that the chronic stresses and acute shocks that cities face going into the future require us to start building more caves. In the end, forces at the surface might become such that tents can no longer withstand them, and caves will provide the resilient habitats for humanity to survive.

6.5. This chapter's core ideas

According to Bloomberg and Pope (2017), 'we will need a greater resilience at all scales' for our cities moving toward the future. They see the changing climate as the primary driver for the need for resilience. The 100 Resilient Cities Campaign, supported by the Rockefeller Foundation, approaches urban resilience from a broader perspective, identifying chronic stresses and acute shocks as drivers.

Underground space and urban resilience have an interesting relationship. On the one hand, the subsurface itself can produce acute shocks or chronic stresses. On the other hand, underground space could prove to be a major asset when it comes to looking at mitigating measures.

Earthquakes are a good example of acute shocks that can act on the urban environment. At the same time, past human activities below the surface, be it mining or storage of waste, could, over time, prove to be chronic stresses, in that, left unchecked, they could cause adverse effects such as sinkholes or contamination of groundwater. The latter could easily lead to drinking water supplies being polluted for years to come. We concluded that it is essential for cities to realise that the subsurface has a role in urban resilience. Good data and mapping of that data are required, to provide insights to urban planners for them to act on.

In accord with Bloomberg and Pope, we believe that climate change is a major threat to our cities. Precipitation, heat, drought and storms are transitioning from freak events to becoming the new normal. Cities have to take measures to cope with these effects. The urban heat island effect and the potential for flooding after intense rainfall are the most worrying threats, in that they are, for the moment, only chronic stresses, and slowly showing their potential disruptive power. Both are caused by the urban fabric itself – overwhelmingly by hardened surfaces and the use of heat-absorbing materials for our buildings.

The use of underground space can help cities in meeting some of these challenges. For one there is a definite need to free up surface space to create new blue and green areas. These areas will help to reduce the urban heat island effect and create additional capacity for the intermediate storage of rainwater. The biggest effect can be found when combining uses – a storm water tunnel also being used for road traffic, or an underground car park that is also a water retention basin. These combinations of uses are, in our opinion, the way forward to finding solutions. We need to leave the era of mono-use of land and look towards a new era where multi-use maximises the use we can make of the available space, both at and below the surface.

Urban resilience is key to creating the cities of the future. Understanding and using underground space is key to achieving it.

References

1   100 Resilient Cities (2017) What is urban resilience? http://www.100resilientcities.org/resources/#section-1 (accessed 14/11/2017).

2   Ahmed A (2017) Hurricane Irma: a week on from the deadly storm and St Martin residents are struggling to survive. _The Independent._ http://www.independent.co.uk/news/world/americas/hurricane-irma-latest-st-martin-caribbean-residents-struggle-to-survive-a-week-on-a7949921.html (accessed 14/11/2017).

3   Begley S (2011) The reality of global climate change is upon us. _Newsweek._ http://www.newsweek.com/reality-global-climate-change-upon-us-67757 (accessed 14/11/2017).

4   Bloomberg M and Pope C (2017) _Climate of Hope._ St Martin's Press, New York, NY, USA.

5   Brown H (2014) _Next Generation Infrastructure: Principles for Post-industrial Public Works._ Island Press, Washington, DC, USA.

6   Diaz J (2012) Hurricane Sandy could really flood the New York subway system. Gizmodo. https://www.gizmodo.com.au/2012/10/hurricane-sandy-could-really-flood-the-new-york-subway-system/ (accessed 14/11/2017).

7   _Everyday Science and Mechanics_ (1931) 'Depthscrapers' defy earthquakes. _Everyday Science and Mechanics_, Nov.: pp. 646, 708.

8   Katz A (2016) That 'unprecedented' sinkhole in Japan? It's already fixed. _Time._ http://time.com/4571934/japan-massive-sinkhole-fixed/ (accessed 14/11/2017).

9   McKie R (2015) Why fresh water shortages will cause the next great global crisis. _The Guardian._ https://www.theguardian.com/environment/2015/mar/08/how-water-shortages-lead-food-crises-conflicts (accessed 14/11/2017).

10 Munich RE (2017) Press release. Natural catastrophe review for the first half of 2017: a series of powerful thunderstorms in the USA causes large losses. https://www.munichre.com/en/media-relations/publications/press-releases/2017/2017-

07-18-press-release/index.html (accessed 14/11/2017).

11 Narang Suri S, Brennan S, Johnson C and Lipietz B (2018) *Developing the Sendai Framework Words into Action: Implementation Guide on Land Use and Urban Planning*. UN Office for Disaster Risk Reduction, Geneva, Switzerland. (In preparation.)

12 Rajagopalan P, Lim KC and Jamei E (2014) Urban heat island and wind flow characteristics of a tropical city. *Solar Energy (Supplement C)* **107:** 159–170.

13 Rockefeller Foundation (2017) Resilience. https://www.rockefellerfoundation.org/our-work/topics/resilience/ (accessed 14/11/2017).

14 The Water Project (2017) Water scarcity & the importance of water. https://thewaterproject.org/water-scarcity/ (accessed 14/11/2017).

15 Tully S (2000) Water, water everywhere. *Fortune*. http://archive.fortune.com/magazines/fortune/fortune_archive/2000/05/15/279789/index.htm (accessed 14/11/2017).

16 UNISDR (2012) *How To Make Cities More Resilient: A Handbook for Local Government Leaders*. UNISDR, Geneva, Switzerland. See https://www.unisdr.org/we/inform/publications/54256 (accessed 14/11/2017).

17 US Environmental Protection Agency (2017) Heat island impacts: compromised human health and comfort. https://www.epa.gov/heat-islands/heat-island-impacts#health (accessed 14/11/2017).

18 US National Research Council (2013) *Underground Engineering For Sustainable Urban Development*. National Academies Press, Washington, DC, USA.

19 Whyte WH (1988) *City: Rediscovering the Center*. University of Pennsylvania Press, Philadelphia, PA, USA.

Chapter 7

Building for people – valued underground spaces

7.1. Loveable spaces

The urbanist William Whyte (1988) was highly critical when it came to underground spaces:

> The war against the street gains force. Not only have planners and architects been lining it with blank walls and garages; they have been levelling blocks of old buildings for parking lots, de-mapping streets for megastructures. Now they are going the next step. They are taking the principal functions of the street and putting them almost anywhere but on street level. They are putting them in underground concourses and shopping malls, in skyways and upper level galleries. Ultimately, they may get the pedestrian off the street altogether.

What Whyte feared was, as he called it, the 'dullification' of the street. In his view, and that of Jane Jacobs, the street 'is the river of life of the city, the place where we come together, the pathway to the center. It is the primary place' (Whyte, 1988). According to him, any actions that take pedestrians from the street will sentence the streets of a city to disuse, to become dull, and, with that, the city will become dull.

When it comes to underground space, the shape of the spaces is very much determined by local geology. Countries such as Sweden, Finland, Hong Kong and, to a large extent, Singapore all share a solid rock geology, allowing them to create human-made caverns of vast dimensions. When boring tunnels through relatively soft soils, as in the Netherlands, the bigger the tunnel-boring machine, the costlier the project. This simple factor then drives engineers to look at the 'envelope of space' that the project requires, often determined by the size of the carriages that have to pass through the system. The size of the tunnel, together with the circular shape, seems to have historically determined the size and shape of the platforms and the station corridors, as we can see from metro systems worldwide. Efficiency in engineering and construction, but also in transiting people as quickly from the surface to the train and vice versa, determine the shape and layout of underground stations (Admiraal and Cornaro, 2017).

As Whyte pointed out,

> The surrogate streets the most rooted in function have been the underground concourses. Originally, they came about as adjuncts to the

underground rail systems. They were geared to the movement of great numbers of people in very short periods of time. They still are, and save for the introduction of escalators – pioneered by the London Underground – their physical characteristics have not changed very much.

For Whyte, there is a natural progression in all of this. The efficient people-moving surrogate street, extending to nearby building developments – what was to all intents and purposes meant to be a 'transportation corridor' – started to feature 'shops along its spine and was connected with a sunken plaza at one end' (Whyte, 1988). These sunken plazas are the basement developments that are now so familiar in cities worldwide. The natural progression continued after this, with 'concourses as ends in themselves – connected with rail and subway stations, perhaps, but providing complete environments, with a range of shops and service facilities, restaurants and meeting places' (Whyte, 1988).

Whyte observed that there is always a specific context within which this all works, for example in cities such as Minneapolis and Montreal. The context of these examples is the foul weather as the primary reason for developing underground. That reason does not always exist for other cities, which, nevertheless, started to copy these underground developments, with the direct result that streets become empty as city life went below the surface within the edifices of consumerism.

On top of all this, Whyte had other issues as well: 'How good is the substitute?', he asked. 'If the planners had to spend some time in their underground utopias, they might have second thoughts. The underground spaces are, among other things, disorienting'. He mentioned the architects' like for symmetry as another problem that these concourses have, as well as controlling the climate within them. According to him, there is an absence of high-end retail shops that do not seem to favour lingering in basements below the surface. But it is not all doom and gloom. Whyte does like Montreal's Place Ville Marie. He specifically mentioned the way that daylight is 'brought into the complex through small courtyards leading to a broad plaza above.'

We feel that it is important to note that development of underground spaces is not a means to an end in itself. We advocate the creation of spaces that add to the city rather than distract. Underground spaces need to become part of the city's fabric rather than being just an 'aggregate of segments' or even an 'encompassing network with every building linked to every other', as Whyte typifies them. We agree in principle with Whyte that the development of underground space should be part of the urban fabric and complement it, even if a new urban tissue is created below the surface. We also agree with his observation that underground spaces should not be disorienting: they need daylight, and climate control is essential. To all intents and purposes, underground spaces need to be loveable spaces that people enjoy using. They should provide individuals with new experiences that bring enjoyment to city life. Even though they have a functional purpose, this should not distract from the sheer pleasure of being in a beautiful space. The design of underground spaces should in that sense look more to the requirements of public spaces – that is, spaces designed for people to enjoy and meet each other. These spaces will then give off a vibrancy that adds to city life. It brings the city to life, and although underground spaces might not be the main river of life the runs through the city, they should be major tributaries adding life to that river.

There is a caveat to all this, and that is that we need to plan in such a way that the balance is maintained between surface and subsurface life. As Whyte put it, 'The biggest problem posed by skyways and concourses is not that they will fail to function but that they will function too well.' We also need to design underground spaces in such a way that they become spaces for people, loveable spaces adding to the liveability and inclusiveness of the city.

The Beurstraverse sunken shopping street in Rotterdam, the Netherlands, is a good example of this. As Figure 7.1 shows, its design incorporates features that people automatically associate with the surface: trees and water. We already saw in Section 4.3 that the layout of the Beurstraverse is such that it is a street that functions irrespective of the opening times of shops or the operating hours of the metro. See how the children are obviously enjoying themselves with the surprise water feature that suddenly pops up and then disappears again. It transforms this underground street into a place of sheer enjoyment, a place where you want to be. It becomes a place that you might make a detour to because the kids demand it, much in the way that playgrounds at fast-food chains or Scandinavian furniture stores are there to attract children and make parents buy as they play. In this case, the point is that, by including some straightforward features, what could have been just a functional passageway is transformed into a public space that adds to the city fabric. The tree, according to Whyte, is one of the best ways to make space more habitable. Research has shown that the absence of greenery, in general, has an adverse effect on health in cities. The lack of being able to connect with nature below the surface has been noted by Lee *et al.* (2017): 'By incorporating greenery into the design of underground structures, the loss of contact with nature can be compromised. Such a measure will promote the physical and psychological well-being of the underground community.'

Figure 7-1 Beurstraverse Rotterdam with tree and water as attractors for public space | Courtesy of G. Lanting (top), reproduced under CC BY-SA 4.0 and courtesy of Tom de Rooij (bottom)

The tree is an essential element of making underground spaces habitable, as is known from the longstanding practice of planting a tree in the courtyard of yaodongs (see Section 3.1, Figure 3.1).

The Metropolitan Transportation Authority in New York City has an extensive programme called Arts for Transit. Whyte (1988) described it as an offshoot of the City Walls programme that came about through the enthusiasm of Doris Freedman, and also led to the Percent for Art programme. Whyte comments on how the Arts for Transit and the Music Under New York programmes were set up to support the notion that the subway was getting better. In his words, 'The subways actually are getting better but this is not enough. People have to think they are.' In our opinion, this might have been the principal reason for starting these programmes, but they do so much more for underground spaces. The art below the surface is not just there to entice people; it does away with the solely functional corridors stemming from the Victorian age. Involving artists in enhancing the habitability of underground spaces is making use of that inherent aspect of underground spaces: blank walls that can act as a canvas for the creative arts (Figure 7.2). It is a tradition that can be traced back to the early cave paintings, when early civilisations discovered that they could express themselves by leaving images on the walls of their underground shelters. The blank canvas is the single biggest difference between underground spaces and buildings, where the use of glass to create transparency has left little or no room to hang paintings or other decorations.

Lee *et al.* (2017) commented on the 'perceived lack of control' that occurs when

using underground spaces. The lack of visible cues that make the spaces recognisable hinder wayfinding and contribute to the general perception of having no control over one's journey. For this reason alone, creating distinguishing features that provide visible cues and add to the enjoyment of underground spaces should be used as opposed to uniform designs of stations along a route, as we already noted in Section 4.4.

Further evidence for the way that art works positively is provided by Storstockholms Lokaltrafik, the Stockholm Public Transport company (SL, 2017):

> The art makes the stations perceived as more beautiful, safer and it helps to make the trip into something more than just a transport between two places. But art is also important to give each station its own identity, and thereby make it easier to navigate in the transport network. We also believe that art helps reduce criminal damage and vandalism.

The Stockholm metro is a world-class example of how art can transform the 'look and feel' of a modern and efficient transport system (Figure 7.3). Since the 19th century, debate has been ongoing as part of Swedish society on making art public and more accessible rather than keeping it inside cosy salons for the happy few. The Moscow Metro was seen as a good example, even though the art it contained and the design were seen as somewhat 'grandiose'. In the 1950s, two Swedish artists – Vera Nilsson and Siri Derkert – started a campaign that led to the adoption of a resolution by Stockholm City Council to introduce art into the metro (SL, 2017):

In 1957 T-Centralen was the first station to gain art, following a competition launched the previous year. The competition was preceded by much talk of cooperation between artists, architects and engineers but when these visions came up against reality, time was running out and although the entries from the twelve winning artists were displayed in the station, they were not integral to the design, as many of those involved had imagined would be the case.

Today, SL can boast of being the longest underground museum. It has created an enormous cultural heritage for the city, and provides us with valuable insight, that making 'art integral to the design' is paramount for creating unique underground spaces.

Where Stockholm looked at Moscow as an example, we need to provide a little more context to unearth what inspired the grand designs of the Moscow Metro. Kettering (2000) demonstrated that for the major part this was a socialist reaction to the dull, drab and uniform systems of the West. She mentioned a speech made by Lazar Kaganovich, the director of Metrostroi, on the occasion of the opening of the first line of the Moscow Metro on 15 May 1935, to illustrate this:

> The subway in capitalist nations, he announced to a cheering crowd, was intended to generate the highest possible profit and its interior was therefore monotonous, dirty, dim, and altogether 'cryptlike'. Such a gloomy atmosphere, he maintained, could in no way offer the worker repose after a long day, but would instead further exhaust the pitiable proletarian in London or New York. Conversely, in a socialist society, with its greater consideration for its workers, the government would naturally choose to build more splendid and therefore expensive structures that would assure the population not only convenience but 'palatial' architecture creating feelings of joy and happiness, or 'zhizneradostnost'.

It was Kaganovich who decreed that each station on the Moscow Metro would have a distinctive look. Besides being a reaction to Western designs, it also served a practical purpose, as Kettering wrote, 'in that even the illiterate passenger could immediately recognize the station from the window of the subway car, and the difference among stations essential to creating the sensation that the traveler was moving through series of grand and richly decorated galleries.'

Apart from anything else, the grand designs served both a propaganda purpose in their explicit grandeur, creating an atmosphere that would negate any negative feelings of being underground. 'If such a sensation could be created in the ground beneath Moscow, the Metro interior would be yet another site demonstrating the widely propagandized ability of Soviet citizens to overcome and transform any natural force, be it darkness, damp, cold, or frozen earth' (Kettering, 2000).

It meant that, from the beginning, a great deal of effort was put into ensuring that the lighting in the stations created a feeling of daylight. This was achieved by creating high-ceilinged halls and floors covered with marble: 'Furthermore,

Soviet planners made mathematical calculations to ensure that the light would reflect from the marble with the desired brilliance' (Kettering, 2000). Apart from concentrating on the lighting, ventilation systems were installed that cleaned the air in the stations eight to nine times an hour.

At the time, Komsomol (now Komsomol-skaya) station was seen to be as the pinnacle of the metro designers' accomplishments (Figure 7.4). It was awarded the Stalin Prize, and the 'station's interior decoration was conceived as a "Hall of Victory," commemorating Russian and Soviet triumphs over past invaders' (Kettering, 2000).

Even though we may now look back with amazement at the rationale behind creating these Soviet stations, it is clear that even in the first half of the 20th century planners, architects and engineers were able to create designs that captivated people using these underground spaces. As such, this provides us with a valuable lesson from history.

Sometimes more down to earth reasons dictate the outcome of the interior of underground spaces. In the city centre, an underground complex was constructed beneath the Grote Marktstraat, designed by Dutch architect Ben van Berkel and called The Souterrain. The complex consists of a tramway tunnel, underground car park and corridors connecting to the basements of nearby shops. During construction, the building pit flooded, and the project was delayed and faced both time and cost overruns. In an attempt to cut costs, it was decided not to use prefab concrete panels to cover the earth-formed walls. In the final design, the walls are now subtly and offset

by a wooden floor that covers the platform. The whole atmosphere is that of a cave, and it creates a unique environment in this underground space (Figure 7.5).

To paraphrase Whyte (1988), whatever the reasons to build underground spaces, there is no need to make them look dull and uninviting. The challenge is to create loveable spaces that will be appreciated by the people using them and to create 'feelings of joy and happiness'.

7.2. Comfortable spaces

In the previous section we discussed the need for loveable spaces in cities and the way that underground space could contribute to this. We see this as a positive approach rather than focus on the idea that we need to somehow overcome the negative associations that people have with the subsurface.

Lee *et al.* (2017) pointed to some of the problems that need to be dealt with when it comes to underground space use and how to solve these (Table 7.1).

Figure 7-4 Komsomolskaya Station on the Moscow Metro | Courtesy of Tim Adams, reproduced under CC BY 2.0

Carmody and Sterling (1993) formulated the basic design objectives for the layout and spatial configuration of underground buildings (Box 7.1).

These authors came from the point of view that people are naturally inclined not to use underground spaces and will only use them if they are attractive enough or overcome their initial inhibitions. Whyte (1988) had an opposing view: 'People adapt to the underground. It's like the simulated blue cheese dressing in the salad bars. Once you get used to it you lose your taste for the real thing.' His primary concern was that people get used to dull and efficient spaces. We feel that this holds true as long as there is a necessity or a compelling reason to use them. When there is no real alternative to underground transport, the choice is limited. In that regard, Whyte's observation makes sense – as does the consideration that people can have inhibitions to going underground.

People fear a lot of things, notably the unknown. Pfeffer and Salancik (1978) have described the basic human instinct to reduce uncertainty. In the resource dependency theory they show that in any situation where people or organisations become interdependent, this interdependency is characterised by uncertainty. Uncertainty causes a desire by both parties to want to reduce it. One way of doing this is by providing information. If, however, the uncertainty remains, it will eventually evolve into fear, causing emotional reactions. Take flying as an example. Many people enjoy flying, some people fear flying, while a third group, when flying, can have certain anxious moments when things happen out of the ordinary. For this reason,

Table 7-1 Potential issues and possible solutions (Lee *et al.*, 2017)

Issue	Solutions
Isolation	■ Additional transit connections ■ Introduction of natural light ■ Intermediary spaces
Lack of control	■ Enhanced landmarks ■ Greenery
Negative associations	■ Emphasis on privacy and safety ■ Increased high-end uses
Perceived security	■ Added surveillance ■ Improved visibility

Box 7-1 Design objectives for layout and spatial configuration (Carmody and Sterling, 1993)

1 Create an interior layout that is easy to understand, thereby enhancing orientation as well as emergency egress.

2 Arrange space to create a distinct image within the building to compensate for the lack of image outside.

3 Develop a layout and spatial configuration that contributes to creating a stimulating, varied indoor environment to compensate for a lack of windows. Create a stimulating environment from the point of view of people occupying the facility as well as people passing through.

4 Provide visual connections between the interior and exterior environments whenever possible.

5 Arrange spaces and building circulation to enhance a feeling of spaciousness through the facility by providing extended interior views as much as possible.

6 Design each space to enhance a feeling of spaciousness by manipulating room size and shape.

7 Arrange spaces to protect privacy as much as possible.

airlines provide public address announcements from the cockpit or by the cabin staff explaining what is going on. A simple screen that shows the flight on a world map with added flight information comforts travellers. It is the lack of information that causes anxiety; the information provided helps to reduce uncertainty, even though there is no actual control over the flight itself. It is this perceived lack of control that is the inhibitor (Lee *et al.*, 2017).

We feel that, when it comes to underground space, we need to distinguish between the various forms that it can take. Not all underground spaces are entirely earth covered and resemble dark caves that only die-hard speleologists would use while providing perfect backdrops for Indiana Jones movies! There is also no need to design underground spaces in such a way that they are unattractive and automatically make people turn back the minute they enter them.

We have seen in previous chapters that there are numerous examples of beautiful underground spaces that are well thought out, appealing and provide a unique user experience. In many ways, an underground space provides both architects and artists with a challenge, to work with the earth in shaping and forming an underground building. In this, Dominque Perrault stands out from his peers. In an interview, when asked what fascinates him about the underground, he said (100 Years Steiner, 2017).

To put it simply, you can increase architectural density not only by going upwards, but by going underground as well. When you build downwards, the architecture disappears and there is room for green areas and public spaces.

Architecture can be put centre stage again by using valleys or clearings in the forest, as with the Women's University of Seoul, which we completed in 2008. This way, daylight arrives underground. Underground construction also offers benefits in terms of energy. The ground keeps things cool in the summer and warm in winter. This means the Women's University has reduced its energy costs by 60 per cent.

As Figure 7.6 shows, the design of the Women's University is not only about creating an underground building housing the university; it is also about achieving a grand public space around and in it. It is this 'void' that carries the whole design, that brings a logic to the whole design and brings together surrounding buildings. As Perrault (2016) explained: 'The void attracts, aspirates, not only because of the distribution of the elements of the program on either side of the fracture, but also because it generates a new public space, a focal point that recenters the entire university, polarizing the existing buildings like a magnet.'

The design has been thought through in such a way that it negates any thoughts of being underground. It has become a beautiful building in its own right, a comfortable building with sufficient daylight entry to take away

Figure 7-6 Women's University, Seoul, South Korea | © André Morin/ Dominique Perrault Architecte/Adagp

the idea of being underground. In this way, it is comparable to the design of the Arnhem Underground School, where it was found that there was so much daylight entering that at some times the daylight had to be tempered. Both examples show that when underground spaces and underground buildings are designed as comfortable spaces for people, many of the issues that may prevent people from using them can be overcome.

Daylight is one of the key design tools that are required to create comfortable spaces. But natural light is not always available, either because the design prevents the entry of light or because it's dark outside. Either way, lighting needs to be addressed, both with regard to daylight and to artificial lighting.

Kettering (2000), in her essay on the Moscow Metro, observed that

> Throughout the Metro's history, lighting was an arena in which designers displayed the greatest ingenuity. Although some stations relied on oversized chandeliers, the majority of the stations offered ingenious solutions to the problem of creating an intensely lit interior while managing to diffuse the light. At the Electric Factory (Elektrozavodskaia) station on the third line, winner of the 1944 Stalin Prize, for example, hundreds of lights were housed in small, recessed spaces to create a uniform diffusion and minimal shadows reminiscent of high noon … In the Dynamo (Dinamo) station on the second line … some of the lighting devices were placed behind thin sheets of the colored marble that sheathed the interior walls and columns. As the light projected through the marble, a rich, diffused golden light fell on the glazed surfaces of Elena Ianson-Manizer's monumental porcelain medallions depicting athletes … To retain the magical quality of this atmosphere, a large group of workers labored from one to five A.M. each night, when the Metro was closed, to polish the marble and bronze, clean the floors, dust light fixtures and the screens covering ventilation shafts, change light bulbs, and even replace marble panels when necessary.

The design for the 'earthscraper' as an inverted pyramid was specifically chosen by the architects to ensure maximum daylight entry into the building, as can be seen in Figure 7.7. In the words of the designers themselves (BNKR Arquitectura, 2011):

> Besides the structural challenges of such a project, it is very important that we have systems in place to make living underground acceptable. Among these is the solution to the need for natural light in the lowest levels. In these levels a system of fibre optic illumination would need to be put into place which would guarantee a natural light even at the greatest depths. We hope that in creating a pleasant environment underground we would convince sceptics of the viability of our scheme.

The use of fibre optics is an interesting proposal. A different way of achieving this is the plan used

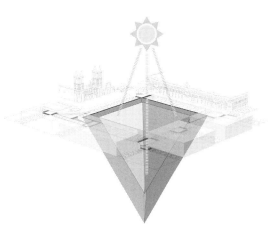

to bring daylight into a former underground tramway depot in New York. The Lowline project aims at turning this terminal into an underground park, providing much-needed green public space to the Lower Eastside. Daylight is essential to achieving this, to stimulate plant growth beneath the surface. One of the founding fathers of the project, James Ramsey, a former NASA engineer, found a solution based on satellite technology to bring daylight into an entirely enclosed space. The Lowline Lab demonstrated the proof-of-concept from February 2015 to February 2017, when a mock-up was created to show and study the feasibility of the plan (Lowline, 2017) (Figure 7.8):

> Co-Founder James Ramsey, his team at Raad Studio, and Korea-based technology company Sunportal designed and installed optical devices which track the sun throughout the sky every minute of every day, optimizing the amount of natural sunlight we were able to capture. The sunlight was then distributed into

the warehouse through a series of protective tubes, directing full spectrum light into a central distribution point. A solar canopy, designed and constructed by engineer Ed Jacobs, then spread out the sunlight across the space, modulating and tempering the sunlight, providing light critical to sustain the plant life below.

What is intriguing in the technology used above is that both through design and use of fibre optics, the same objective can be achieved. Daylight can penetrate spaces where it cannot enter naturally. This could ultimately prove to be a breakthrough technology when used in underground space design.

Artificial lighting will also play the same role underground as it does above ground. When there is no daylight, artificial lighting is needed to create the right atmosphere for the environment, whether the purpose of that environment is transit, shopping, recreation, working or living. Modern LED technologies make it possible to achieve this and even to go as far as projecting images on the blank canvasses provided by underground buildings to show surface imagery, both to connect with the surface and aid navigation, as was part of the Amfora project proposal for an extensive underground space complex beneath the City of Amsterdam in the Netherlands (see Section 4.4).

Climate control in underground spaces and buildings is essential, contributing to a comfortable environment. As we can grasp from Perrault's quote, the Earth has an inherent quality in that the constant temperature that exists in the shallow subsurface has a natural ability to keep the temperature inside underground spaces constant. This means less energy is required to heat and cool these facilities. On the other hand, the absence of natural ventilation does require active ventilation to refresh the air inside the underground space. From previous examples, we have seen that this could also be achieved through natural ventilation using shafts that reach the surface and double as daylight entrance portals. Creating a natural flow of ventilation through the design will lower the dependency on mechanical ventilation. As we will see in the next section, ventilation also performs a vital role when it comes to smoke control in the event of fire.

In a study into climate control, Blesgraaf et al. (1999) concluded that outside climatological conditions have little effect on buildings below the surface. It is the local geology that actually influences the climate inside. There is a difference between a building that is actually constructed below the groundwater table and one that is constructed in a more impermeable soil such as clay. In the first case, Blesgraaf et al. found that humidity could be an overarching factor that needs to be dealt with. In the second case, we saw from the example of the London Underground that heat produced inside the underground system can dissipate into the soil over time, and thus change the characteristics of the soil (see Section 5.2).

Interestingly, Blesgraaf et al. mentioned that the spatial design of an underground building needs to be considered when looking at climate control. Figure 7.9 shows how climate requirements can affect the distribution of uses within an underground building.

Blesgraaf et al. also pointed to the use of ground-source heat pumps. They observed that although this could be a good way to heat and cool underground buildings, care needs to be taken to ensure that the soil surrounding the building is part of the energy mass requiring heating and cooling. The thinner the outer skin of the building, the more this applies. A good combination would be to use this form of heating and cooling in combination with a surface building. For the larger part of the year, cooling might be required in the subsurface building as opposed to the surface building. The cooling water that extracts heat from the subsurface building could then be used to heat the surface building before being returned to the subsurface.

Van der Voorden (1999) noted the fact that, from a building engineering physics point of view, the aforementioned aspects should also be considered in combination. When talking about daylight entry, we need to consider that this is directly related to heat as well. As we saw previously in the case of the Underground School in Arnhem, a covered atrium solution allows sunlight into the building – but as a direct consequence the building is also heated. This needs to be taken into account when looking at climate control. If daylight is to penetrate as deep as possible into an underground building, this would require linked spaces with a certain transparency. This transparency could cause acoustic problems, in terms of noise filtering from one space to another. Acoustics requires specific consideration as, in contrast to surface buildings, outside noise is unlikely to penetrate underground, making underground buildings potentially very quiet. Apart from the combination light–acoustics, the combination ventilation–acoustics needs to be considered as well. Allowing entry of air from outside the underground building permits ambient noise from outside to enter as well. Mechanical ventilation in itself can be a source

of noise. Both aspects need to be considered, specifically in regard to the inherent quiet nature of underground buildings. The combinations humidity–ventilation and humidity–heat need to also be taken into account. As Van der Voorden pointed out, humidity can occur in underground buildings, both through ventilation or as part of heating. This requires more attention in subsurface buildings than in surface buildings.

Creating comfortable underground spaces need not be too different from the way this is achieved at the surface. Controlling the underground climate, be it in spaces or buildings, does require specific attention. The fact that the construction is either partially or totally enclosed by soil does require attention in terms of the total energy mass being more than just the walls and floors of the building itself. Spaces created inside rock mass are different again, in that they have no walls as such – the mass itself acts as a wall. The main observations made above still apply in that case, specifically in relation to controlling humidity.

7.3. Safe and secure spaces

We start this section by categorically stating that underground spaces and buildings need not be less safe or secure than spaces or buildings at the surface. There are, however, specific characteristics that require more attention in the case of underground spaces and buildings. One of these is that, when underground, emergency egress is always – as in any building – towards the surface. What is different is that, in this case, the emergency egress route is in the same direction as the propagation of smoke. In high-rise buildings, smoke travels up, and evacuees

Figure 7-9 Climate requirements versus building layout

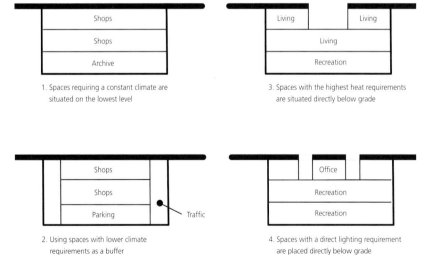

1. Spaces requiring a constant climate are situated on the lowest level

2. Using spaces with lower climate requirements as a buffer

3. Spaces with the highest heat requirements are situated directly below grade

4. Spaces with a direct lighting requirement are placed directly below grade

move downwards – that is, away from smoke. To look at safe and secure spaces from a broad perspective, we will examine physical, public and external safety, and the issue of security.

We define physical safety as all those measures that are taken to ensure that people can safely exit underground spaces in circumstances that are outside normal operational activities. There are two types of events we will look at: fire and overcrowding.

Dealing with fire is an important consideration, given that smoke propagation in an underground building needs to be controlled in such a way that emergency egress is possible without coming into contact with the smoke. This smoke control requires, just as in buildings on the surface, fire compartmentation, use of smoke screens, use of mechanical ventilation, and smoke-free emergency escape routes. The main strategy is to prevent the smoke from escaping from one compartment to another, to keep the emergency escape routes free from smoke by using overpressure ventilation. Smoke control needs to consider the natural air flow present in facilities that can carry smoke to the surface. In the absence of air flow, smoke will propagate along ceilings until it cools and then de-stratifies, filling up the compartment as it does so.

Another strategy actively used in underground car parks is the use of sprinklers or water mist systems (fixed firefighting systems), ensuring that the fire cannot grow or spread while at the same time containing smoke. These systems can offer protection against fire for civil construction as well. In many countries, these types of systems are mandatory for underground car parks.

Consideration also needs to be given to how the emergency and rescue services can access the underground facility. This access is not just for firefighters – medical emergency teams also require use of these routes to get to the injured and bring them out on stretchers. When buildings go well below the surface, the availability of water is something that also has to be considered, although this does not differ in concept from high-rise buildings.

Underground shopping plazas can have large concentrations of people in them at any one time. Crowd control can in certain situations become an issue, especially when the facility needs to be evacuated. Again, this does not differ from surface facilities other than the fact that walking up takes more effort than walking down.

A vital element for normal operation and emergencies is wayfinding. Navigation in underground spaces and buildings differs from how people move about on the surface. The absence of specific landmarks or the ability to look outside through windows to determine where you are makes navigation below the surface more difficult.

In Section 4.4 we looked at the importance of signage in relation to wayfinding. Bélanger (2007) has pointed to the balance that needs to be struck between commercial signage (often competing for the attention of people) and signs that are part of the wayfinding scheme with the objective of creating flow through the facility. As Paul Mijksenaar, responsible for the wayfinding concept and design at Amsterdam Schiphol Airport, has stated: 'wayfinding is about offering the right balance of means of

Figure 7-10 A colour-based scheme using the distinctive Frutiger typeface for wayfinding at Schiphol Airport | © Mijksenaar – mijksenaar.com

Figure 7-11 Wayfinding signage in the recently renovated Forum des Halles in Paris, France

orientation, information and navigation to let users find their way'. In his eyes, a good wayfinding scheme depends on the five Cs: 'comprehensiveness, clarity, consistency, conspicuous and catchy' (Mijksenaar, 2017a). The Schiphol scheme is based on the flow of passengers through the terminals to and from the gates, as well as intermediate stops they may want to make to use the restrooms or for shopping or eating. The concept depends on a simple colour scheme (Figure 7.10). 'At Schiphol, colors are coupled to certain types of information. Yellow signs provide information on arrivals and departures, for example, while blue signs refer to shopping and restaurant-café facilities, anthracite to waiting areas, and green to escape routes' (Mijksenaar, 2017b).

A particular category of users of underground spaces needs to be considered when looking at safety. People who are mobility impaired will also be using underground facilities, especially those combined with transport infrastructure. In the case of emergency evacuation, care must be taken that security staff are present to assist the mobility impaired towards emergency exits.

It is interesting to see how the wayfinding scheme used at Schiphol Airport compares with the more subtle scheme in the Forum des Halles

in Paris, France (Figure 7.11).

Toronto Parks and Recreation produced a guide for creating safer parks and open spaces (Project for Public Spaces, 2009). The guide states that

> The design of a park can have a direct impact on people's perceptions of safety and their willingness to use a space. The physical characteristics which park users associate with high-risk environments include:

- Poor lighting
- Confusing layout
- Physical and aural isolation
- Poor visibility
- No access to help
- Areas of concealment
- Poor maintenance
- Vandalism
- Presence of 'undesirables'.

We find that what holds true for safer parks also holds true for underground spaces, whether they are underground shopping malls or underground stations. Areas of concealment, no access to help and the presence of undesirables are issues that we need to address in addition to what has already been discussed (see Table

7.1 and Box 7.1). Typically, underground spaces contain columns or pillars. Designs need to be made in such a way that these do not offer areas of concealment. A good example of how to achieve this is the Laakhaven underground car park in The Hague (Figure 7.12). Rather than using straight columns, the columns are angled, making it impossible to conceal a person.

Another approach can be to limit the use of columns and to create a bright ambiance, as has been achieved in the case of the Sechseläutenplatz underground car park in Zürich, Switzerland (Figure 7.13).

Underground train platforms can be intimidating as well in this respect. To ensure that there is maximum eye contact between travellers, the dividing wall between platforms in the Rotterdam Blaak railway station has large holes in it. The resulting effect reduces the feeling of confinement (Figure 7.14).

No access to help is another issue that needs to be considered. Emergency points need to be accessible so that contact can be made with the facility operator or security control room. The Second Heinenoord Tunnel near Barendrecht in the Netherlands has one tunnel bore for cyclists and pedestrians. At times there can be a high volume of use, but at other times there may be only one or two cyclists. Constant CCTV monitoring made no sense given the infrequent use of the tunnel. It was decided instead to use an intelligent CCTV system that would activate an alarm if no movement was detected. If a person stood still inside the tunnel or if a cyclist fell and was unable to reach the emergency point, CCTV detection would activate an alarm, and the operator could use the public address system to make contact. The presence of this scheme satisfied the local community that public safety had been dealt with and that the tunnel would be safe to use.

The presence of undesirables in public spaces can be intimidating to other users. When discussing PATH in Toronto (see Section 4.4), the ability for private entities to decide on who enters the system or not using security guards was seen as a dynamic that needed to be addressed. If underground spaces are to be part of the urban fabric, they need to include public spaces that, by definition, are accessible for all.

Whyte (1988) was extraordinarily clear on this issue, and devoted an entire chapter in his book to undesirables: 'They are themselves not

Figure 7-12 The Laakhaven underground car park in The Hague, the Netherlands | Courtesy of Joeri van Beek/Atelier Pro – The Hague

Figure 7-13 The Sechseläutenplatz underground car park in Zürich, Switzerland | © Michael Erik Haug

Figure 7-14 The Rotterdam Blaak railway station in the Netherlands

too much of a problem. It is the actions taken to combat them that is the problem.' In his opinion, defensive designs based on distrust mostly get what was anticipated – they attract undesirables as they are not attractive to others. He concluded that, 'With few exceptions, plazas and small parks in most central business districts are as safe a place as you can find during the times that people use them.'

Whyte's vision of public spaces that are appealing will attract people to use them. The more people frequent them, the less chance of undesirables using them, as they favour quieter places.

Feeling safe in public spaces and in underground spaces requires the presence of people. The more we create them as open spaces, as opposed to restricted spaces segregating users, the less likely they are to attract undesirables.

Up to now, we have discussed internal safety in relation to underground spaces or buildings. These are all safety aspects that need to be dealt with from the viewpoint of a facility used by people. External safety looks at the possible effects of an emergency in an underground facility for the surrounding environment.

If we consider high-pressure gas transport pipelines, it is immediately clear that these can pose a risk if they pass nearby to communities. For this reason, specific legislation is usually in place, requiring risk analysis to show that these pipelines do not present a high risk in terms of explosion or leakage. Conversely, placing new objects such as wind turbines or wind farms near these pipelines needs to be reviewed as well. Breakage of a turbine blade coupled with the

possibility of it hitting the pipeline and causing a leakage or explosion needs to be mitigated.

Underground rail lines or stations could also pose an external safety risk if the transport of hazardous goods is allowed through them. Flooding of underground metro lines could also lead to impacts in other areas, as the subway system starts acting as a large sewer and water erupts from stations down the line.

In the case of fires below the surface, smoke can escape and cause side effects on the surface, from disrupting traffic to potentially the evacuation of nearby buildings. The same holds true in the event of leakage of hazardous goods, if this were to occur.

External safety is very much part of the urban planning process in the sense that these safety considerations need to be made at the time when specific uses of areas are planned. This holds true for both planning at the surface and below the surface. In particular, when considering planning in layers, the specific use of the layers needs to be addressed with external safety in mind, to avoid potential cascading effects (i.e. an emergency in one facility also causing emergencies in other facilities).

The most extreme case would be the collapse of an underground structure leading to the collapse of buildings on the surface. Passive and active fire protection of structural elements must therefore be provided to prevent this from occurring.

The question of the security of underground spaces is one that is increasingly being raised. In the past, underground transport systems have been targeted by terrorists. From the sarin attacks in the Tokyo Metro (1995) to the

London Underground bombings (2005) and, most recently, the Brussels Metro (2016), the main question to be asked is: do we need to take additional measures that take these events into account?

From an engineering point of view, safety and security are risk-driven processes. The difference is that safety deals with the aftermath of events in terms of emergency management. Security is far more pre-emptive, in the sense that it is based on information analysis and determining whether or not a credible risk exists. In most Western nations the terrorist risk level is high, which in itself means that people are asked to be more vigilant. At railway stations and airports, luggage left without an owner is enough to shut down the facility. Specific threats to underground facilities require a response by the authorities that is proportional to the risk, and require operational staff to resort to specific operational procedures. What is characteristic is that this is information driven, and the security response is aimed at preventing the risk event from occurring. Once an attack has happened, the safety measures in place should prevent the event from further escalating, and an emergency and rescue response is started.

From the users' perspective, visible safety measures in terms of CCTV cameras, emergency points and security staff provide sufficient proof of security. Additional security measures, such as screening at entrances or the presence of the military guarding the facility, will not heighten the perception of security but rather alert the user to the fact that something could potentially happen. It is not until these measures are present over a long period, much like in airports,

that they become accepted as a necessary but disruptive measure. In this sense, people do adapt to situations, even if they are far from perfect.

Security, in our opinion, does not require additional measures in terms of more equipment or designs different from those we have already mentioned. However, it does require the owners and operators of underground spaces to liaise with the appropriate authorities, and to prepare for potential events by developing specific procedures. An example of this approach is the Counterterrorism Alert System used in the Netherlands. The Netherlands National Coordinator for Security and Counterterrorism (NCTV) is responsible for organising and maintaining this system, which is based on collaboration between the security and intelligence communities, the national police, and owners and operators of infrastructure that has been deemed to be of vital importance (NCTV, 2017). The NCTV evaluates and determines both the national generic threat level as specific levels for identified sectors and objects.

An information-driven approach using threat levels, in combination with procedures specifying cooperation between authorities and operators, ensures that pre-emptive measures (that only disrupt normal services when escalated to the highest threat level) can be taken.

Underground spaces and buildings are, in this sense, part of a national approach, and are not selected on the basis of being subsurface facilities. They are instead selected for their specific use or the role they play within the national economy. To us this seems a sensible approach, providing the appropriate level of security when this is required without singling out underground facilities as being particularly vulnerable to terrorist attacks and therefore requiring additional measures.

7.4. This chapter's core ideas

We started this chapter by looking at William Whyte's objections to underground spaces. Part of his criticism comes from the fact that plazas created below the surface subtract from the streets above the surface. He feared that the process of 'dullification' of the streets will continue to drive people to use underground shopping plazas that in themselves are unattractive and not laid out as public spaces.

When creating underground spaces, we argue for the creation of loveable spaces that add to the urban fabric rather than subtracting from it. City life should not move to below the surface but extend to below the surface, creating tributaries to the river of life in the city: its streets. Underground space is not competing with the surface, but rather it is complementing it and in some ways maybe even completing it.

For underground spaces to achieve this, they need to be attractive and appeal to the people using them. To do so requires specific approaches when it comes to climate control and lighting. These spaces must also be safe and secure. In many ways, the same safety regulations that apply to surface facilities apply to subsurface facilities. Given the specific circumstances of the underground, certain aspects require more attention, for example dealing with fires, emergency egress and emergency access.

We saw that the perception of users is important as well. The perception of lack of control (identified as an inhibitor for using underground facilities) stems from uncertainty, and can be reduced effectively by providing information to users. Wayfinding in that respect is of utmost importance, as it provides people with information on where they are and how to reach their destination.

Security is often seen as a critical concern. We feel that underground spaces and buildings need no special consideration and should be part of national procedures that apply to all spaces, buildings and infrastructures.

Developing underground spaces and buildings in this way will provide valued spaces for people that will become an essential part of the urban fabric and further enhance it.

References

1   Admiraal H and Cornaro A (2017) The impact of urban planning on the design and operation of stations and interchange hubs. In *Forschung und Praxis*, vol. 49. *U-Verkehr und Unterirdisches Bauen*. Studiengesellschaft für unterirdische Verkehrsanlagen, Cologne, Germany.

2   Bélanger P (2007) Underground landscape: The urbanism and infrastructure of Toronto's downtown pedestrian network. *Tunnelling and Underground Space Technology* **22:** 272–292.

3   Blesgraaf P, Smienk E, Spangenberg W, Van Dam H and Van Hulst H (1999) *Techniek van ondergrondse ruimten verkenning en oplossingsrichtingen*. Centrum Ondergronds Bouwen, Gouda, the Netherlands, Report O-104. (In Dutch.)

4   BNKR Arquitectura (2011) *Stop: Keep Moving – An Oxymoronic Approach to Architecture*. Arquine, Mexico City, Mexico.

5   Carmody J and Sterling R (1993) *Underground Space Design*. Van Nostrand Reinhold, New York, NY, USA.

6   Kettering KL (2000) An introduction to the design of the Moscow Metro in the Stalin period: 'the happiness of life underground'. *Studies in the Decorative Arts* **7(2):** 2–20.

7   Lee EH, Christopoulos GI, Kwok KW, Roberts AC and Soh C-K (2017) A psychosocial approach to understanding underground spaces. *Frontiers in Psychology* **8:** 452.

8   Lowline (2017) http://thelowline.org/lab/ (accessed 14/11/2017).

9   Mijksenaar P (2017a) Less signs but better flows: how does wayfinding design improve the travel experience? Flows. Modelling Mobility. http://www.flowsmag.com/en/2017/06/15/less-signs-but-better-flows/ (accessed 14/11/2017).

10 Mijksenaar P (2017b) A promise of happiness. http://www.mijksenaar.com/project/amsterdam-airport-schiphol-2/ (accessed 14/11/2017).

11 Netherlands National Coordinator for Security and Counterterrorism (2017) The terrorist threat assessment: Netherlands versus the counterterrorism alert system. https://english.nctv.nl/organisation/counterterrorism/TerroristThreatAssessmentNetherlands/The-Terrorist-Threat-Assessment-Netherlands-versus-the-Counterterrorism-Alert-system/index.aspx (accessed 14/11/2017).

12 Perrault D (2016) *Groundscapes: Other Topographies*. HYX, Orléans, France.

13 Pfeffer J and Salancik GR (1978) *The External Control of Organizations: A Resource Dependence Perspective*. Harper and Row, New York, NY, USA.

14 SL (2017) Art walks. http://sl.se/en/eng-info/contact/art-walks/ (accessed 14/11/2017).

15 100 Years Steiner (2017) Dominique Perrault. http://100yearssteiner.ch/partners-and-pioneers/dominique-perrault (accessed 14/11/2017).

16 Toronto Parks and Recreation (2009) *Planning, Designing and Maintaining Safer Parks*. Toronto Parks and Recreation, Toronto, Canada. See https://www.pps.org/reference/what-role-can-design-play-in-creating-safer-parks/ (accessed 14/11/2017).

17 Van der Voorden M (1999) *Bouwfysische knelpunten bij de realisatie van ondergrondse ruimten*. Centrum Ondergronds Bouwen, Gouda, the Netherlands, Report TUD-10. (In Dutch.)

18 Whyte WH (1988) *City: Rediscovering the Center*. University of Pennsylvania Press, Philadelphia, PA, USA.

Chapter 8

Governance and legal challenges of underground space use

8.1. Oversight and insight

A typical discussion on the merits of the use of underground space often follows the same pattern and consists of three distinct questions. The first is why would we even want to use underground space? The second is about whether it is possible. The third that immediately follows, and is typically posed as the final hurdle against the madness of the scheme: what about land ownership? This last question usually brings a smirk to the face of the person asking it, as if to say, 'Try and get yourself out of this one!' Apart from illustrating that not everyone is enthusiastic about the idea of using underground space, and that people seem to have a preconceived vision of what it entails, it does – rightly – throw up the aspect of governance and legal challenges. In this chapter, we will take a closer look at these issues. We start by looking at the oversight of underground space, followed by the regulatory controls governing land ownership, liability, building codes and the environment. The final section will discuss the question of managing underground space use.

The Government of the Netherlands (2016) has instigated a large-scale programme called Subsurface and Underground Space as part of an effort to take responsibility for oversight on what is going on below the surface:

> It is becoming increasingly congested below the surface. Authorities, therefore, need to make choices on where what type of activities can take place. They may also need to decide how groundwater can be protected at the same time. Or on how authorities need to deal with contaminations when new activities take place in such a location. These choices cannot be made without taking all aspects into consideration.

The programme consists of three pillars. The first is the development of the Subsurface Spatial Planning Vision (in Dutch: Structuurvisie Ondergrond – STRONG). The strategy aims at reaching agreement at the national level on the use of the subsurface. The second pillar addresses the issue of utilisation of the subsurface at the regional and local levels with the appropriate authorities. In practice, this seems a logical step, as in practice the planning process follows levels of scale appropriate to the area of responsibility of the planning authority. When it comes to the subsurface, this approach fails in that the third dimension comes into play. During extensive public consultation rounds, this became apparent. It led to the conclusion that STRONG would need to focus on those areas and aspects of the use of the subsurface that are deemed to be of national interest. Further strategies would need to be developed at the regional and local levels, taking into account the specific responsibilities of each level of government but also the interaction with other levels of government. In practice, STRONG looks primarily at the deep subsurface and drinking water and (renewable) energy.

The third pillar acknowledges that more knowledge and data are required to gain a full understanding of the subsurface. A new research programme was set up for this purpose, closely linked to the Baseline Register Subsurface (in Dutch: Basisregistratie Ondergrond – BRO), and is one of a total of 12 registers created by the Government of the Netherlands. These registers aim at providing open-source data for future decision-making. As such, this can be seen as the Netherlands' implementation of regulations stemming from the EU's INSPIRE programme, aiming at creating a spatial data infrastructure for the EU's environmental policies and policies or activities that may have an impact on the environment. The BRO will collect and contain all relevant data relating to the subsurface, limiting itself to geology, hydrology and mining activities in the deep underground. Data on underground car parks, basements,

tunnels or cables and pipelines will be part of one or more of the other 12 baseline registers. The reason for doing this lies in that it was found too complicated to create new legislation focusing on the subsurface as an independent entity, given the way it is already part of various acts of Parliament.

Governmental oversight of the subsurface is not only required to regulate the use of underground space but also to protect those ecosystem services that are vital to life on the surface. The example of the Netherlands shows that it requires a comprehensive approach. The acquisition of knowledge and data for a better understanding is an ongoing dynamic process, and as such needs to be part of the oversight mechanism. It also shows that it is possible to develop a methodology that can be part of an existing regulatory framework. It does, however, require more cooperation and coordination between levels of government and policy departments, as the typical approach of levels of scale linked to areas of responsibility will not work below the surface.

8.2. Land ownership

The Dutch Logistics Corridors report for the first time includes pipeline transport as a modality of transport (Netherlands Ministry of Infrastructure and Environment, 2017). This is, firstly, based on the enormous benefits that pipelines offer society in the transport of dangerous substances. These benefits include a transport capacity that cannot be matched by any other modality. Secondly, this form of transport of dangerous goods is inherently safer than other modalities. As such, pipelines contribute to both the national economy and provide a higher level of safety to the community.

From a historic perspective, these types of transport pipelines have always been placed below the surface in purposely created pipeline corridors, planned alignments or negotiated alignments. One dedicated pipeline corridor runs between the Port of Rotterdam and the Port of Antwerp in Belgium, along an 80 km alignment and carries 230 million tonnes of oil, gas, chemicals and water between the ports on an annual basis. It would require 16 000 daily trucks between the two ports to transport this. Pipelines, in general, have one major advantage: continuity in service. Industrial complexes many kilometres apart are connected as though they form one physical private network.

The pipeline corridor provides space for owners to place their pipelines and operate them. It was created through an act of parliament enabling the government to expropriate land to create the corridor. The corridor's management and maintenance is ensured by a purposely created separate legal entity: a foundation. The pipeline corridor is firmly anchored in both national spatial policies and local zoning plans.

This example illustrates one way of acquiring the land necessary for underground space development: through expropriation. Before looking more closely at this we need to consider how ownership of the subsurface is regulated in general. The basis for this can be traced back to Roman law and the principle 'superficies solo cedit' – 'the surface yields to the ground'. This principle implies that anyone who holds the ownership of a piece of land by default also owns anything that is added to that land.

During Medieval times, a second principle of law became common, namely 'cuius est solum, eius est usque ad coelum et ad inferos' – 'whoever owns the soil, holds title all the way up to the heavens and down to the depths of the Earth'. It is this principle that gave way to the common perception in property law that land ownership extends unlimited both upwards and downwards.

These principles still apply today, and they mean that, in order to develop underground space either through public law or civil law, exceptions to the general rule must be created. In the previous example, the Netherlands Government exercised its legal power to expropriate land to take over its ownership on behalf of public interest. This type of compulsory acquisition has to be laid down in law, and requires certain conditions to be met. The European Convention on Human Rights (ECHR) states in Article 8 that any deprivation of the rights of the owner of a property must be in accordance with the law, necessary in a democratic society and proportionate.

The ECHR always requires the original holder of the land to be compensated for the loss of property. In the UK, specific legislation is often created in the form of a hybrid bill for a project that includes the power to acquire land for the project. In the case of London Underground's Elizabeth Line (the Crossrail Project), the Crossrail Act 2008 (Her Majesty's Government, 2008) states that

> The Secretary of State may acquire any land mentioned in the Act after the passage of the Crossrail Act 2008. Although there is a five-year limit on land

acquisition, the Secretary of State may extend this power for up to another five years. In addition, private rights of way may be extinguished upon the passing of the Crossrail Act 2008 and the loss of these rights must be compensated.

The principle of land ownership in relation to underground space use has been discussed in the past by Thomas (1979), Barker (1991) and Admiraal and Cornaro (2016), among others. One conclusion is that, over the years, it is possible to observe a trend that limits the extent of ownership upwards. Not only air rights but also the creation of condominiums are ways in which shared ownership of a plot of land upwards is both limited and regulated. The same practice extended downwards for the subsurface does not occur as a similar trend, but it is emergent in the sense that as the awareness and appreciation of the subsurface grows, so does the realisation that a new legal approach may be required.

The power of expropriation is a power limited in general to public bodies. An interesting exception to this is the Mining Construction Act in the Netherlands. This act deals with the extraction of minerals and energy from the subsurface. It not only states that these minerals and energy are property of the state, thereby de facto limiting the ownership rights of the land owner, but also that any works that are required for the purpose of extraction also qualify for use of the power of compulsory acquisition. The act does limit these powers to the extraction of minerals and energy from at least 100 m below the surface for minerals, oil and gas, and from 500 m below the surface in the case of geothermal heat extraction.

The second way that pipeline transport can come about is through private negotiations and reaching agreement on rights of way. This is usually the approach taken by private parties, whereby one party holds the land and allows use of the subsurface beneath that land under specific conditions and compensation. In Anglo-American law this is covered by several categories, most notably easements and equitable servitudes. In civil law this is usually covered by servitudes. In the case of pipelines, it requires a private contract between the parties regulating the placement of the pipeline, access to the pipeline, restricting use of the surface above the pipeline and compensation to the land owner. These rights are legally drawn up and registered. The specifics vary depending on the legal tradition of a country – either common or civil law. It is also worth noting that these agreements are civil in nature. Additional requirements may need to be met stemming from public law in terms of meeting planning regulations, external safety regulations and building regulations.

Although this is a legal and practical way to achieve the placement of a pipeline along an alignment, especially in the case of long alignments, the number of agreements that need to be reached can be very high. When talking about cross-border projects, the complexity becomes even higher, as it can involve different jurisdictions. Also, the rights are often obtained by a private company and cannot be transferred to a third party without renegotiations. This makes the transfer of ownership, or reuse of the pipeline for a different purpose, difficult.

Another possible scenario that effectively limits land ownership beneath the surface is the case of CERN's Large Hadron Collider (LHC). The Swiss approach is based on the common position that land ownership is limited to the depth of its economic usage. This approach, codified in Article 664 of the Swiss Civil Code, is unique in Europe, as it not only limits land ownership but also deems the space below it to be part of the public domain – the use of which is for the cantons forming the Swiss Federation to define/regulate. It is also up to the owner to demonstrate that they have a vested interest in a layer of the Earth in order for it to remain part of their ownership (Boermans and Ten Have, 2000). In practice, this is a somewhat ambivalent position that is open to challenge. For this reason, the Swiss Government is now looking into modifying the approach in such a way that the ambivalence is avoided in future proceedings. It is part of the effort that the government is taking to make the underground transport of goods possible, for example in the Cargo sous terrain project. Given that this project is based on private investment, investors will want assurance that the project will not be delayed or become hostage to extortionate compensation claims by land owners whose land the project will pass under.

An observation made by Durmisevic (1999) is that the way that underground space is regulated also shapes its use. Durmisevic compared underground space use in Toronto (Canada) and Japan (Figure 8.1). The fact that the Municipality of Montreal had already acquired the land on which surface development took place, and subsequently led to the creation

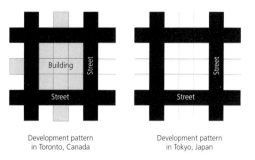

Development pattern in Toronto, Canada

Development pattern in Tokyo, Japan

Figure 8-1 Underground space development patterns in Toronto and Tokyo showing how strict land ownership rules shape development

of the Underground City, is in stark contrast to the development of underground infrastructure in Japan that follows the limits of public ownership. Property laws in Japan were formerly so restrictive that even compulsory acquisition was impossible due to the high compensation linked to high land value. Inevitably, this led to new legislation in Japan limiting the depth of land ownership to 40 m below a basement or 10 m below foundation piles. The space beneath property is deemed to be space that can be used in the public interest (Admiraal and Cornaro, 2016). Zhou and Zhao (2016) have reported changes in legislation in Singapore that make development of underground space possible:

In Feb 2015, the Singapore Parliament passed two significant legislations aimed at addressing the issue of ownership and acquisition of underground space, the State Lands (Amendment) Act 2015, and the Land Acquisition (Amendment) Act 2015. The State Lands (Amendment) Act 2015 defines ownership of the subterranean space as 'land includes only as much of the subterranean space as is reasonably necessary for the use and enjoyment of the land.' It further defines reasonable use as being: a) such depth of subterranean space as stated in the State title for that land; or b) if no such depths is specified, subterranean space to −30m below the Singapore Height Datum.

In terms of defining the limits of ownership, we can see a parallel with the Swiss approach. The change to the Land Acquisition (Amendment) Act 2015 interestingly allows the compulsory acquisition of a 'specific stratum of underground space' (Zhou and Zhao, 2016).

A new appreciation of the use of underground space requires an evaluation of existing policies and legislation. As Sandberg (2003) concluded:

> Subsurface development, just like the development of surface space, requires the formulation of a broad planning strategy that targets in advance areas for subsurface use, and prepares the appropriate infrastructure over many years … As soon as the axiomatic property impediment to three-dimensional subdivision is removed, planning restrictions and planning supervision will be of decisive importance in shaping the relationship among the three-dimensional units. The importance of long-term planning for subsurface use will increase.

Solving land ownership issues is possible within most legal systems. It requires either a lot of negotiation or public acquisition. In whatever way the use of the subsurface is achieved, it calls for some form of agreement and compensation.

8.3. Easement and right-of-way compensation

In the previous section we touched on how in legal terms through easement and right-of-way agreement can be reached on the use of underground space below someone else's property. We also saw that, whether it is through private agreement or through public expropriation, the actual use of the space needs to be compensated to the owner.

Carmody and Sterling (1993) have argued that the development of underground space is connected with land value prices or easement cost. Although this seems a fair comparison at first, the compensation cost for easement could actually be significant.

Lea (1994) has provided a thought-provoking insight into the way that easements are valued, as in the case of the Los Angeles Metro. He argued that the use of the subsurface below someone's property without requiring surface access has little or no economic effect for the land owner. Things change, however, when the impact on potential future development is considered (Lea, 1994):

> The potential problem areas for future development fall under the following four general categories:
>
> ■ Is construction above the tunnels legally or physically possible?
>
> ■ Do the tunnels and their easements limit the potential density or scale of future development?
>
> ■ Will construction costs be measurably increased as a result of the presence of the tunnels?

- Will limitations on subterranean parking negatively affect construction costs or building appeal and operations?

It is these considerations that will rapidly increase the cost for easement, as the easement for underground transport systems is often perpetual. As we saw in Section 5.2 in the case of Helsinki, the local geology plays an important role too. Future surface development could take place free of any subsurface development in the case of rock conditions. In softer soils, future surface development could be severely limited in the case of subsurface use. Especially when we touch on private ownership versus public needs for transportation, this can lead to substantial easement costs to compensate the owner for future loss of income from development restrictions caused by the subsurface development.

The development of the London Underground ran into this problem in its extensions during the first half of the 20th century: 'With the extensions of the tubes from 1913 until the 1940s, the railways began passing under property, but as with the City & South London, this was subject to the purchase of easements, which could considerably drive up costs of delivering the new railway' (Darroch, 2014).

What this means is that, apart from legal instruments in terms of settling easement and rights of way, instruments are required to appraise the cost of an easement.

8.4. The principle of tort

Before we can discuss the issue of tort, we need to point to the fact that legal systems worldwide vary. This variance is as rich as the Earth's geology, and requires different solutions in different locales. Just as there is no universal design for a tunnel, there is no universal legal system. In general, we can distinguish between the Anglo-American system of common law and the European model of civil law, or coded law. The latter stems from Napoleonic times and the French Code Civile. The main difference between the two systems is that civil law is a codified law. Common law is based much more on the interpretation of cases within the principles of law. In the English and American courts, cases and rulings are cited to argue a point of law, and this in itself can lead to a new ruling, clarifying the case put before the court. In civil law, interpretations can be made, but they are always based on a law or part of the law and how to interpret the law rather than the case.

According to Uff (2013), 'Tort can be defined as a civil wrong independent of contract; or as a breach of a legal duty owed to persons generally.'

Within common law countries, tort involves many categories, and its application is solely based on interpretations of cases that have been brought to the courts. In civil law countries, the principle of tort is codified but based on the same notion that people must be protected from the civil wrong inflicted through actions of others. In the Netherlands Civil Code, tort is dealt with in Article 6:162, which states that the party that commits a tort towards another is obliged to compensate the losses that the other party suffers as a result of the civil wrong inflicted (Government of the Netherlands, 2017).

Governance and legal challenges of underground space use

The principle of tort is relevant to the use of underground space as an often overlooked consequence. A parallel can be drawn with the rise of condominiums in the USA in the late 1960s as a new way of dealing with housing issues: this required the property of house owners to be distinguished in one building at various levels. As Rohan (1967) wrote:

> Enabling acts, designed to provide a legislative foundation for the condominium format and to fit it into the existing legal system, have been enacted by the federal government, District of Columbia, and forty-nine states. However, perfection should not be anticipated in such a broad undertaking; drafting flaws are certain to appear as experience is gained with various condominium uses. One such imperfection has recently come to the writer's attention, namely, failure to clarify the unit owner's posture (and

that of his household) with respect to tort liability and insurance. What is the nature and extent of the risk assumed as co-owner of the project and its facilities? What policies are available to neutralize this exposure and should protection be purchased on an individual or community basis, or perhaps both? Conversely, is a participant permitted to sue the group (or a fellow unit owner) if negligently harmed? Would such a judgment be covered by a master liability policy?

These questions are as relevant for the layered ownership or use of underground space as they are for layered ownership inside one building. An illustration of this can be found in the centre of the City of Rotterdam. The Willems Rail Tunnel is a four-track-wide rail tunnel running through the Rotterdam city centre. It is the main north–south rail line in the Netherlands. Construction works for the partially immersed tunnel and partially cut-and-cover tunnel started

Figure 8-2 The elevated rail line through Rotterdam (below) and redevelopment on top of the Willems Rail Tunnel (below right) | Courtesy of https://beeldbank.rws.nl, Rijkswaterstaat and Aeroview respectively

on 28 April 1987, exactly 110 years after the opening of the elevated railway. The railways in the Netherlands were very much a royal initiative, with King William I personally pushing for rapid development of the rail system. In 1993, the elevated rail line started being demolished, and the first two tracks of the tunnel, named after King William I, were inaugurated (Figure 8.2). The project was completed 3 years later, in 1996. To allow the connection of the immersed part beneath the Maas River to the cut-and-cover parts, a building pit was created on the banks of the river. The plans called for the area's redevelopment after completion of the tunnel. For this purpose, the tunnel construction was additionally strengthened to allow for building on top of the tunnel roof after its completion. The historic houses that had been built in the 19th century, and were in or near the tunnel alignment, had to be demolished brick by brick. The famous White House, built in 1898 and considered the first skyscraper in Europe, was saved, alongside seven other shipping merchant houses. These houses were later rebuilt in the 1990s; however, one large building dating from 1917 – The Insurance House – was not rebuilt. This left a large hole waiting for a new development. Finally, in 2009, permission was obtained to start this development (Van Haastrecht, 2009). Part of the legal battle that took place between 1996 and 2009 concerned with issue of tort. Not unlike previous questions posed about ownership of condominiums, this was about who would be liable for damages during construction, and further damages incurred if rail operation were interrupted as a result of construction or future surface use

above the tunnel. ProRail, the network operator, had cold feet at first. Demanding numerous reports and using safety as a reason, it wanted reassurance that construction and use would not lead to disruption of services. Conversely, ProRail also wanted assurance that any movement in the soft soil of the tunnel would not lead to damages in the building on top, and tort claims as a result.

This case clearly illustrates that apart from dealing with land ownership and using instruments such as easements or right of way, any servitudes that result from multiple and layered use of the subsurface need to be judged in terms of tort and potential liability. This also holds true for the original land owner, who can still be held liable by third parties for use of their land by other parties, after everything has been settled in contracts. Such a situation can be prevented by ensuring there are proper indemnification clauses in contracts.

The principle of tort applies to the use of the subsurface, as it does in any other situation. With the advent of growing use of urban underground space, it will be interesting to see how tort law and its interpretation will develop.

8.5. Building codes

The town of Coober Pedy in South Australia is one of the hottest places on Earth, with summer temperatures often exceeding 40°C. This town is well known for two reasons: firstly, it is seen as the opal capital of the world, with this gemstone being mined in the town since 1915; secondly, it is known for its extensive underground dugouts – dwellings where people live below

the surface, taking advantage of the yearly constant temperature well below the outdoors temperatures. The town also has several hotels, one of which, the Desert Cave Hotel (Figure 8.3), advertises as being the only international-class underground hotel in Coober Pedy. Visitors can choose to sleep above or below ground (Desert Cave Hotel, 2017):

> Visitors can stay underground, or if they prefer, above ground rooms are also available. Sleeping underground is a unique experience. Quiet, cool, dark and airy - the rooms are spacious with high ceilings. Most visitors say that sleeping underground gives them the best night's sleep they have ever had!

For us, Coober Pedy is interesting in that it has for a long time had specific requirements in its building code dealing with underground habitats. Known as the *Guidelines for the Construction of Underground Buildings in Coober Pedy* and released by the District Council of Coober Pedy, the guidelines effectively continue where the Building Code of Australia (BCA) ends. In other words, the BCA is applicable to underground buildings as much as it is to underground dwellings in Coober Pedy. In specific areas, local guidelines provide further guidance in cases where the BCA does not cover them. A typical example is clause 1.4, which gives the minimum width a wall must have when it is dividing underground rooms (Figure 8.4).

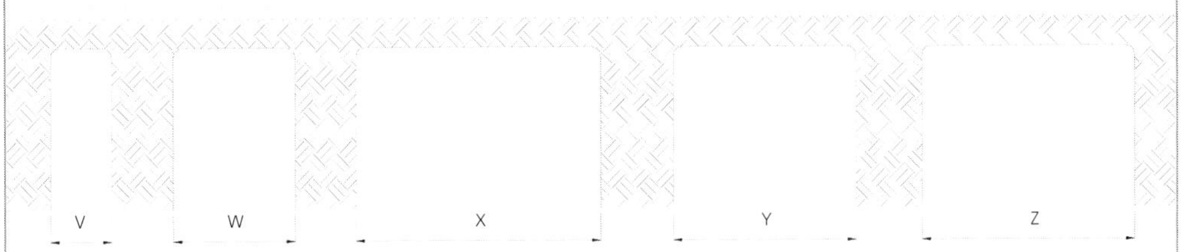

Figure 8-4 Clause 1.4 of the Coober Pedy Building Code

1.4 The combined span of an opening either side of a supporting internal wall of an underground dwelling must not exceed a ratio of six times the thickness of the wall.

Explanatory information

The ratio of the combined width of tunnelled rooms to the width of the dividing wall must not exceed 6:1. For example, the width of wall dividing two rooms each with a 3.6m width would be based on 7.2m/6 = 1.2 metres. (Clause 1.3 takes precedence in the case of a conflict with this requirement). See Figure 1.4

Minimum width of wall between rooms:

v and w $\quad \dfrac{v+w}{6} = \dfrac{3.6}{6} = 0.6$ (1.5m required *refer Clause 1.3*) $\qquad$ **x and y** $\quad \dfrac{x+y}{6} = \dfrac{8.4}{6} = 1.4$ (1.5m required)

w and x $\quad \dfrac{w+x}{6} = \dfrac{7.2}{6} = 1.2$ (1.5m required) $\qquad$ **y and z** $\quad \dfrac{y+z}{6} = \dfrac{7.8}{6} = 1.3$ (1.5m required)

V   W   X   Y   Z

Coober Pedy serves as an example of how underground construction can be regulated in building codes. We also point to an observation made by Papageorgiou that the building code in Greece effectively limits the ownership of the subsurface as it does not allow development below a certain depth on account of the many archaeological artefacts that are present in the Greek subsurface (Admiraal and Cornaro, 2016). Article 2:127 of the Netherlands Building Regulations highlights a different approach, by stating that in the case of fire safety (Government of the Netherlands, 2012), 'A building being constructed that contains a floor of a useable area higher than 70 metres above or lower than 8 metres below datum is designed in such a way

that the building remains safe in event of fire.'

Effectively, this means that although in these instances no specific guidance exists the appropriate authorities must be informed and shown that high-rise or underground buildings are just as safe as other buildings. It follows the principle that codes should cover the most general cases but not hinder future development.

The Kansas City Building and Rehabilitation Code has a specific section on underground spaces. The Code consists of the International Building Code as compiled by the International Code Council together with relevant standards of the National Fire Protection Association (NFPA, 2016). In addition, local amendments apply, as is the case for underground spaces.

When looking at the local amendments, it becomes clear that these are based on the local underground industrial complex SubTropilis (see Section 5.1.5). This can be seen from the occupancy requirements given in section 18-231: 'Group US occupancies shall be a subsurface structure formed out of a horizontal layer of solid limestone by the room-and-pillar method of mining when such underground space is developed into community housing, manufacturing, offices, warehousing, storage facilities and other classes of occupancy.'

Kjelshus (1984) has reported on how a task force was set up to specifically adapt both the building codes and zoning ordinance of Kansas City, to further stimulate the use of underground space, based on the initial success of what is now known as SubTropilis.

More generic requirements are found in the International Building Code, in section 405 on underground buildings. As such, the Kansas City example follows what we saw with the Coober Pedy case, and stimulated further adaptation of their locally developed codes into generically applicable codes.

Both codes reference the NFPA 520 standard when it comes to fire safety in underground buildings. The NFPA (2016) described the scope of NFPA 520 as follows:

> _NFPA 520: Standard on Subterranean Spaces_ covers the unique fire and life safety considerations that exist in subterranean spaces, including means of egress issues such as orientation and excessive travel distances, poor ventilation, communication difficulties, and non-traditional behavior of fire. The Standard

allows the following occupancies within new and existing subterranean space buildings: public assembly, business, educational, detention and correctional, health care, board and care, residential, industrial, mercantile, and storage uses.

Requirements include the latest criteria for:

- Construction features
- Means of egress
- Fire alarm, detection, and suppression systems
- Emergency preparedness
- Fire department provisions.

In general, we can say that, when it comes to building codes, whether adequate guidance is developed is entirely dependent on the local state of underground space use. In areas where underground development has not taken place or is not foreseen, local or national building codes will not contain any specific requirements that need to be met. The International Building Codes are, in that sense, an exception to the rule, as they proactively provide requirements. In terms of life and fire safety, the NFPA standards provide specific guidance as well. In the absence of national guidance on underground buildings or facilities, the combination of the International Building Codes and NFPA standards provide comprehensive guidance.

A practice that is often seen is to use existing guidance developed for buildings at the surface and apply it to underground buildings. We strongly recommend that this tactic is not undertaken. The reason for this is that underground buildings require a specific approach, as has been demonstrated by the case of Coober Pedy. Rather than applying existing guidance that was not developed for this purpose, it would be better to look at the guidelines quoted in this chapter.

8.6. Environmental control

Any human intervention in underground space is also an intervention that, in some way, is going to influence the environment. As we saw earlier, the future development of buildings or infrastructure, constructed either partially or entirely below the surface, needs to be developed in harmony with nature. Sustainable development requires an awareness of the services that the subsurface provides. Constructing physical objects below the surface is not just about creating space for various uses; the act of construction itself is also about extracting materials from the Earth. It is a human intervention that potentially interferes with the ecosystem services while at the same time removing resources.

In many countries there will be a degree of regulation and control of these processes. As the awareness of the environment grew, so did the measures to prevent unwanted and unnecessary damage. Brownfields in many western European cities are leftovers from an industrial past that have left a legacy of contaminated soils and groundwater. Redevelopment of these sites is a formidable challenge, where public authorities and private developers point at each other when it comes to the cost of rehabilitation.

Environmental legislation usually requires an environmental impact assessment to be carried out for particular categories of projects. Large infrastructure projects fall into this category, as do pipeline projects when carrying dangerous goods. A typical office building, even if it includes a large basement, usually falls outside this category. This omission brings up the question whether, in the case of the subsurface, the depth to which an activity extends itself should be the determinant for whether or not some environmental assessment needs to take place.

In the Netherlands, in the city of Terneuzen, which is located along the Ghent–Terneuzen shipping canal, a plan was conceived for a spatial reservation for a pipeline corridor to connect the port of Ghent with the Western Scheldt Estuary. This corridor would run from the industrial cluster along the Western Scheldt, parallel to the canal to Ghent, and a spatial reservation would make it easier in the mid-term to place pipelines required as part of the industrial symbiosis between clusters in the Netherlands and Belgium (Flanders). An environmental impact assessment was required by the city council, to approve a local spatial strategy for a pipeline corridor. The basis of the assessment focused on the sustainability effects of the project. Interestingly, a matrix was used to assess the sustainability effects, concentrating on the 'when', 'where' and 'what'. The aspect of time (when) looked at how the present, future and intermediate were affected. The last category came about from the idea that the present and future could be defined, but that the intermediate effects needed to be looked at as well. There is quite a difference between constructing a whole corridor at once versus it coming about over a period of 10 years – the former requiring only the excavation of one trench, the latter requiring repeated trenches over a period of years. Agriculture was the primary use of the land below which the corridor was projected, and while topsoil removal was once a process that was deemed to be reversible, doing this more than five times in 10 years would make the land virtually barren and unusable.

The aspect of location (where) looked at the effects *in situ* and *ex situ*. Doing so allowed a distinction between benefits directly affecting the region and those that were of more national interest. The third aspect (what) allowed a distinction between people, the planet and profit, the three determinants of sustainability (Jumelet *et al.*, 2012).

What this case illustrates is that when we call for a holistic approach to urban planning that includes the subsurface, we need to do the same when it comes to environmental control. In the case of the example given here, 'planet' was further subdivided into the subsurface, water, landscape, nature, use of mineral resources and fossil fuels, and carbon dioxide emissions. It allowed a total assessment of the impact of the project and a weighting of benefits to support the decision-making process.

Even though these evaluations are important for making strategic decisions, controls that regulate water quantity and quality, extraction of mineral resources, extraction or storage of energy, and use of the subsurface for storage of carbon dioxide are needed as well. It goes without saying that when creating projects such as the 57 km-long Gotthard Base Tunnel passing under the Swiss Alps, which, as we saw in Section 5.2, created a spill of 28.7 million tonnes of rock,

a degree of control is required to regulate the disposal, preferably through recycling as part of a circular economy, as indeed happened in the case of this project.

8.7. Managing the subsurface

Webster (1914) – as we saw in Section 3.3 – pointed to the problems that could arise if no planning of what he called the subterranean street has taken place. Even if we could plan in the sense that we have a vision and strategy regarding the use of underground space, this also needs to be managed in some way. This management requires not only an in-depth knowledge of the natural environment below the surface but also requires knowledge of the physical objects present in underground space.

Before we look at the question on how to achieve this, we need to look at the subsurface from a perspective of scale. We can do this by comparing the subsurface with the sky. When looking up at the sky, we can see planes overhead flying into airports or having just taken off. On clear days, we can observe condensation trails of jets flying at high altitudes. At night, while gazing at the stars in outer space, we can spot satellites as they follow their trajectory around our planet. What the casual observer fails to notice is the planning of the sky and its complex regulations, ensuring not only safety through separation of air traffic but also providing noise avoidance as planes approach the ground to land at an airport.

Planning the sky is achieved by dividing the sky into flight information regions, consisting of a lower and an upper part. Within the lower parts, we find further subdivisions into sectors

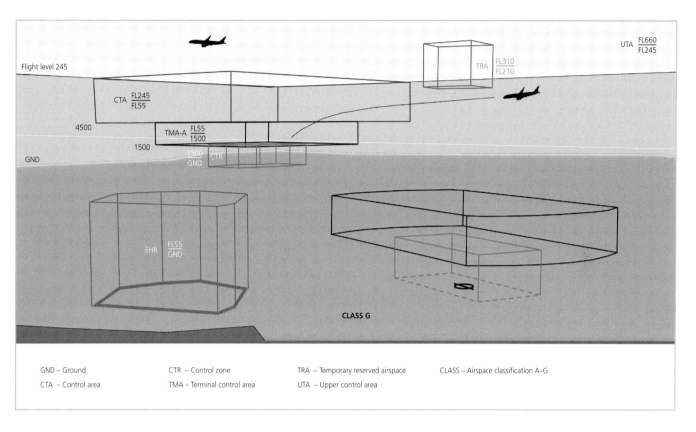

Figure 8-5 within image:

Flight level 245

UTA FL660/FL245

TRA FL310/FL210

CTA FL245/FL55

4500

TMA-A FL55/1500

1500

GND

1500/GND CTR

EHR FL55/GND

CLASS G

GND – Ground   CTR – Control zone   TRA – Temporary reserved airspace   CLASS – Airspace classification A–G

CTA – Control area   TMA – Terminal control area   UTA – Upper control area

for en route traffic, and terminal control zones and control areas for traffic landing and taking off from airports. There are radio beacons and reporting points. Flying into danger zones is prohibited because of objects at the surface or because they are reserved for training purposes (Figure 8.5).

One thing we can learn from this is that height is a determining factor in being able to manage airspace. Secondly, we learn that as we get closer to the ground, airspace becomes more congested, which means it is increasingly regulated – not only because of the volume of use but also because of the interdependency that exists between the surface and the sky. The presence of cities with high-rise buildings influences flight paths. The presence of airports with radar coverage and instrument landing systems require an absence of buildings. As we move up into the sky and climb into the upper areas, traffic density decreases, and we see new types of free airspace, where flights can choose routes between entry and exit points (Eurocontrol, 2003).

If we use this analogy for managing and regulating underground space, then we can

Figure 8-5 Schematic three-dimensional visualisation of German airspace

see how the concept of levels translates into what we have called layers. The idea of sectorisation is the same as zoning. We can reserve underground space for particular uses, or prohibit activities taking place in certain areas. As we approach the surface, the use of the subsurface densifies and requires different kinds of regulation and control than for the subsurface at greater depth.

The City of Rotterdam uses a model for its urban planning that distinguishes the following layers: ground elevated, ground level, shallow subsurface (0–15 m), civil construction layer (15–50 m), water layer (50–500 m), deep subsurface (>500 m). Interestingly, it limits the influence of municipal planning to the level of the civil construction layer. Regional planning should take the water layer into account, and the deep subsurface requires national planning. This is an attempt to fit the concept of volumetric underground planning into the standard two-dimensional planning practice, combined with the governance layers that exist within the country (Van Campenhout et al., 2016).

From the way that airspace is organised, we can learn that control of the skies can take place across national boundaries and that, in certain areas, multiple national airspaces are monitored by a transnational entity, such as Eurocontrol.

The need to manage underground space requires us to look outside our traditional ways of thinking and, maybe, learn from the structuring and regulating of airspace (or even outer space!) in an attempt to find a suitable methodology for underground space planning. The concepts of layering, zoning and density of use near the surface, as well as the interdependency with

uses at the surface, are good starting points to achieve this.

The challenge, once again, is data acquisition. The skies have become not only safer in recent years but also more heavily used due to there being a reduction in the vertical separation between flights. This was only possible because of advances in positioning technology. Modern aircraft are equipped with independent navigation systems that accurately determine their position and transmit this information to ground stations. They are equipped with collision avoidance systems that talk to other aircraft in the vicinity and determine collision avoidance actions in such a way that mid-air accidents are avoided. The parallel with underground space is that there is now more information available than ever before. Geologists are upping their game and refining their models. The advent of building information modelling (BIM) provides a data container with unlimited amounts of information on construction works. The challenge is to sort out the real data from noise in this abundance of data, and to find formats that allow the exchange of data. Visualising this data in such a way that the underground space controller can make sense of it is the biggest challenge that remains.

When it comes to airspace management, every nation on this planet has its own national civil aviation authority. All these national bodies are members of the International Civil Aviation Authority, a United Nations agency. For controlling and regulating outer space, the UN has an agency called the Office for Outer Space Affairs (Admiraal and Cornaro, 2013). Yet, when it comes to underground space, there is no governance, no regulation and no international oversight, even though the actions of one nation could seriously affect other nations. We believe that, when it comes to underground space, leaving it up to local governments to sort things out might be a solution in the short term. The implications of a more intensive use of underground space require a national if not international debate. A national body that regulates and manages underground space may be needed, even if only to ensure that data acquisition and exchange of information becomes mandatory. International agreements may very well be needed on the extent to which human intervention is allowed below the surface, and limiting the depth to which nations can claim territorial rights. This would also ensure no activities taking place at great depth endanger life at the surface across international boundaries.

8.8. This chapter's core ideas

We started this chapter by stating that government oversight of the subsurface is not only required to regulate the use of underground space but also to protect the ecosystem services that are vital to life on the surface. The balancing act we wrote about in Chapter 2 can only come about if this is recognised and covered by regulations.

Regulating land ownership of the subsurface in such a way that the concept of ownership to the centre of the Earth is limited in the same way that it does not extend upwards into outer space is vital to achieving this balance. It does not mean that land ownership ceases at the surface

or that we should not regulate and compensate any loss of use or loss of property.

The principle of tort could prove to be a limiting factor when it comes to the development of underground space. Where existing regulations regarding land ownership provide possibilities for private settlement or public expropriation of land, the principle of tort is a more difficult concept to address. It can hinder new projects in the context of unplanned development of underground space. Whether this applies or not depends on the type of geology, the ownership of the land and the legal status of the party developing the project, as illustrated in the Helsinki example.

Building codes vary from a global approach to underground construction to quite detailed requirements. The level of detail depends on the actual use of underground space. As we saw from both the Coober Pedy and Kansas City examples, extensive underground space use also drives the development of regulations in that respect. International building codes present a comprehensive approach, and are a good starting point in the absence of any local building regulations for underground space.

Construction in underground space requires environmental control: not just from the aspect of assessing the impact on the environment – part of the balancing act between preservation and exploration of the subsurface – but also regulating the spill from the underground works in such a way that there is no negative impact on the environment. Recycling this spill as building material rather than just dumping as waste seems a more sensible option that also fits in with the concept of a circular economy.

Governance of the subsurface also requires active management to ensure the achievement and safeguarding of what was planned. Managing requires the usual balancing act between preservation and exploitation. It also requires thinking in terms of volume rather than in area. Depth becomes a determining component. To find a methodology for managing the subsurface we looked at the skies and at how airspace is organised and structured. We feel that this analogy is valid, in that a comparison between airspace and underground space shows some very distinct similarities. Rather than extending area-focused planning and management as used at the surface, the more volumetric approach used for both airspace and in outer space and defined as outside national interests could also point a way forwards when it comes to the planning and management of underground space.

References

1 Admiraal H and Cornaro A (2013) From outer space to underground space – helping cities become more resilient. In *UN Inter-Agency Meeting on Outer Space Activities: Space and Disaster Risk Reduction: Planning for Resilient Human Settlements, Vienna, Austria*. http://www.unoosa.org/oosa/en/ourwork/un-space/ois/10th.html (accessed 14/11/2017). (Microsoft PowerPoint presentation.)

2 Admiraal H and Cornaro, A (2016) Why underground space should be included in urban planning policy – and how this will enhance an urban underground future. *Tunnelling and Underground Space Technology* **55**: 214–220.

3 Barker M (1991) Legal and administrative issues in underground space use: a preliminary survey of ITA member nations. *Tunnelling and Underground Space Technology* **6(2)**: 191–209.

4 Boermans R and Ten Have T (2000) *Privaatrechtelijke aspecten van ondergronds ruimtegebruik*. Centrum Ondergronds Bouwen, Gouda, the Netherlands, Report B100. (In Dutch.)

5 Carmody J and Sterling R (1993) *Underground Space Design*. Van Nostrand Reinhold, New York, NY, USA.

6 Darroch N (2014) A brief introduction to London's underground railways and land use. *Journal of Transport and Land Use* **7(1)**: 105–116.

7 Desert Cave Hotel (2017) http://www.desertcave.com.au (accessed 14/11/2017).

8 Durmisevic S (1999) The future of the underground space. *Cities* **16(4)**: 233–245.

9 Eurocontrol (2003) *Eurocontrol Manual for Air Space Planning*, vol. 2. Eurocontrol, Brussels, Belgium. See https://www.icao.int/safety/pbn/Documentation/EUROCONTROL/Eurocontrol%20Manual%20for%20Airspace%20Planning.pdf (accessed 14/11/2017).

10 Government of the Netherlands (2012) Bouwbesluit 2012. Government of the Netherlands, The Hague, the Netherlands. http://wetten.overheid.nl/BWBR0030461/2017-07-01 (accessed 14/11/2017).

11 Government of the Netherlands (2016) *Ontwerp Structuurvisie Ondergrond*. Ministry of Infrastructure and Environment and Ministry of Economic Affairs, The Hague, the Netherlands. See https://www.rijksoverheid.nl/documenten/

rapporten/2016/11/11/ontwerp-structuurvisie-ondergrond (accessed 14/11/2017). (In Dutch.)

12 Government of the Netherlands (2017) Burgerlijk Wetboek Boek 6. Government of the Netherlands, The Hague, the Netherlands. http://wetten.overheid.nl/BWBR0005289/2017-09-01 (accessed 14/11/2017).

13 Her Majesty's Government (2008) Cross Rail Act 2008. The Stationery Office, London, UK. https://www.legislation.gov.uk/ukpga/2008/18/contents (accessed 14/11/2017).

14 Jumelet H, Elings C and Van Ginkel M (2012) *Milieueffectrapportage: Multi Utility Providing*. Zeeland Seaports, Terneuzen, the Netherlands. (In Dutch.)

15 Kjelshus B (1984) Encouraging underground space development: modifications to Kansas City's building code and zoning ordinance. *Underground Space* **8(5–6):** 320–330.

16 Lea R (1994) Subway tunnel easements in metropolitan areas. *Appraisal Journal* **62(2):** 310. See https://www.thefreelibrary.com/ents+in+metropolitan+areas.-a015409723 (accessed 14/11/2017).

17 Netherlands Ministry of Infrastructure and Environment (2017) *MRT onderzoek goederenvervoercorridors Oost en Zuidoost. The Dutch Logistic Corridors*. Ministry of Infrastructure and Environment. https://www.rijksoverheid.nl/documenten/rapporten/2017/07/07/mrt-onderzoek-goederenvervoercorridors-oost-en-zuidoost (accessed 14/11/2017). (In Dutch.)

18 NFPA (2016) *NFPA 520: Standard on Subterranean Spaces*. NFPA, Quincy, MA, USA. See http://catalog.nfpa.org/NFPA-520-Standard-on-Subterranean-Spaces-P1329.aspx?icid=D729 (accessed 14/11/2017).

19 Rohan PJ (1967) Perfecting the condominium as a housing tool: innovations in tort liability and insurance. *Law and Contemporary Problems* **32:** 305.

20 Sandberg H (2003) Three-dimensional partition and registration of subsurface land space. *Israel Law Review* **37(1):** 119–167.

21 Thomas WA (1979) Ownership of subterranean space. *Tunnels and Underground Space Technology* **3(4):** 155–163.

22 Uff J (2013) *Construction Law*, 11th edn. Sweet and Maxwell, London, UK.

23 Van Campenhout I, De Vette K, Schokker J and Van der Meulen M (2016) *Rotterdam: TU1206 COST Sub-Urban WG1 Report*. COST, Brussels, Belgium. See https://static1.squarespace.com/static/542bc753e4b0a87901dd6258/t/577a622146c3c4b3877d44 2d/1467638323226/TU1206-WG1–013+Rotterdam+City+Case+Study_red+size.pdf (accessed 14/11/2017).

24 Van Haastrecht R (2009) ProRail staat bouwen op spoortunnel toe. *Trouw*. https://www.trouw.nl/home/prorail-staat-bouwen-op-spoortunnel-toe~a73e9fbe/ (accessed 14/11/2017). (In Dutch.)

25 Webster GS (1914) Subterranean street planning. *Annals of the American Academy of Political and Social Science* **51:** 200–207.

26 Zhou Y and Zhao J (2016) Advances and challenges in underground space use in Singapore. *Geotechnical Engineering Journal* **47(3):** 85–95.

Chapter 9

Investing in underground space is all about value capture

9.1. The cost conundrum

There is a legend that is often used by consultants called the 'boiling frog' that, although it has been disproven by biologists, illustrates that people seem to have a natural inability or unwillingness to react to or be aware of threats that arise gradually and can have undesirable consequences. In case of the frog legend, the story goes that if you attempt to put a frog into a pan of hot water, it will immediately jump out, as the high temperature makes it aware of life-threatening danger. But if you place the frog in a pan of cold water and then gradually increase the temperature, the frog will sit in it until it's too late to jump and it's boiled. Schneider *et al.* (2013) observed this in the context of climate change, citing Anthony Giddens's paradox:

> since the dangers posed by global warming aren't tangible, immediate or visible in the course of day-to-day-life, however awesome they appear, many will sit on their hands and do nothing of a concrete nature about them. Yet waiting until they become visible and acute before stirred to serious action will, by definition, be too late.

It was Diamond (2005) who first introduced a term for this: 'creeping normalcy'. Creeping normalcy is not only a challenge when it comes to climate change: it influences decisions taken on the non-use of underground space too. What sometimes appears to be politicians' short-sightedness can actually, in our opinion, be attributed to the creeping normalcy phenomenon. When it comes to our cities and the available space, the sorites paradox seems to apply. Consider a heap of sand. Now imagine taking away a grain of sand one at a time from that heap. When does the heap stop being a heap? When politicians are asked to choose between two options, a surface solution and a subsurface solution, the former requiring less initial investment and less initial disruption than the latter, the usual reaction would be to choose the former as long as it is possible. The depletion of urban space, and with it all that makes cities liveable, is a creeping normalcy. 'When does a city stop being a city?' is thus answered by 'When all the space runs out.' However, this should not be the way we look at our cities, the projects they need, and the way we appraise and fund these projects. It is this normalcy that is proving to be the second reason why the use of urban underground space has stagnated. Once surface space does run out or becomes very sparse, such as in the case of Singapore, land prices rocket sky high. Only then are we willing to turn away from skyscrapers and, metaphorically speaking, consider 'earthscrapers'.

When it comes to climate change, Green (2015) found that the cost of doing nothing outweighs by far the cost of doing something. Humankind is showing no sense of urgency, and even apocalyptic visions of the future of humans and this planet cannot move us away from our presumption of safety as the climate gradually heats up. What we now perceive as comfortable warmth, so to speak, could be tricking us into feelings of wellbeing grounded on nothing more than creeping normalcy. We need to act now, and when it comes to the question of using a city's underground space, it is not a case of waiting until needed but acting while it is still possible.

9.2. Creating societal value

Heertje (2000) has discussed a common misconception spreading through Europe: economics is all about money. He pointed out that economics deals with scarcity, among other things. When we look at how we can justify investment in underground space projects, a frequently used instrument is a cost–benefit analysis. The cost–benefit analysis is, in essence, an economic model that compares the cost and benefits of one or more projects. The common metric used to make the comparison is, of course, money. Heertje quoted a colleague who once said to him that the biggest abstraction introduced by humankind is money. It is essential that we understand that there is a difference between the economic models we use to justify a decision in favour of a project and the financial models that will eventually determine the budget required to develop these projects. The fact that both use money as a primary abstraction does not help in making things clearer when it comes to making this distinction.

The most rudimentary way of comparing projects is to look at the initial investment cost required to build a project. When it comes to comparing a bridge to a tunnel, these comparisons most often favour the bridge as the least costly option. Such comparisons are limited in that not only is the comparison done by financial cost, it is also limited to the initial investment – that is, capital expenditure. For a more unbiased comparison, it is necessary to look at the total life-cycle of a project and the total cost of ownership – the latter being the sum of the capital expenditure and the operational expenditure. However, even when doing this it was found that underground solutions often failed to reach the next stage of the planning process. As was observed by the UK Parliamentary Office of Science and Technology (POST, 1997): 'Proponents of tunnel options see the current situation as unsatisfactory because current appraisal methods largely fail to take account of the costs to the environment, health and quality of life of pursuing surface options.'

Kotsareli et al. (2013) reached more or less the same conclusion as above:

> The decision making process between underground or above-ground alternatives sometimes favors conventional surface solutions and penalizes underground projects on

the grounds of their high initial costs. Though, as it has been demonstrated in the present paper, this decision should consider the benefits of increased long-term social and environmental improvements and related economic development. This is true especially in the case of underground rapid transport systems. Metros are large infrastructure projects that are built in the context of contemporary urban areas, they are expected to have a long lifetime service and their impact on urban development is quite significant.

Even though the appraisal schemes look at the direct and indirect costs, they fail to take into account the direct and indirect benefits. These benefits usually translate into societal benefits. In the guidance given on cost–benefit analysis (CBA) by the Netherlands Government (Romijn and Renes, 2015), CBA is characterised as follows:

> The essence of a CBA is weighing up different project or policy alternatives by comparing their welfare effects on society as a whole: the economic and social costs and benefits calculated at the national level. The CBA therefore addresses the question 'How does total social welfare change?' An additional important question is 'How are the costs and benefits distributed?' The role of CBA in decision-making is to make discussions about policy as objective as possible.

Core to making policy decisions as objective as possible is therefore looking at both the economic and social costs and benefits. Brown (2014) makes the case for justification for infrastructure ecology by introducing the metrics in Box 9.1. The sum of all these metrics then gives the total benefits and cost savings for the project. The metrics provide us with a thought-provoking indication of effects that can be considered.

It is important to note that cost and social benefits in Brown's approach can be gained through site co-location, as we saw in the example of the Croton Water Filtration Plant in New York (see Section 2.4). An example of eliminated redundancies in maintenance and operation is the use of multi-utility corridors, as will be discussed later.

When it comes to societal benefits, these are no more evident than when elevated

Box 9-1 Justification for infrastructure ecology

- Site optimisation through multiple land use (co-location)

- Economies of scale

- Elimination of redundancies in maintenance and operation

- Synergistic cascading of energy and/or resources

- Reduced environmental impact/resource conservation

- Reduced construction disruption

- Community benefits

- Job creation and new tax revenue

- Increased resilience

Investing in underground space is all about value capture

Figure 9-1 Transformation of the Rio de Janeiro waterfront | (right, far right) © Porto Maravilha – RJ (below right) Courtesy of Mario Roberto Duran Ortiz, reproduced under CC BY-SA 4.0

infrastructures, cutting through urban areas, are removed by placing them below the surface in road or rail tunnels. The Congress for New Urbanism (CNU, 2017) makes the case quite clearly when it stated that 'In the 20th century, the American era of highway-building created sprawling freeways that cut huge swaths through our cities. Too often vibrant, diverse, and functioning neighborhoods were destroyed or isolated by their construction, devastating communities and economies alike.'

In recent years, urban planners have been looking at new ways to revitalise areas that have fallen prey to elevated highways and railways, often considering their replacement with underground solutions. A good example is the Elevado da Perimetral that used to dominate the Rio de Janeiro waterfront in Brazil. The area had become run down, and consisted of old warehouses. By constructing two road tunnels, the Rio 450 Tunnel and the Prefeito Marcello Alencar Tunnel, the capacity of the former elevated Perimetral was sufficiently compensated for its removal. In doing so, the city centre and the urban waterfront were reconnected, which now also includes the Museum of Tomorrow

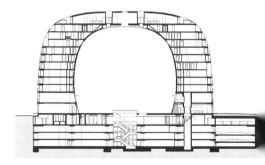

designed by architect Santiago Calatrava. The project itself was part of the Porto Maravilha transformation of the old port area. It also included the construction of a boulevard that created new public spaces, a light railway and plenty of trees (Figure 9.1). The CNU's slogan 'Highways to boulevards' is certainly applicable to this vast urban regeneration project.

In Section 8.4 we saw how the elevated railway line in Rotterdam, the Netherlands, was replaced by a rail tunnel. In doing so, it was possible to create new space for further redevelopment of the city centre. One of the new developments was the Markthal or Market Hall project. Similar to the Museum of Tomorrow, the project would never have taken place if the elevated railway had still been there. The Markthal now contains a permanent covered market, food courts, housing in the outer shell and, in the underground space, a supermarket and three floors of parking. The design cleverly uses the vista onto the city that is now visible as a backdrop from inside the hall: a view that came about through the demolition of the railway viaduct (Figure 9.2).

The Alaskan Way Viaduct has dominated the urban waterfront of Seattle, Washington, since the 1950s. The viaduct, carrying State Route 99 through the city, has been a prominent part of the cityscape, offering drivers a beautiful view of Elliott Bay. Unfortunately for everyone else, the viaduct was an eyesore, hiding Elliott Bay from the city and effectively cutting the city off from its waterfront: as Seattle's city engineer said on completion of the viaduct, 'It's not beautiful' (Washington State Department of Transportation, 2017). It did, however, serve its purpose, providing a better flow of traffic.

Renner (2018) has pointed to the value of the urban waterfront:

> Green strips along rivers have the highest potential for successful recreational areas. When activated with programmes, they can be qualitative, local recreation areas for all city dwellers. Green systems have an impact on our perception of the city. They increase the perceived quality of life and increase the attractiveness of their location. In the competition for the most livable city and

Figure 9-2 MVRDV's Market Hall in the centre of Rotterdam, the Netherlands | Illustration © MVRDV. Photograph courtesy of Scagliola and Brakkee, Rotterdam.

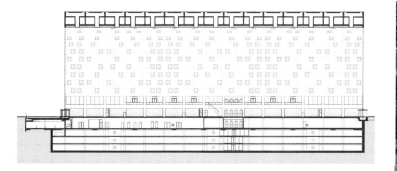

the resulting influx of talented workers, that have an economic impact as well.

The replacement of the Alaskan Way Viaduct became a necessity, as it was reaching its end of life, hastened by earthquakes in the region. By placing State Route 99 in a 3.2 km-long tunnel, the opportunity arose to regenerate the city's waterfront (Figure 9.3). Waterfront Seattle (2017) described its vision as follows:

> Waterfront Seattle will create a new public space that reconnects Seattle to Elliott Bay. Once the aging Alaskan Way viaduct is removed in early 2019, the program will build a new, multimodal surface street along Alaskan Way and Elliott Way providing access in and out of downtown, create eight acres of new public parks, and improve east-west street connections from Seattle's retail core, Pioneer Square and Belltown to the waterfront. The program is led by the City of Seattle's Office of the Waterfront, and builds on the construction currently underway to replace the Elliott Bay Seawall.

It is a clear demonstration of how societal benefits are gained and value is created by developing underground space. As we will explore later on, the challenge is capturing this societal value, to create funding for the project. Combining infrastructure replacement with urban regeneration is one approach that can be followed.

Renner (2018) sees the city not as a living entity, but rather as an 'urban being'. Considered in this way, the city itself does not live – but humans bring it to life. The urban being in his thinking refers to the whole urban entity or the people themselves. His observation that the 'many urban beings do not possess large green systems' is a poignant one. Green areas are, in our opinion, as vital to the urban being as lungs are to human beings. In Section 2.4 we discussed the need for green spaces in urban areas. It is not just that green increases the 'perceived quality of life' as Renner sees it: green gives a direct contribution to the wellbeing of the urban being. Green infrastructure makes our cities more liveable and pleasant. Green is a pleasant colour to our eyes. Plants, trees and greenery in general are a pleasant contrast to

Figure 9-3 Alaskan Way in Seattle (right) with the viaduct and (far right) after traffic has been moved to the tunnel | Courtesy of Joe Mabel (right) and the Washington State Department of Transportation (far right)

the built environment we are surrounded by in cities. Wong *et al.* (2010) argued that vertical greenery systems not only provide advantages in terms of energy savings but also contribute to spatial quality, and to lessening noise and air pollution in cities, such as Singapore. Possible health benefits of creating attractive landscapes in cities can be expected based on past research by Ulrich (1984) and Hartig *et al.* (2003). Ulrich observed that patients were more likely to leave hospital sooner after an operation when they had a view of a green park, while those looking at buildings or walls overall took longer to recuperate.

KPMG (2012) reported on the economics of ecosystems and biodiversity. One of its findings was that substantial benefits could be gained by increasing the amount of green by 10% in the Bos and Lommer area of Amsterdam. These benefits were a reduction in direct health costs and an increase in the productivity of workers. The report states that if the results were scaled up to a city with 10 million inhabitants, basically the size where we start talking about mega-cities, these benefits could annually be €400 million (based on a reduction in doctor visits accounting for €65 million, and a further €328 million savings for employers by reducing sickness levels and increased productivity). Interestingly, during the Netherlands Public Health Congress in 2012, the first results of the study were presented during the workshop 'Green = free medicine'.

The findings by KPMG show us not only the importance of green to the wellbeing of the urban being but also the value creation through freeing up surface space by going underground and greening the vacant space on top.

9.3. Capturing created value

Peltier-Thiberge (2015) expressed the opinion of many when he wrote the following on the World Bank Transport for Development blog:

> As urbanization continues all over the world, many mega-cities are desperately looking for credible solutions to improve urban transport systems and reduce traffic congestion. Sophisticated but expensive systems like underground subways are economically out-of-reach for many large cities in the developing world. The good news is that there are some excellent alternatives that the World Bank Group and other international partners have been promoting.

His thinking on underground subways contains a fundamental flaw, namely that these systems are 'sophisticated but expensive': solutions should never be judged on cost alone. As we saw in the previous section, projects should be justified and appraised by the value they create. Value creation, however, is the economics of the project, the justification, why it's worth investing in it in the first place. We also need to look at value capture. Value capture is about the financing of the project; it is about acquiring sufficient funds for the project to be built. What we need to understand is that these are two entirely different things. We also need to appreciate that any proposal made that only delivers on justification is never going to get agreement from any decision-maker if you cannot at the same time show how to fund the project.

Investing in underground space is all about value capture

Figure 9-4 The Sijtwende tunnel complex and development | Courtesy of Van Hattum en Blankevoort BV

A second flaw is that often, as is the case with public transport, the focus is on solving just one issue. We do not doubt that other solutions are probably cheaper in terms of initial investment, but without considering all the benefits, as we saw in the previous section, comparisons make little sense. The real question, as Brown (2014) put it, is how can any one solution solve multiple challenges?

In 2016 the Australian Government released the *Smart Cities Plan*. In it is written that 'Cities are first and foremost for people. Their function is to serve humanity, so they must have a human form' (Australian Department of the Prime Minister and Cabinet, 2016). The plan also points to how this can be achieved:

> Smart investment that enables partnerships between governments and the private sector will deliver better infrastructure sooner, and within budget constraints. However, funding is not enough. The global lesson is that cities collaborate to compete. Success requires all tiers of government, the private sector, and community, to work together towards shared goals.

When it comes to developing underground space, we feel that this approach is the only way forward. It is about working together towards shared goals. It is also about smart investments that can capture the value that is created by projects to make them feasible from a financial point of view. 'Value capture uses a share of this increased value to help finance the infrastructure responsible for the uplift' (Australian Department of the Prime Minister and Cabinet, 2016).

Gurran and Lawler (2016), citing the *Smart Cities Plan*, gave a more detailed explanation of value capture. They distinguished transit value capture, tax increment financing and value capture through the planning process as three variants.

Transit value capture occurs when packaging a new railway with a new town development (Gurran and Lawler, 2016):

> Commercial holdings along the railway line deliver an ongoing revenue stream as does long term investment in residential development. In Hong Kong, a significant program of public rental and subsidised home ownership has also been delivered as part of this model.

A further example of this is the Sijtwende development in the towns of Voorburg and Leidschendam in the Netherlands (Figure 9.4). The project consisted of building a road and public transport tunnel in combination with the development of 700 high-level residences. Three public parties (the national government acting as the road operator, the regional transport authority and the local municipality) and one private property developer joined forces to make the project feasible (Van Beek *et al.*, 2003). Apart from the residential development, a further 10 000 m^2 of office space was developed (International Tunnelling Association, 2017).

What these examples show is that transit value capture is possible if public and private parties can collaborate in reaching a common goal, while at the same time meeting their own individual aims. In this sense, value capture needs to not only address the overall financing but also the contributions that the parties will make. Each party will then need to decide on whether to maximise or minimise its individual value capture, with obviously no agreement reached if all sides want to maximise their own value capture. In this sense, transit value capture calls more for the formation of alliances than typical joint-venture-type collaborations. It requires moving away from the initial 'What's in it for us?' to a more strategic consideration of the mutual benefits that the alliance can achieve in the long term (Doz and Hamel, 1998).

Tax increment financing aims to capture some of the value that is created by increased business revenues or rents in areas where an incremental value uplift is anticipated. Value capture is affected by levying a special property tax (Gurran and Lawler, 2016). Although simple enough in concept, raising additional taxes is always a politically sensitive issue. As Jens Kramer Mikkelsen, the CEO of CPH City & Port Development and former Lord Mayor of Copenhagen, said (Katz and Noring, 2017):

> We knew the city was in a desperate situation and we needed to come up with something to address this situation. However, to pay for the grand infrastructure project we needed serious money. We could not raise taxes. Also, we needed agility and flexibility to operate.

The project that Kramer Mikkelsen is referring to is the Copenhagen Metro – part of the Ørestad redevelopment. This case is a prime example of what Gurran and Lawler (2016) referred to as 'value capture through the planning process'. Ørestad is interesting as it not only demonstrates how to capture value in the context of underground development but also in the larger context of city redevelopment in general.

Ørestad was an area outside Copenhagen that consisted mostly of marshland and land

Investing in underground space is all about value capture

Figure 9-5 The Copenhagen model

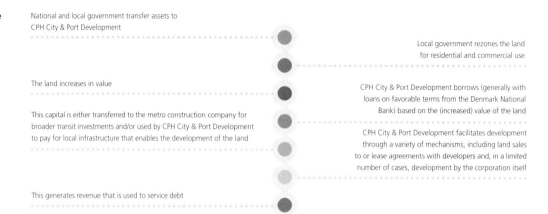

National and local government transfer assets to CPH City & Port Development

Local government rezones the land for residential and commercial use

The land increases in value

CPH City & Port Development borrows (generally with loans on favorable terms from the Denmark National Bank) based on the (increased) value of the land

This capital is either transferred to the metro construction company for broader transit investments and/or used by CPH City & Port Development to pay for local infrastructure that enables the development of the land

CPH City & Port Development facilitates development through a variety of mechanisms, including land sales to or lease agreements with developers and, in a limited number of cases, development by the corporation itself

This generates revenue that is used to service debt

owned by the Danish state. It was wedged between the airport and the city, but lying in a crucial location. With the completion of the Øresund connection, linking Denmark with Sweden, the area became directly linked to Malmø. In 1990, the Würtzen Committee was asked to outline a plan for future transportation investments in Copenhagen. Although the committee considered several options, the development potential of the land outside the city was seen as having the highest potential. The total area measured 3 km². The idea that the committee came up with was to use the development potential of this land, given its strategic location, to finance the much-needed transport solution. This idea was received with enthusiasm, and led to the Danish Parliament passing the Ørestad Act in 1992. Critical to the whole plan was that the land was brought into the specially conceived Ørestad Development Corporation that would then be responsible for developing both the area and the first two lines of the Copenhagen Metro. The development authority would generate revenue not only

through selling the land but also by levying taxes associated with land use within the area (Kampmann, 2002).

Katz and Noring (2017) showed how the model, in later years, led to a merger between the Ørestad Development Corporation and the Port of Copenhagen, creating the new CPH City & Port Development Corporation. The financing mechanism was described by them as 'simple and effective', and is shown in Figure 9.5.

Value capture through the planning process is effectively levying a charge on the property transactions that take place after a change that creates new value has taken place. This allows for capturing part of the increase in house or land values. In addition, a levy could be added to existing taxes being paid. The idea behind this way of value capture is that it seems unfair that public investments would lead to immense profit by some, rather than benefiting all (Gurran and Lawler, 2016). The Ørestad model in this sense maximises value capture, as it can take all revenues from the area through land sales and property tax.

A final example of value capture is one that we call 'value capture through private initiative'. To all intents and purposes the car park built in Boston's Post Office Square in Massachusetts was functional but drab looking – typical of the monstrous buildings we see worldwide, providing a much-needed service but at the same time destroying any sense of spatial quality (Figure 9.6). An alternative use for this space was proposed (Norman B. Leventhal Park, 2017):

> In 1982, a group of civic and business leaders discussed the possibility of creating a new public park on the site of the Post Office Square parking garage in the heart of Boston's Financial District. After extensive technical and legal analyses, the group incorporated a new civic entity in June of 1983, Friends of Post Office Square, Inc.

The idea was that this park would provide much needed green public space in the heart of the Boston central business district, creating value for the businesses and property owners around the square. This could be achieved by placing the car park below the surface, creating double the original space and allowing more cars to park.

The Friends of Post Office Square succeeded in buying out the leasehold interest of the operator of the parking garage, and paid the city $1 million for ownership of the land. The purchase agreement contained a clause – that park and garage would be returned to the city after 40 years. This time was needed to pay back the $80 million acquisition and redevelopment cost. The $80 million was partially financed through a bank loan. The remainder was

Figure 9-6 Post Office Square, Boston, Massachusetts, as it was with the car park on top | © Bill Horsman

Figure 9-7 Post Office Square with the car park below the surface and the park on top | © Ed Wonsek

financed by capturing the value that would be created through the underground car park with a park on top. The Friends of Post Office Square offered stock in the parking structure. It sold individual shares for $65 000 to local businesses. A share gave the right to a monthly parking space and a cumulative 8% dividend to be paid out when the debt relief was completed. The entire lot of 450 preferred shares was sold out in 6 weeks, raising $29.25 million. The underground car park opened in 1990, and the park in 1992 (Project for Public Spaces, 2009).

Most importantly, the whole project was privately financed, and sparked an enormous transformation for the area. It brought back spatial quality, allowing workers in adjacent offices to enjoy lunch breaks in the park (Figure 9.7).

Value capture is possible when development of underground space is integrated into urban planning, and seen as a way in which to achieve the city's goals. At the same time: 'unless value capture opportunities are explicitly identified and attended to, value capture is unlikely to take place' (Doz and Hamel, 1998). Over the years, advocates for the use of underground space have used value creation as an argument to prove the feasibility of these projects. Value creation, however, only justifies the plans, whereas value capture enables building them. But value capture requires as much innovation in terms of governance as is sometimes asked from engineers and planners. The Copenhagen model of an innovative institutional vehicle – a publicly owned, privately run corporation – could well prove to be instrumental in terms of the innovation required.

9.4. Investing in underground space

Bielenberg *et al.* (2016) opined that 'Infrastructure choices determine whether we have clean power, compact cities, and energy-efficient buildings and whether infrastructure will be resilient to a changing environment and climate.' They gave an interesting definition of sustainable infrastructure: it is socially inclusive, low carbon and climate resilient. According to them, this is the only type of infrastructure that will be able to deliver on the demands that cities have for infrastructure. It is also the only type of infrastructure that will help cities, and thereby nations, meet the Intended Nationally Determined Contributions (INDCs) acceded to in the Paris climate agreement.

One of the findings highlighted by Bielenberg *et al.* is that large infrastructure projects are more often publicly financed, and therefore they and the dynamics of politics are interdependent. Large infrastructure projects are often the first to be shelved when there is a funding crisis within national governments. On top of that, many countries have no means of publishing the infrastructure pipeline linked to long-term plans. This does not enable the right climate for investors. Bielenberg *et al.* quoted the World Bank's Bertrand Badré, who said: 'The challenges are as much on the side of projects as on supply of capital. There are simply not enough viable projects out there.'

The demand for sustainable infrastructure in the coming years is such that there are not enough public funds to finance all these projects. There is a gap between what can be funded and what needs to be funded.

Not to mention that things need to change to enable private investment in projects. We agree with Bielenberg *et al.* when they stated, 'And we believe a "triple win" is within reach: infrastructure that reduces emissions and climate risk, spurs economic development, and increases returns for investors.'

Infrastructure projects require as much recognition from urban planners as they do from engineers; it is not just about justifying projects in terms of value creation, it is also about identifying value capture and ensuring that the right climate is enabled for private investors to become interested in investing in projects.

One infrastructure project that seems uniquely able to do just that is Cargo sous terrain in Switzerland. Cargo sous terrain (2017) is a planned automated logistics system that will use underground tunnels to transport driverless vehicles to urban areas, where they surface and continue to deliver the goods (Figure 9.8). The project has just moved to the next stage, and enough private funding has been secured to enable this. What makes the project unique is that it is wholly funded by private sector investors. Although supported by the Swiss Government, the project receives no direct public financing. So, what makes this a viable project? Firstly, working with the federal government and the regional cantons ensured that sectorial policies and institutions were aligned to enable the project's development. This included a proposed change in the land ownership legislation, to avoid ambiguity and possible project delays through legal action by surface land owners (see also Section 8.2). Reducing uncertainty and avoiding delays in

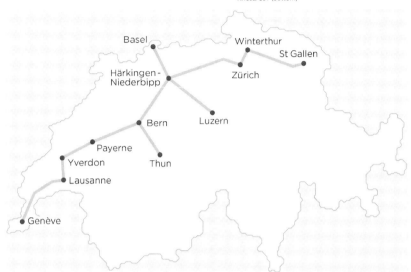

Figure 9-8 The Cargo sous terrain (top) project alignment and (bottom) proposed driverless cargo vehicle I Courtesy of Ben Fürst/CST (top) and Nitin Khosa/CST (bottom)

this way is paramount to get private investors on board (Bielenberg *et al.* have identified lack of transparency and potential project delays as major obstacles to private investment). Secondly, a delivery vehicle was created in the form of an association that, as the project progressed, became a corporate entity. The members of the association, and later the company, included the users of the system, who will be paying for the services provided. These services include the automated goods distribution but also the use of space inside the tunnels for the medium-distance delivery of parcels, cables and pipelines. In bringing together the users who would benefit from the project and are willing to pay for it, the investors became aware that there was not only a willingness to pay charges for using the system but also to do so over an extended period of time. This further reduces concerns that any investor may have in terms of the project not being able to fully recover the costs or providing the return on investment they are seeking. Lastly, the first stage of the project consists of a 67 km alignment, significant enough to warrant an investment, and further stages provide a perspective for future investments. The investment pipeline in that sense is visible and generates sufficient confidence that the project will be achieved. In this way, value creation and value capture are combined, and a climate is enabled that attracts private investors.

Brown (2014) has looked specifically at the infrastructure market in the USA. Her concerns were that massive investments are required not only for new infrastructure but also for refurbishment and replacement of the ageing and mostly neglected roads and structures. According to her, the scale of the task has become such that the traditional approach will not be able to cope with the challenge, specifically because public funding is insufficient. She suggested moving to a new post-industrial paradigm that is based on an ecological model of interdependency, rather than the industrial model of segregation. For her, the criteria are clear, and public works should be 'multipurpose, low-carbon infrastructure that is tightly coordinated with natural systems, well integrated into social contexts, and capable of adapting to a changing climate'.

Brown echoed the findings of Bielenberg *et al.* while also underlining why Cargo sous terrain can attract private funding where others fail. We need to move away from single-purpose infrastructure – not just because it has proven to be a waste of space but because it does not deliver sufficient benefits to warrant a long-term investment by private parties. Brown quotes Ausubel, who said that 'There are sufficient resources to retrofit cities, if we practice integrative infrastructure management … if we begin to manage the city as if it really were a living ecosystem, which of course it is, or was, and should be.'

Those sufficient resources are out there. Bielenberg *et al.* have pointed out that institutional investors allocate 5.2% of their portfolios to infrastructure on average. Their target is, however, 6%, which would amount to an additional $120 billion annually not being used through lack of viable infrastructure projects in which to invest. Overall, Bielenberg *et al.* estimated that as much as $1.5 trillion of private institutional investment could annually be available, given the right incentives.

The urban metabolism, urban being or the living ecosystem urgently needs these types of investments in projects: projects that utilise underground space as much as they use surface space; projects that deliver socially, economically and environmentally. As such, it is not so much about the cost of these projects as it is about how to make them bankable for investors.

9.5. Political will empowers

Frederic Peter Salvucci was born in Boston, Massachusetts, in 1940, and grew up in a close-knit Italian family. When he was a child, his mother would take him and his sister to the city centre to buy shoes. Back there and then, you could still see the dome of Massachusetts Institute of Technology (MIT) across the river. Frederic's mother would tell him, 'If you study hard, you'll be able to go there.' And going there is exactly what Salvucci did, starting an architecture degree but later switching to civil engineering. Danigelis (2004) continues the story:

> While Salvucci was an undergraduate, Massachusetts state officials started clearing space for the Massachusetts Turnpike. They evicted his grandmother from her home in Brighton, gave her a dollar down payment on the purchase of her house, and then demolished it … 'At the time, it was a pretty impressive experience for me to watch: the theory of transportation at MIT and the ugly reality of what was happening,' Salvucci says. His mentors at MIT were

teaching him that transportation should nonintrusively serve the local community and be respectful of the environment, but his family witnessed the opposite.

The elevated Central Artery, a green-painted steel and concrete monster, was constructed in 1951. It cut Boston and Charlestown off from their waterfronts. In doing so, businesses moved away, and, in the end, the capacity of the structure proved to be inadequate to handle all the traffic.

Salvucci was taught by one of his professors, A. Scheffer Lang, that 'engineers have a moral obligation to think about how and why a structure should be built' (Danigelis, 2004). It was that lesson and the experience of his grandmother being evicted that shaped his thinking and made him the 'man behind the Boston Big Dig'.

In 1970, he became transportation advisor to the Boston mayor, and in 1975 the newly elected governor Michael Dukakis asked him to become state secretary of transportation for the Commonwealth of Massachusetts. Dukakis was an anti-highway crusader, but Salvucci, who himself had become convinced of the benefits of moving the highway underground, persuaded Dukakis that the Central Artery/Tunnel Project – informally called the Big Dig – would be worth every dollar that was spent on it.

Salvucci had to put his plans on hold, due to politics being politics, when in 1978 Dukakis lost his re-election bid. He went back to teach at MIT, while the new governor abandoned the project and instead concentrated on a new tunnel to connect Interstate 90 to Boston's Logan Airport.

In 1982, Dukakis was re-elected, and Salvucci once more returned as secretary of state for transportation. His masterstroke was to revive the old project and combine it with the airport tunnel. As both Interstate 93 and Interstate 90 were eligible for federal funding and would preserve neighbourhoods, improve the environment, and alleviate traffic jams, it proved to be a winning combination (Danigelis, 2004).

It did come, however, at a price: 'The benefits of the largest highway construction project in the United States are about to become visible and real,' Salvucci wrote in 2003, 'but the cost has escalated from a $6 billion estimate in 1990, as construction was about to begin, to a current estimate of $15 billion, creating both national concerns and problems for other large underground projects.'

Salvucci believed in the project and maintained that belief throughout his days in public office. He also did something else: he reached out to the public from the project's get go, meeting with people and explaining to them the many benefits of the project. As he himself clarified (Salvucci, 2003):

> Only by understanding the extremely high benefits of the project and sheer necessity to the regional economy is it possible to understand how, in the usually fractious political environment of Boston, broad bipartisan political, business, labour and community support have continued in the face of serious increases in cost most of which are borne by the City and the State.

In 2004 *The Boston Globe* illustrated some of those benefits that had become apparent (Palmer, 2004):

> since the Central Artery tunnel project began, the value of commercial properties along the mile-long strip that this year will become the Rose Kennedy Greenway increased to $2.3 billion, up 79 percent. That's almost double the citywide 41 percent increase in assessed commercial property values in the same period.

Furthermore, in 2015 *The Boston Globe* confirmed what Salvucci had known from the beginning:

> Rush hour brings what radio reporters refer to as heavy volume. But the traffic moves, and for 1.5 miles through downtown Boston, it moves out of sight, underground. Above those famously expensive tunnel boxes is some of the most beautiful and valuable urban real estate anywhere in the nation, if not the world. Getting to and from Logan Airport has never been easier, whether picking up grandma or getting an executive to a startup in Fort Point or along Route 128. (Flint, 2015)

Salvucci identified six lessons from the Big Dig by underlining the enormous effects the project has had on the city itself (Salvucci, 2003): 'First, the enormous benefits of the Big Dig to the economy of the Boston metropolitan area, and the policy of taking full responsibility for "external" project costs through mitigation have created the bipartisan community support needed to see the project through.'

Secondly, he pointed out the serious consequences that delay can have on the costs of a project. By 'delay', he does not mean time schedules slipping during construction, but rather the delay brought about by the decision-making process. With that in mind, he thirdly pointed to the difficulty of managing transitions between political administrations and the transition from planning to construction.

The fourth learned lesson was the 'excessive privatization of project management without maintenance of adequate public sector management capacity' (Salvucci, 2003). In Salvucci's opinion, this point alone led to a large increase in the overall cost of the project. His fifth observation was that Boston faced a major challenge in that 'prudent use of this major investment, both the proper operation and maintenance of these assets, and fulfilling the commitments to "smart growth" policies' required a further focus after completion of the project. Lastly, he observed that

> Federal and State funding mechanisms and environmental oversight processes need to be revisited if the large infrastructure renewal and new investments required to support sustainable economic growth in the 30 major metropolitan areas of the United States … are to be planned and implemented both effectively and efficiently.

His sixth and last observation is still valid a decade later, and reinforces the ideas discussed in Section 9.2, and Hillary Brown's new post-industrial paradigm.

Projects can be empowered by political will. This is not limited to Boston's Big Dig, and can be seen in many projects around the world, as was the case with the Madrid M30/Madrid Rio project (see Section 2.4) (Time Out, 2013):

> Former mayor and PP politician Alberto Ruiz Gallardón was the real driving force behind many of the grand urban renewal project that has come to define the capital, and left large swathes of the city in a state of permanent roadworks for much of the noughties. But while many – in particular the city's taxi drivers – swore and cursed about the disruption this caused, there's now almost unanimous approval for the changes, in particular the €3.5-billion project to move part of the M-30 ring road underground and build the Madrid Rio park on top. Locals now have a new park that stretches for ten kilometres along the banks of the Manzanares River, complete with cafés, fountains, bike lanes, skate parks, football pitches, tennis courts and even a BMX track. Once derided as a Pharaoh, due to his apparent desperation to leave his imprint on the city, Gallardón has been lavished with praise for his efforts to modernise Madrid – a city that, unlike Barcelona and Seville, has never had the excuse of an Olympics or Expo to indulge in a spot of cosmetic surgery.

Political championship of projects can be decisive in shaping their outcome. According to

Flyvbjerg et al. (2003), this is not all that mega-projects require. They identify three shortfalls when it comes to projects failing or costs overrunning – as already pointed out by Salvucci (2003):

1. Under-involvement of the general public and of stakeholder groups concerned by outcomes; over-involvement of business lobby groups;

2. Lack of identification of public interest objectives to be met by the project;

3. Lack of clearly defined roles for government and involved parties.

As we saw in the previous sections, the development of underground space requires participatory planning, transparency in the decision-making process, value creation ident-ification, value capture identification and a funding mechanism. Above all, it needs the political will to support these projects in creating the cities of the future. As Salvucci (2003) so pointedly observed: 'If we want to see sustained investment in the re-development of our urban infrastructure systems, we need to begin by supporting broadly-based local planning processes rooted in environmental sustainability principles.'

9.6. This chapter's core ideas

In our work, we always meet engineers who have great ideas. They attempt to demonstrate that underground solutions have a massive positive impact on society. An impact that, if valued, makes any underground project exceed a surface project any day. When asked how to finance these projects, these engineers have no answer.

For us, this is the second largest obstacle to the large-scale use of underground space – the first being our inability to plan in such a way that urban underground corridors are created to connect the basements and networks we develop and shape a new urban tissue below the surface.

To solve this, we need to appreciate that there is a difference between economics and finance. We need to become more aware of how projects can be funded rather than solely focusing on justification and using money as an abstraction to do so.

Justification of projects requires us to highlight the benefits the project will bring. These advantages can then be monetised and used in economic models to compare the project with others or to determine sufficient social return. There are various methods to do this, but they only serve one purpose: comparison and justification. They demonstrate value creation and nothing more.

Projects require sectorial policies and institutions to not only promote them but enable them, by ensuring legislation that allows construction of a project, seamless land acquisition, and obtaining permits and licences.

Finally, projects require the financing structures that enable them to be constructed and operated. These structures need value capture but also the right environment to allow private investment.

To achieve these kinds of projects we need a larger goal. Projects that are multipurpose, targeting low-carbon infrastructure that is tightly coordinated with natural systems, well integrated into social contexts and capable of adapting to a changing climate have such a goal. All efforts need to concentrate on delivering sustainable infrastructure to maintain the focus on these goals. To do so requires that, from the early planning stages to final delivery and operation, value creation and value capture should be part of the project process as much as planning, engineering and construction are. Only in this way will projects become viable and bankable. As such, projects in underground space do not differ from those at the surface. They need not be 'economically out of reach' for any city, whether in the developing or developed world. All they require is the foresight of decision-makers to create the right environment for them to become possible. The best way to do this is to work together with the private sector in finding bankable ways of meeting the challenges we face. In that way, we can use underground space to create the cities of the future that are sustainable, resilient, socially inclusive and, above all, liveable and loveable for their citizens.

References

1   Australian Department of the Prime Minister and Cabinet (2016) *Smart Cities Plan*. Commonwealth of Australia, Canberra, Australia.

2   Bielenberg A, Kerlin M, Oppenheim J and Roberts M (2016) *Financing Change: How to Mobilize Private Sector Financing for Sustainable Infrastructure*. McKinsey Center for Business and Environment, Washington, DC, USA.

3   Brown H (2014) *Next Generation Infrastructure: Principles for Post-industrial Public Works*. Island Press, Washington, DC, USA.

4   Cargo sous terrain (2017) http://www.cargosousterrain.ch/de/en.html (accessed 14/11/2017).

5   CNU (2017) Highways to boulevards. CNU. https://www.cnu.org/our-projects/highways-boulevards (accessed 14/11/2017).

6   Danigelis A (2004) The man behind the big dig. *MIT Technology Review*. https://www.technologyreview.com/s/402867/the-man-behind-the-big-dig/ (accessed 14/11/2017).

7   Diamond JM (2005) *Collapse: How Societies Choose to Fail or Succeed*. Viking Press, New York, NY, USA.

8   Doz YL and Hamel G (1998) *Alliance Advantage: The Art of Creating Value Through Partnering*. Harvard Business Review Press, Boston, MA, USA.

9   Flint A (2015) 10 years later, did the Big Dig deliver? *The Boston Globe*. https://www.bostonglobe.com/magazine/2015/12/29/years-later-did-big-dig-deliver/tSb8PIMS4QJUETsMpA7Spl/story.html (accessed 14/11/2017).

Investing in underground space
is all about value capture

_____

10 Flyvbjerg B, Bruzelius N and Rothengatter W (2003) *Megaprojects and Risk: An Anatomy of Ambition*. Cambridge University Press, Cambridge, UK.

11 Green F (2015) *Nationally Self-interested Climate Change Mitigation: A Unified Conceptual Framework*. Centre for Climate Change Economics and Policy, Leeds, UK; Grantham Research Institute on Climate Change and the Environment, London, UK.

12 Gurran N and Lawler S (2016) Explainer: what is 'value capture' and what does it mean for cities? *The Conversation*. https://theconversation.com/explainer-what-is-value-capture-and-what-does-it-mean-for-cities-58776 (accessed 14/11/2017).

13 Hartig T, Evans GW, Jamner LD, Davis DS and Garling T (2003) Tracking restoration in natural and urban field settings. *Journal of Environmental Psychology* **23(2):** 109–123.

14 Heertje A (2000) *Economie in een notendop*. Promotheus, Amsterdam, the Netherlands. (In Dutch.)

15 International Tunnelling Association (2017) Sijtwende Tunnel. https://cases.ita-aites.org/search-the-database/project/23-tunnel-trace-sijtwende (accessed 14/11/2017). (In Dutch.)

16 Kampmann N (2002) The free selection of solutions for a friendly metro – project finance. In *Proceedings of the Copenhagen Metro Inauguration Seminar, Copenhagen*. COWI, Lyngby, Denmark, pp. 33–36.

17 Katz B and Noring L (2017) The Copenhagen City and Port Development Corporation: a model for regenerating cities. Brookings Institution. https://www.brookings.edu/research/copenhagen-port-development/ (accessed 14/11/2017).

18 Kotsareli M, Mavrikos A and Kaliampakos D (2013) Social cost–benefit analysis of the western expansion of the Athens Metro. In *Advances in Underground Space Development* (Zhou Y, Cai J and Sterling R (eds)). Research Publishing, Singapore, pp. 202–203.

19 KPMG (2012) *Groen, gezond en productief: The Economics of Ecosystems & Biodiversity*. KPMG Advisory, Amsterdam, the Netherlands. (In Dutch.)

20 Norman B. Leventhal Park (2017) History of Boston's Post Office Square. http://www.normanbleventhalpark.org/about-us/history-of-post-office-square/ (accessed 14/11/2017).

21 Palmer T (2004) For property owners, parks mean profits property values soar on mile-long swath. *The Boston Globe*, Jun. 14. See http://archive.boston.com/news/local/massachusetts/articles/2004/06/14/for_property_owners_parks_mean_pro64257ts/ (accessed 14/11/2017).

22 Peltier-Thiberge N (2015) Lagos' bus rapid transit system: decongesting and depolluting mega-cities, The World Bank. http://blogs.worldbank.org/transport/lagos-bus-rapid-transit-system-decongesting-and-depolluting-mega-cities-0 (accessed 14/11/2017).

23 UK POST (1997) *Tunnel Vision. POST Report Summary 90*. POST, London, UK.

24 Project for Public Spaces (2009) Garage below supports park above in Boston. https://www.pps.org/reference/posquare/ (accessed 14/11/2017).

25 Renner R (2018) *Urban Being: Anatomy & Identity of the City*. Niggli, Salenstein, Switzerland.

26 Romijn G and Renes G (2015) *General Guidance for Cost–Benefit Analysis*. Netherlands Bureau for Economics and Netherlands Environmental Assessment Agency, The Hague, the Netherlands.

27 Salvucci FP (2003) The 'big dig' of Boston, Massachusetts: lessons to learn. In *Proceedings of The ITA World Tunnelling Congress, Amsterdam* (Saveur J (ed.)). Balkema, Amsterdam, the Netherlands, vol. 1, pp. 37–41.

28 Schneider V, Leifeld P and Malang T (2013) Coping with creeping catastrophes: national political systems and the challenge of slow-moving policy problems. In *Long-term Governance of Social-Ecological Change* (Siebenhner B, Arnold M, Eisenack K and Jacob KH (eds)). Routledge, New York, NY, USA, pp. 221–238.

29 Time Out (2013) *Time Out Madrid*, 9th edn. Time Out, London, UK.

30 Ulrich RS (1984) View through a window may influence recovery from surgery. *Science* **224(4647):** 420–421.

31 Van Beek J, Ceton-O'Prinsen NM and Tan GL (2003) *Tunnels in Nederland: een nieuwe generatie*. Bouwdienst Rijkswaterstaat, Utrecht, the Netherlands. (In Dutch.)

32 Washington State Department of Transportation (2017) Viaduct history. http://www.wsdot.wa.gov/Projects/Viaduct/About/History (accessed 14/11/2017).

33 Waterfront Seattle (2017) What is Waterfront Seattle? http://waterfrontseattle.org/Media/Default/pdfs/2017_April_WFS_11x17.pdf (accessed 14/11/2017).

34 Wong N, Tan AYK, Tan PY, Sia A and Wong NC (2010) Perception studies of vertical greenery systems in Singapore. *Journal of Urban Planning and Development* **136(4):** 330–338.

Chapter 10

How disruption is creating new paradigms for an urban underground future

According to Poleg (2017),

> Traditional hotel companies have high operating costs and require heavy investment in design, fit-out, and (sometimes) the acquisition of whole buildings. Their business is built on strong branding, proprietary management tools, and a global network that caters to diverse needs. Airbnb offers a comparable value proposition without owning or fitting-out a single building. It does so by aggregating millions of under-utilized rooms under a single, reliable, and easy-to-use platfor.

Poleg considers the same model to apply to unused cars and their drivers. Uber is globally challenging the familiar concept of the taxi, offering clients an easy to use app on their phones to arrange transportation and payment through a credit card. Poleg sees unused assets becoming more used through aggregators. The victims are the established companies, which are caught like rabbits in the headlights of the aggregator companies. When looked at from a more abstract level, what aggregators are doing is using new technology to shift to a new paradigm on accommodation or mobility. The aggregators are disruptive, and the disruption itself is causing a transition to what will inevitably become the new normal.

The renowned physicist Stephen Hawking recently proposed that humankind has about 100 years to escape the Earth and move to a new planet in another solar system: 'He thinks humanity needs to become a multi-planetary species within the next century, revising his hopes for our species down from an earlier warning which gave us 1000 years' (BBC, 2017a).

In order to do so, we need to overcome some obstacles, among them the fact that the closest eligible planet, Proxima b, is about 4.2 light years from Earth. It would take about 120 000 years to get there using our conventional rockets. In view of this, scientists are looking at new forms of space travel that will cut the journey time, such as using plasma propulsion. Chang Diaz, a former astronaut, is confident that his engine will be in production within a few years for use in outer space – which, if successful, will dramatically cut the time required to reach Mars from around 8 months to 39 days (Clash, 2017).

Diaz calls it a paradigm shift for transportation in outer space, but this is only the precursor to further shifts that are needed if we are to go to planets such as Proxima b – which would still take 2000 years to reach even with plasma propulsion (BBC, 2017b). Humankind apparently requires the ability to travel at speed to evolve, adapt and, ultimately, survive as a species.

One system that could deliver a paradigm shift and disrupt the way we look at travel is Hyperloop. Hyperloop is not just a system that proposes high-speed travel, it also proposes to create a physical internet for mobility: people moving about in the same way that data packets now flow through the internet, coming together at the destination (Earle, 2017).

If we are able to create such a physical internet, then the way we move about, and the way we ship our goods, will change dramatically. Not only that, but, potentially, it would reshape the habitation layer. We now see a large migration to our cities from rural areas. People want to be in the city because that is where the work is. Travel takes too long from rural areas to the city, so people migrate to the city, or at least its fringes. The fringes then become suburbs, and new fringes cause sprawl. When the sprawl moves outside a limit of about 30 minutes to travel to work, it stops as it is not attractive to live that far from the city centre. This idea is based on Marchetti's constant, which states that 'personal travel appears to be much more under the control of basic instincts than of economic drives'. This constant was formulated by Cesare Marchetti, and is based on earlier research undertaken by Yacov Zahavi that shows, on average, we spend one hour commuting each day (Turner, 2012):

The Japanese salaryman on the Shinkansen bullet train, the Amazonian hunter-gatherer, the Canadian sub-urbanite stuck in rush-hour traffic: all of them, left to their own devices (or lack thereof), will aim to spend about an hour commuting each day. Marchetti looked at the historical record and determined that the mean held true all the way back to Neolithic cave sites. He refers to this as the quintessential unity of traveling instincts around the world'.

If the distance over which we can travel in 30 minutes could be extended in much the same way that Hyperloop aims to do, this would give a totally new meaning to the concept of satellite cities – which could once more become fashionable. But it goes further than that. Living in Berlin and working in Amsterdam would become quite normal, as it would only take 30 minutes when travelling at 1200 km/h. What's more, the actual concept foresees a pod on call that allows for seamless travel without waiting times, beating the aeroplane that can cruise at these speeds but loses out because of the time required for transport to and from the airport, as well as security and check-in requirements.

This, at least on a European scale, would make a vast difference and disrupt travel patterns and habitation patterns massively. It would also be the ultimate way in which to bring cohesion to the EU, as it would realise the vision of a united Europe without boundaries, through a disruptive form of travel outpacing all other modalities of transport.

Bélanger (2017) points us to 'ecologies of scale' that confirm the way that this infrastructural disruption could shape the urban landscape:

> The Athenian Oath which has restrained urban designers for the past two thousand years can finally loosen its grip and make room for new instruments and methods for intervening at geospatial scales, beyond the city and into contemporary urban territories. The linear, fixed, and closed mechanisms of the industrial economy are quickly fading in the background of more flexible, circular and networked systems of urban economies. Releasing the pristine ideals of the city from the crutches of security, permanence, and density opens a horizon of new social equities and regional synergies – a whole range of projects beyond that of a few exceptional precedents.

Hyperloop has come about through the vision of one person: Elon Musk. Musk has already disrupted the way that financial transactions take place on the internet through setting up PayPal that earned him the millions he is now using for further disruption. Apart from Hyperloop, Musk has started Tesla, to deliver electric cars ahead of the traditional manufacturers. He has also set up Space X, to create the ability to colonise Mars. What is interesting about Musk is that he not only has foresight and vision, he also has the ability to inspire others and to create a movement. This movement engages with the theme and organises worldwide disruption by enthusing students, fostering the spirit to carry out alignment studies, and to create start-up companies that compete with each other to be, say, the first to deliver a pod that can successfully enable Space X to colonise Mars.

The reactions from the establishment to UK entries for potential Hyperloop routes are predictable: 'Sources close to Innovate UK, the government's blue-sky thinking agency, insisted that none of the four shortlisted bids had official support. "They've not had a penny from us", the source said. "It's safe to say this isn't going to happen any time soon"' (Paton, 2012). This reaction is typical, and it shows a total miscomprehension of what disruption is about. It is the same way that taxi companies react to Uber, and how hotel chains respond to Airbnb. They look at them from the safety and comfort of a long-existing practice without recognising what they truly are: disruptive movements creating a new paradigm that will reshape the way that people travel and acquire temporary living space at their destinations.

Hyperloop is currently visualised as resembling a large elongated tube carried on columns through the landscape and urban areas. As such, it bears a striking resemblance to the elevated structures of the past that cities around the world are taking down to reunite neighbourhoods and cities with their waterfronts. As promising as Hyperloop may be, it is hard to see how it will be accepted if this is the ultimate design. Creating Hyperloop at the surface makes it highly vulnerable to exogenic forces. These could be natural forces, but also intentional human forces, that could disrupt the disruptor. We feel that the power of Hyperloop would be further enhanced if a radical decision was taken to turn it into an underground

**How disruption is creating
new paradigms for an urban
underground future**

concept: Hyperloop as the ultimate solution to travel at high speed through underground space. In doing so, Hyperloop would not be susceptible to those forces mentioned, and would in the event of earthquakes be better protected – as underground structures in earthquake regions have demonstrated over the years. This fact is acknowledged by The Boring Company, another Musk-inspired venture: 'Fast to dig, low cost tunnels would also make Hyperloop adoption viable and enable rapid transit across densely populated regions, enabling travel from New York to Washington DC in less than 30 minutes' (The Boring Company, 2017).

The basic premise behind this latter venture is that we need to speed up the time required to bore tunnels and reduce the cost by at least a factor ten. In itself, if achievable, this would be a giant leap forward. The company states, 'To solve the problem of soul-destroying traffic, roads must go 3D, which means either flying cars or tunnels' (The Boring Company, 2017). It continues to unfold plans to create a network of tunnels to allow cars to be moved rapidly below urban areas. As traffic increases, just dig more tunnels at a lower level, stacking them downwards.

Although looking at speeding up construction time is a good way forward, it is actually less disruptive than we think. Looking at the overall time it takes to move a project from inception to operation, the planning and design stages – including the licence and permit stages of a project – take up almost 70% of this time. In a drastic move to reduce the time it takes to deliver infrastructure projects, the Netherlands Government introduced new legislation and streamlined the planning process. In doing

so it was suggested that rather than taking 20–30 years to deliver, this could be cut back to 10 years, with the planning and design stages taking 7 years, and construction and commissioning, 3 years. If we really want to be disruptive when it comes to infrastructure projects in general, we need to start coming to terms with the toll that democracy has on our projects.

To survive, humankind must adapt. To adapt we need to fundamentally change the way we do things. Industrial symbiosis is the process through which industries exchange waste products, and is core to the circular economy that many are striving for. It is also central to our efforts to reduce carbon emissions. Yet, creating the connectivity required for this symbiosis through pipelines is stuck in a discussion on who is responsible and who is willing to finance, and even if these problems are solved, the entire process threatens to sink in a swamp of bureaucracy. Much of this is caused by legislation initially introduced to protect the public, yet now hindering the developments that will save the future of that same public. Industries have very short response times and are looking for connectivity through pipelines that are as capable and flexible as the internet is for data transmission. For the internet, data is simply data, and it makes no difference whether this data becomes speech, video, graphics or text. In that sense, the internet created an absolute disruption in society. It has led to entirely new ways of communication, access to information, and enabled the appearance of providers that are competing with the traditional telephone and cable TV companies and their products. These older technologies are now most likely integrated into the services of internet providers, with glass-fibre cables creating the backbone, making copper wire and coax cables obsolete. We have become an on-demand society, which is shaping the way we want future services delivered. This is the concept that lies at the core of all of Musk's initiatives.

Space, time and speed: all three are of essence if we are to achieve the much-needed disruptions and paradigm shifts that will challenge our conceptions of where we live, where we work and how we travel. And when we do travel to those far-away planets, we may find the need to create underground dwellings there to be protected from the harsh environments that may be encountered. As German architect Arina Ageeva of ZA Architects said, 'It seems pretty logical to use caves as the main protective structure of the colony.' ZA Architects have developed a concept for underground dwellings on Mars to enable those first colonisers to survive (Prigg, 2013). According to a recent article in *The Times*, we might yet find underground spaces on the Moon inside enormous lava tubes to accommodate our insatiable need for settlement space. The tubes are naturally formed tunnels with a diameter of 1 km or more and a length of hundreds of kilometres, and 'are shielded from cosmic radiation and protected from meteorites, potentially providing safe habitats for humans' (Leake, 2017).

We live not in an era of change but in a change of era. The coming 20 years will require more work on infrastructure and mobility than the past 200 years. Humankind needs to adapt if it is to survive. It needs to change. If not because technology is making it possible, then at least because we cannot continue in the way we have. The human population is growing at such a rate that we are now questioning the way we traditionally produce our food. The effects of climate change are such that we are questioning the way we design and construct our houses. Regions that were cold are becoming hotter, regions that were dry are becoming wetter, and regions that had hurricanes once every 10 years will experience them annually or even more often. Hurricane Irma in 2017 and those that followed left a path of destruction in the Caribbean. These changes can no longer be met with traditional solutions, or by solutions that fit within administrative models offering only comfort to the elite. There is a need to change, and if we only learn one thing from the disruption brought about by new technologies (and bear in mind that technologies are being shaped as you read this), it will be that they will challenge our thinking about how we can achieve our goals and fulfil our needs. Rather than looking at these schemes as far-fetched and futuristic, we need to embrace them for the potential they offer: the potential to adapt, the potential to survive.

If we are to leave this planet within 100 years, we still have five times 20 years to go. That means at least another five generations and five investment cycles to go through. In that time, new paradigms will shape our cities in a process that, according to Bélanger (2017), has already started: 'Whether in slums, suburbs, or skyscrapers, paradigms are changing, dispersal substitutes density, pace instead of space, sequence over speed, design instead of technology, concurrency over control, culture instead of growth.'

How disruption is creating new paradigms for an urban underground future

And an urban underground future: how will that feature in all this? We believe it offers as yet untapped potentials. And not just in terms of spatial development and physical use. Underground space will become vital for our survival in that it offers heat for energy and storage for water. It provides shelter, and the ability to create connections that bypass obstacles that we have created on the surface. As such, it allows for efficient, straight-line networks, minimising distance and maximising connectivity. It does require imagination, it does require adapting legislation, and it might need more-advanced and faster technologies.

But in the end, it is our belief that the uses of underground space will prove to be as disruptive, as challenging initially and as successful in the end as PayPal, Tesla, Uber, Airbnb, Hyperloop, The Boring Company, Space X and the eventual colonisation of other planets.

We hope that what we have written in this book has given a glimpse into the possibilities that the future holds for underground space, and how to potentially achieve these visions. We hope that we have shown what needs to be adapted to allow it to happen. But, above all, we hope that this book will inspire future generations to look at the world below our feet in a different and appreciative way, and make them tap into the as yet unforeseen opportunities that will allow humankind to survive and prosper on this planet.

References

1   Bélanger P (2017) *Landscape as Infrastructure: A Base Primer*. Routledge, New York, NY, USA.

2   BBC (2017a) *Newsday*: How long do we have left on Earth? http://www.bbc.co.uk/programmes/p052d6g1 (accessed 14/11/2017).

3   BBC (2017b) *The Search for a New Earth*. http://www.bbc.co.uk/programmes/b0953y04 (accessed 14/11/2017). (Video.)

4   Clash J (2017) A plasma rocket engine may get us to Mars in 40 days (Elon Musk, are you listening?). *Forbes*. https://www.forbes.com/sites/jimclash/2017/07/06/a-plasma-rocket-engine-may-get-us-to-mars-in-40-days-elon-musk-are-you-listening/ (accessed 14/11/2017).

5   Earle N (2017) 'A physical version of the Internet': how Hyperloop could be the broadband of transportation. Global Infrastructure Initiative. http://www.globalinfrastructureinitiative.com/article/physical-version-internet-how-hyperloop-could-be-broadband-transportation (accessed 14/11/2017).

6   Leake J (2017) Giant tunnels in moon could give us a home. *The Times*. https://www.thetimes.co.uk/article/giant-tunnels-in-moon-could-give-us-a-home-vdjvxbfqk (accessed 14/11/2017).

7   Paton G (2017) British experts on track to make 750mph travel a reality. *The Times*. https://www.thetimes.co.uk/article/british-brains-on-track-to-make-750mph-travel-a-reality-lctjv7w88 (accessed 14/11/2017).

8   Poleg D (2017) What might kill WeWork? Rethinking Real Estate. https://www.poleg.net/2017/01/15/what-might-kill-wework/ (accessed 14/11/2017).

9   Prigg M (2013) Could we live in underground caves on Mars? Architects propose concept to carve homes beneath the red planet's surface. *The Daily Mail*. http://www.dailymail.co.uk/sciencetech/article-2423309/Could-live-underground-caves-Mars-Architects-propose-concept-carve-homes-beneath-red-planets-surface.html (accessed 14/11/2017).

10 The Boring Company (2017) FAQ. https://www.boringcompany.com/faq/ (accessed 14/11/2017).

11 Turner C (2012) For pedestrians, cities have become the wilderness. CityLab. https://www.citylab.com/transportation/2012/11/pedestrians-cities-have-become-wilderness/3878/ (accessed 14/11/2017).

Underground Spaces Unveiled Planning and creating the cities of the future

Index

100 Resilient Cities Campaign, 115

access
        to help, 145
        mobility and, 78
Accessing Subsurface Knowledge (ASK) Network, 109
acoustic requirements, 142
acute shock, 118, 119, 121, 125
ACUUS (Associated Research Centers for Urban
        Underground Space), 55, 56, 85
aeroponic farms, 87
Ageeva, Arina (of ZA Architects), 197
aggregators, 193
agriculture (farming), 86–87, 90, 91, 164
Airbnb, 193, 195
airspace (sky), comparing management of subsurface with,
        164–165, 166
Alaskan Way viaduct (Seattle), 175–176
Almere, 51–52
Alps, railway tunnels though
        first (19th C.), 46–47
        Gotthard Base Tunnel, 98, 164
Amsterdam
        Amfora project, 77, 141
        greenery in Bos and Lommer area, 177
        Schiphol Airport, 144
Anna, Kofi UN Secretary-General, 27–28
anthropogenic interventions see interventions
Antwerp, pipeline corridor between Ports of Rotterdam and,
        152–153
aquifers, 17, 36, 88
        thermal energy storage/extraction (ATES), 5–6, 8, 14,
        61, 88, 101, 104, 107, 117
architects and engineers, bridging the gap between, 93,
        134
architecture (urban), 17–18, 138
        comfortable space and, 138
Arnhem, 6, 8, 13, 32, 107, 139, 142
        school (Artez Faculty of Dance and Music), 44–45,
        139, 142
art, 132–134
        cave paintings, 43, 132
Artez Faculty of Dance and Music (school in Arnhem,
        Netherlands), 44–45, 139, 142
ASK (Accessing Subsurface Knowledge) Network, 109
Associated Research Centers for Urban Underground Space

(ACUUS), 55, 56, 85
attractive (loveable) spaces, 129–135, 148
Australia
        Coober Pedy, 159–161
        Smart Cities Plan, 178
Austria–Italy transalpine railway (19th C.), 46–47
autonomous scattered objects, 5, 6

Baltard, Victor, 66, 67
Ban Ki-Moon (UN Secretary-General), 3
Bangkok mass rapid transit system (MRT), 121
Barendrecht, Heinenoord Tunnel near, 145
BART (Bay Area Rapid Transport System), 31–32, 121
Baseline Register Subsurface (Basisregistratie Ondergrond),
        152
basement developments, 6–8, 130
Bay Area (San Francisco)
        earthquake (1989), 121
        Rapid Transport System (BART), 31–32, 121
        Transbay Transit Center, 31–32
Beurstraverse (Rotterdam), 62, 72–73, 131
bicyclists (cyclists), 145
Big Dig (Boston's Central Artery/Tunnel Project), 185–187
biodiversity, economics of, 177
BNKR Arquitectura, 96, 96–97, 139, 139–140
boiling frog legend, 171
Boring Company, The, 196
Bosphorus tunnel, 47, 48
Boston, 185–188
        Central Artery/Tunnel Project, 185–188
        Post Office Square, 181
        waterfront, 185
Brazil
        Rio de Janeiro waterfront, 174–175
        São Paulo, 123
British Geological Survey and Glasgow, 25, 104, 109
Bronx (New York), Croton Water Filtration Plant (Bronx, New
        York), 32–33
brownfields, industrial, 25
Brundtland Commission, 23
Brunel, Marc, and son (Isambard Kingdom), 47–48
building
        codes, 159–163, 167
          international, 161, 162, 167
        for people, 129–149

Canada
    Jean Chrétien (former prime minister), 123
    Montreal, 71, 122, 123, 130, 155
    Toronto see Toronto
Canary Wharf Underground station, 65–66
car parks, 123, 135, 143, 145, 181
carbon dioxide reduction measures, 90, 104
    capture/storage, 95–96, 164
Cargo sous terrain project, 155, 183–184
Carrousel du Louvre, 8–9
caves/caverns and cave-like dwellings
    historic, 43–47, 125, 132
    hotels, 160–161
    yaodong, 43–46, 124
CCTV, 79, 145, 147
Centers for Disease Control and Prevention, 122
Central Artery/Tunnel Project (Boston), 185–187
CERN Large Hadron Collider (LHC), 11, 155
Charlestown waterfront, 185
China
    Jinping laboratory, 13
    Wuhan, 16
    yaodong, 43–46, 124
Chrétien, Jean (former Canadian prime minister), 123
cities
    future see future
    needs of, 2–3, 17, 18, 93
    resilience, 115–127
    satellite, 194
    smart see smart cities
    sustainable, 93–94
    Wuhan (China), 16
    see also entries under urban
civil law, 153, 154
civilisations, early, 34–35, 43, 133
climate (city), 122–123
    control, 141–142, 148
climate change (and global warming), 86, 94–96, 110, 118,
    125–126, 171, 172, 197
    action on, 94–96
        lack of (not responding), 171, 173
    disasters relating to, 118
    subsurface and, 101
coal extraction, 25–26
COB (Netherlands Centre for Underground Construction),
    107, 108
codes (building) see building
collapse of structures, 147
comfortable spaces, 135–142
commitment, definite, 2, 55, 61
common law, 157
communities, sustainable, 93–94
commuting time and Hyperloop, 194

compensation, 154, 155
    right-of-way, 156–163
compulsory acquisition of land, 153, 154, 155, 156
concealments, areas of, 145
congestion, 6, 12, 13, 151, 165
connectivity, 18, 91–92, 196
    see also networks
conservation, 24, 26, 29, 100
Coober Pedy (South Australia), 159–161
cooling, 141–142
Copenhagen metro, 64, 81, 179–180
corridors, 71, 74–82, 92
    pipeline, Netherlands, 152–153, 163–164
cost–benefit analysis, 172, 173
counterterrorism, 147–148
Covent Garden Market Hall, 9–10, 62
creeping normalcy metaphor, 171–172
cross-discipline (interdisciplinary) approach, 19, 96, 104,
    108, 110
Crossrail Project, 153–154
Croton Water Filtration Plant (Bronx, New York), 32–33
crowd control, 143
crust (Earth's), 13
CTIPUS (International Permanent Committee of
    Underground Technologies and Planning), 55
cultural ecosystem services, 27, 28
cyclists, 145
cyclones (hurricanes) and other storms, 86, 119, 121,
    123–124, 124, 197

data
    need for/acquisition of, 108–109, 166
    Netherlands large-scale programme, 152
    presentation in 3D models, 109
daylight (natural light), 32, 120, 130, 139–140, 141, 142
decision-making (underground or aboveground
    alternatives), 172–173
Deep City Project at École Polytechnique Fédérale de
    Lausanne, 109
deep subsurface, 17, 28, 37, 101, 152, 166
    top vs, 13–14, 17, 18
defensive stance/designs, 2, 17, 146
definite commitment, 2, 55, 61
delays (project), impact, 187
Denmark
    Copenhagen metro, 64, 81, 179–180
    Sweden link (Øresund), 47, 48, 180
depthscraper, 120
    see also Earthscraper
design (urban), 17–18, 137
    basic objectives, 136
    defensive, 2, 17, 146
    spatial, 59–83, 137, 141

dialogue, spatial, 13, 18, 96, 101–102, 110
Dinamo station, Moskow Metro, 139
directive plan, 81
disasters, natural see natural disasters
disruption, 193–199
Dokhaven Waste Water Treatment Facility (Rotterdam), 33–34
Doublet, Maurice, 55, 57
drinking water, 17, 25, 36, 87, 88, 123, 125
drought, 119, 123
Dukakis, Michael, 184–185
dullification of the street, 129
Dusseldorf Wehrhahn-Linie, 77
Dutch... see Netherlands
Dynamo station, Moskow Metro, 139

Earth
    climate changes see climate change
    crust, 13
    humankind escaping from, 192–193, 195, 197, 198
earth-covered housing, 124, 137
earthquakes, 125
    human-induced, 26, 37, 93, 117
    rapid transport systems and, 121, 196
    San Francisco Bay Area (1989), 121
    Tokyo (1923), 120
Earthscraper (Mexico City), 96–97, 120, 139–140
    see also depthscraper
easement, 157–158
ecology (ecologies)
    infrastructure, justification for, 173
    of scale, 194–195
economics, 26
    Big Dig (Boston) and its impact on, 187
    of ecosystems and biodiversity, 177
    finance and, difference between, 188
    growth, 89–91
    societal value and, 172
ecosystems
    economics of, 177
    services, 23–24, 27–31, 36, 39, 97, 117, 152
        cultural, 27, 28
Ecuador (Quito), Habitat III conference, 3, 93
Electric Factory (Elektrozavodskaia) station, Moskow Metro, 139
Elizabeth Line (London), 153–154
emergency and rescue services, 61
    fire, 143
    terrorism, 147
emergency points, 145, 147
employment, decent, 89–91
empowerment of projects by political will, 185–188
energy/power (storage and extraction), 88–89, 101, 117–118
    affordable, 88–89

clean and renewable, 16, 61, 81, 88–89, 101, 106
fossil-based, 89, 91, 101, 104
geothermal, 14, 16, 61, 82, 88, 98, 101, 117, 154
thermal see thermal energy
wind (wind power from turbines), 91–92, 136
engineering, 188
    19th C., 46–50
    bridging the gap between architects and engineers, 93, 134
environment
    control, 163–164, 167
    humans and, 23–40
    see also nature
Europe, Hyperloop travel, 194
European Convention on Human Rights (ECHR), 153
existing systems and structures, 6, 37
expropriation of land, 153–154, 156
extension of part of urban surface to below surface, 16
external safety, 146–147

farming (agriculture), 86–87, 90, 91, 164
fear, 136–137
fibre optics, 139–140
financing/financing/investing, 171–191
Finland see Helsinki
fire safety, 143, 146, 161, 162
flooding, 86, 94, 121, 125, 147
food security, 86–87
Forum des Halles (Les Halles), 66–70, 81, 144
fossil-based energy, 89, 91, 101, 104
Foster, Norman (Lord Foster) and Foster + Partners, 46, 55, 65
France
    French Geological Survey, 25
    Large Hadron Collider and, 11
Fréjus (Mont Cenis) Tunnel, 47
French Geological Survey, 25
Fukuoka sinkhole, 117
funding/financing/investing, 171–191
future cities, 49–52
    spatial designs, 63–66
future generations, 198
    considering the impact on, 24, 26, 28

Gallardón, Alberto Ruiz, 187–188
gardens, paving over, 119
    see also parks and recreational spaces
gas
    distribution/transport, 50, 61, 146
    exploration/extraction, 13, 25–26, 27, 117, 146
GECUS (Groupe d'Etude et de Coordination de l'Urbanisme Souterrain), 53–54, 55, 67, 68, 69, 81
geology, 13–14, 19, 25, 36, 39, 43–44, 129
    London, 97, 98

Index

planning and, 98, 104, 108–109
surveys (national), 109
    British, and Glasgow, 25, 104, 109
    French, 25
geothermal energy, 14, 16, 61, 82, 88, 98, 101, 117, 154
Germany, Dusseldorf Wehrhahn-Linie, 77
Ghent–Terneuzen shipping canal (Netherlands), 163–164
Glasgow, 25, 104, 105–106, 109
global warming see climate change
Gotthard Base Tunnel, 98, 164
governance and government, 151–169
    local and regional, 17, 116, 151–152, 167
green infrastructure/greenery, 63, 123, 131, 175–177, 179
    absence, effects of health, 131
    trees, 7, 62, 131, 132, 175, 177
Grote Marktstraat (The Hague) 135
groundwater, 6, 37, 97, 104, 123
    table, 97, 119, 141
Groupe d'Etude et de Coordination de l'Urbanisme
    Souterrain (GECUS), 53–54, 55, 67, 68, 69, 81
Growing Underground, 86, 87

Haarlem, 6
Habitat III conference, 3, 93
habitation see housing
Halles Centrales, 66
Haussmann, Georges-Eugène, 49–50, 50, 67
Hawking, Stephen, 193
heat island effect, 32, 35, 116, 119, 122, 125, 126
heat map, Scotland, 106
heat pumps, 141
heating, 141–142
Heerlen (Netherlands), Minewater project, 89
Heinenoord Tunnel near Barendrecht (Netherlands), 145
help, access to, 145
Helsinki (Finland), 98, 98–99, 108, 157, 167
    Orthodox Uspenski Cathedral, 30–31
    Viikinmaki waste water treatment plant, 46
Hénard, Eugène Hénard, 51, 62, 67
high-speed travel by Hyperloop, 92, 194–196
historical perspectives, 24–25, 43–49, 132
    housing/homes/dwellings, 43–47, 124, 125, 132,
    158, 159
holistic approaches, 39, 41, 164
homes see housing
Hong Kong, 175
    sewers and sewage treatment, 11, 46
hotels, 160–161, 193
    Airbnb and, 193, 195
housing (homes and dwellings and habitation), 7, 46, 88,
    124
    cave-like see caves/caverns and cave-like dwellings
    historic, 43–47, 124, 125, 132, 158, 159

iceberg mansions, 4–5, 6–7, 8
in layered approach, 99–100
humans, 23–40
    cave-like dwelling see caves/caverns and cave-like
    dwellings
    early civilisations, 34–35, 43, 133
    interplanetary travel, 192–193, 195, 197, 198
    interventions underground see interventions
    mass migration from rural to urban areas, 2, 3, 94,
    194
    nature and, 23–40
    prehistoric society, 24
humidity, 141, 142
hunger, zero, 86–87
hurricanes (cyclones) and other storms, 86, 119, 121,
    123–124, 124, 197
hydroponic farms, 87
Hyperloop, 92, 194–196

iceberg mansions, 4–5, 6–7, 8
industrial era
    brownfields, 25
    infrastructure, 116
    symbiosis, 91, 92, 163, 196
Industrial Revolution (late 17th to 18th C.), 25
    engineering, 46–50
industry, 91–92
infrastructure, 91–92
    ecology, justification for, 173
    green see green infrastructure
    industrial, 116
    sustainable, 182, 183, 189
innovation, 91–92
    UK's agency for (Innovate UK), 195
insight, 151–152
interdisciplinary (cross-discipline) approach, 19, 96, 104,
    108, 110
International Building Codes, 161, 162, 167
International Congress for Urban Underground
    Development, 1st (Paris), 54, 55
International Permanent Committee of Underground
    Technologies and Planning (CTIPUS), 55
International Tunnelling Association (ITA - becoming the
    International Tunnelling and Underground Space
    Association), 55–56
    Committee on Underground Space (ITACUS), 56, 85
internet, physical, 184
interplanetary travel, 192–193, 195, 197, 198
interventions (underground), human/anthropogenic, 24–27,
    36, 39, 98, 117, 163
    earthquakes due to, 26, 37, 93, 117
inverted pyramid design, Earthscraper, 97, 139
investing/financing/funding in spaces, 171–191

ITA see International Tunnelling and Underground Space
    Association
Italy–Austria transalpine railway (19th C.), 46–47

Japan
        plant factories, 86–87
        sinkholes (Fukuoka), 117
        Tokyo see Tokyo; Tokyo Declaration
Jeanneret, Charles-Édouard (Le Corbusier), 52, 62
Jinping laboratory, China, 13
jobs (work), decent, 89–91

Kaganovich, Lazar, 134
Kansas City
        Building and Rehabilitation Code, 161–162
        SubTropolis facility, 90, 162
Kensington and Chelsea (Royal Borough), 6–7, 8
Kiev Metro, 12
knowledge and the Netherlands large-scale programme,
        152
Komsomol (now Komsolmolskaya) station (Moskow Metro),
        135
Kongens Nytorv Station, Copenhagen Metro, 64, 81
Kramer Mikkelsen, Jens, 179
Kuala Lumpur (Malaysia), Stormwater Management and
        Road Tunnel, 94, 121

Laakhaven underground car park (The Hague), 145
land ownership, 152–156, 167
landscape (underground)
        networks see networks
        objects see objects
        physical, 5, 6, 10
Large Hadron Collider (LHC), 11, 155
Lausanne, Deep City Project At École Polytechnique Fédérale
        de Lausanne, 109
lava tubes on the Moon, 197
law see legislation and regulations
layered approach to subsurface use, 99–101, 159
        ownership, 101, 159
Le Corbusier, 52, 62
Lee Tunnel, 60–61
legislation (law) and regulations, 12, 91, 107, 151–169
        civil law, 153, 154
        common law, 157
        ecosystem services, 28
        public law, 153, 154
Leidschendam, Sijtwende development, 179
Les Halles (Forum des Halles), 66–70, 81, 144
lighting, 139–141
        artificial, 139, 141
        natural (daylight), 32, 120, 130, 139–140, 141, 142
local and regional government, 17, 116, 151–152, 167
Logan Airport (Boston), 186

Loma Prieta earthquake (1989), 121
London
        basement developments, 4–5, 6–7
        Covent Garden Market Hall, 9–10, 62
        geology, 97, 98
        Lee Tunnel (for waste water), 60–61
        policing, 70
        Rectory Farm, 90–91
    warehouses and storage space, 89–90, 97
London Clay, 97, 98
London Underground (Tube), 11–12, 48–49, 65–66, 70,
        157
        climate control and, 141
        Covent Garden Market Hall, Canary Wharf, 65–66
        easements, 157
        Elizabeth Line (Crossrail), 153–154
        Metropolitan Line, 11, 59
        policing, 70, 79
        South Kensington Station subway to museums,
        74–75
Louvre museum, 8–9, 10
loveable (attractive) spaces, 129–135, 148
Lowline project (New York), 140

Maastricht, 107
Madrid Rio, 35, 187–188
Making Cities Resilient – My City is Getting Ready!, 116
Malaysia
        Kuala Lumpur, Stormwater Management and Road
        Tunnel, 94, 121
        Maura, 122
Malmö and the Øresund link to Denmark, 180
mapping, 80
Markthal (Market Hall) project, Rotterdam, 175
Mars, reaching and colonisation, 193, 195, 197
mass migration to urban areas from rural areas, 2, 3, 94,
        194
Massachusetts Institute of Technology (MIT), 185, 186
Maura (Malaysia), 122
megacities, 121–122
metro systems see rapid transit and transportation systems
Metropolitaine (Paris), 11, 50, 63–65
Metropolitan Line (London), 11, 59
Mexico City, Earthscraper, 96–97, 120, 139–140
migration from rural to urban areas, mass, 2, 3, 94, 194
Mijksenaar, Paul, 144
Mill, John Stuart, 23
Millennium Ecosystem Assessment, 28, 29, 39
Minewater project (Heerlen, Netherlands), 89
mining activities (extraction of resources), 13, 25, 153, 154,
        162
        coal, 25–26
mist systems, 143
mobility, 118, 145, 194, 197

access and, 78
Mont Cenis Tunnel, 47
Montreal, 71, 122, 123, 130, 155
Moon, 48, 197
Moscow Metro, 77, 134–135, 139
Museum of Tomorrow (Rio de Janeiro), 175
Musk, Elon, 195, 196, 197

National Fire Protection Association (US), 161, 162
natural disasters, 94, 118, 123–125
    climate change-related, 118
Natural History Museum–South Kensington Station subway,
    74–75
nature
    humans and, 23–40
    subsurface as natural habitat, 43–46
    see also environment
needs of cities, 2–3, 17, 18, 93
negative volumes, 68, 69
Netherlands (Dutch…), 17, 99–104, 107–108, 157–159
    Almere, 51–52
    Amfora project (Amsterdam), 77, 141
    Arnhem see Arnhem
    Centre for Underground Construction (COB), 107,
    108
    coal and gas extraction, 25–26
    Counterterrorism Alert System, 147–148
    Ghent–Terneuzen shipping canal, 163–164
    Haarlem, 6
    historical perspectives, 24–25
    nature and sustainability, 26–27, 28–29, 36
    pipeline corridors, 152–153, 163–164
    planning, 107–108, 108
    Rotterdam see Rotterdam
    Schiphol Airport (Amsterdam), 144
    Second Heinenoord Tunnel near Barendrecht, 145
    Sijtwende development in Voorburg and
    Leidschendam, 179
    Spatial Explorations 2000, 99–100
    spatial planning process (incl. Subsurface Spatial
    Planning Vision), 17, 28–29, 37, 88, 151
    subsurface in, 99–104
    Subsurface and Underground Space program
    (government), 151–152
    The Hague see The Hague
    thermal/geothermal energy schemes, 5–6, 88–89
    tort, 157–159
    tunnelling, 26–27
    Vision of the Subsurface (Municipality of Zwolle),
    104
networks, 5
    in layered approach, 99–100
    private, 11
    public see public networks

rail, 47
    see also connectivity; physical internet
New York, 121
    Croton Water Filtration Plant (Bronx), 32–33
    former underground tramway depot, 140
    subway, 121, 132
Next City website, 64
noise, 142, 164
North Korea, Pyongyang metro, 12

objects
    autonomous scattered, 5, 6
    private, 5–6
    public, 8–10
    of spatial planning, 16–18
Oklahoma, rush to, 4
open spaces, public see public open spaces
operating hours, synchronisation of, 80
Optics Valley Central City (16
Oregon, Pioneer Courthouse Square (in Portland), 79
Ørestad redevelopment, 179–180
Øresund (Denmark–Sweden) link, 47, 48, 180
Orthodox Uspenski Cathedral (Helsinki, Finland), 30–31
Osmose competition, 63, 64
outer space travel, 192–193, 195, 197, 198
oversight, 151–152, 167
ownership
    land, 152–156, 167
    layered, 101, 159
    private, of public open spaces (POPOS), 70–74,
    81–82, 88

paintings, caves, 43, 132
Paris
    Hausmann and, 49–50, 50, 67
    International Congress for Urban Underground
    Development (1st in 1937), 54, 55
    Les Halles (Forum des Halles), 66–70, 81, 144
    Louvre museum, 8–9, 10
    Metro (Metropolitaine), 11, 50, 63–65
parks and recreational spaces, 91, 122, 144–145, 175,
    181–182
    see also gardens
paving over gardens and its effects on rainwater, rainfall,
    119
pedestrian networks, 70, 71, 72, 75, 76, 80, 82
    Toronto PATH system, 71, 75–79, 80, 108, 146
    see also corridors
people see users
perceptions of users, 148
    green systems and, 175–176
    lack of control, 132–133
    parks, 144–145
physical internet, 184

physical landscape, 5, 6, 10
Pioneer Courthouse Square (Portland, Oregon), 79
pipelines, 93, 99, 152–153, 154, 163
      gas, 61, 146
      Netherlands pipeline corridors, 152–153, 163–164
Place Ville Marie (Montreal), 130
planets (extraterrestrial), humankind escaping to, 192–193,
      195, 197, 198
planning, 1, 2, 16, 17, 19, 96–108
      Arnhem, 13
      case studies, 104–108
      integration of surface and subsurface into, 65–66,
      70, 78, 79, 104, 108, 109, 117
      methodology, 96–104
      policy see policy
      Royal Borough of Kensington and Chelsea Basement
      Planning Policy, 7
plant factories, Japan, 86–87
plasma propulsion, 193–194
plazas, 73, 79, 122, 130, 146, 148
      shopping, 143, 148
policing
      London Underground, 70, 79
      privately owned public open underground spaces,
      70
policy, 12, 85–96, 110
      objectivity in decisions on, 173
      Royal Borough of Kensington and Chelsea Basement
      Planning Policy, 7
political will, empowerment of projects by, 185–188
Portland (Oregon), Pioneer Courthouse Square, 79
Post Office Square (Boston), 181
power see energy
power-to-X, 81, 96
prehistoric society, 24
pressure, 14
private funding and investment, 183–184, 189
private networks, 11
private objects, 5–6
private space, 5, 70, 71, 79
      partially open to the public (POPOS), 70–74, 81–82,
      88
privatisation of projects, excessive, 187
projects empowered by political will, 185–188
provisioning ecosystem services, 28
public law, 153, 154
public networks, 11
      pedestrians see pedestrian networks
public objects, 8–10
public open spaces, 62, 66, 81
      privately owned (POPOS), 70–74, 79, 81–82, 88
Pyongyang (North Korea) metro, 12
pyramid, inverted, Earthscraper design, 97, 139
Pyramide du Louvre, 8

Quito, Habitat III conference, 3, 93

railways, 146
      Crossrail (London), 153–154
      rapid transit see rapid transit
      Rotterdam rail tunnel, 159–160, 175
      train platforms, 145
      transalpine see Alps
rainfall, 119, 121
      see also flooding
Ramsey, James, 140
rapid transit and transportation systems (underground/tube/
      metro/subway), 11, 63–66, 81, 92, 121, 132–135,
      173, 177, 195–196
      BART (Bay Area Rapid Transport System), 31–32,
      121
      Copenhagen, 64, 81, 179–180
      Dusseldorf, 77
      easement, 157
      historic, 46–47, 48–49
      Hyperloop, 92, 194–196
      Kiev, 12
      London see London Underground
      Moscow, 77, 134–135, 139
      New York, 121, 132
      Paris (Metropolitaine), 11, 50, 63–65
      Pyongyang (North Korea), 12
      Rotterdam, 62, 145
      Stockholm, 77, 133–134
      terrorism, 147
recreational spaces and parks, 91, 122, 144–145, 175
recycling, 164, 167
regional and local government, 17, 116, 151–152, 167
regulations see legislation and regulations
renewable and clean energy, 16, 61, 81, 88–89, 101, 106
resilience, 115–127
resources
      extraction see mining
      resources model, 14–16
Rietveld, Gerrit, 44–45
right-of-way compensation, 156–163
Rio+20 conference, 3
Rio de Janeiro waterfront, 174–175
Rio project (Madrid), 35, 187–188
rivers, green strips along, 175–176
road and streets, 18, 26, 50–51, 129–130
Rockefeller Foundation, 115, 118, 125
Rotterdam (Netherlands), 167
      Beurstraverse, 62, 72–73, 131
      Dokhaven Waste Water Treatment Facility, 33–34
      environmental control, 167
      pipeline corridor between Ports of Antwerp and of,
      152–153
      rail tunnel, 159–160, 175

underground stations, 62, 145
water storage basin, 95, 96
Royal Borough of Kensington and Chelsea, 6–7, 8
rural areas, mass migration to urban areas from, 2, 3, 94, 194
Russia
Kiev metro, 12
Moscow metro, 77, 134–135, 139

safety and security, 142–148
external, 146–147
fire, 143, 146, 161, 162
food, 86–87
policing see policing
Toronto PATH network, 80
Salvucci, Frederic Peter, 185–187
San Francisco
Bay Area see Bay Area
privately owned public open spaces (POPOS), 73–74
Transbay Transit Center, 31–32, 62
sanitation, 87–88
São Paulo, Brazil, 123
Sargans (Switzerland), Waferfab factory, 37–38
satellite cities, 194
scale
ecologies of, 194–195
in planning, 17
Schiphol Airport (Amsterdam), 144
Science City (Singapore), 89
Scotland, Glasgow, 25, 104, 105–106, 109
Seattle, Alaskan Way viaduct, 175–176
Sechseläutenplatz underground car park (Zürich), 145
sectorisation, 166
security see safety and security
Semmering railway see Austria–Italy transalpine railway
Sendai Framework, 116, 124–125
Seoul (South Korea), Women's University, 138–139
sewers, 11, 51, 59, 88, 95, 119, 146
see also waste water treatment
Sha Tin Sewage Treatment Works (Hong Kong), 46
shock, acute, 118, 119, 121, 125
shopping plazas, 143, 148
signage, 73, 77, 144
Sijtwende development in Voorburg and Leidschendam, 179
Singapore, 107–108
land ownership, 155–156
planning, 107–108, 108
Science City, 89
sinkholes, 117
sky (airspace), comparing management of subsurface with, 164–165, 166
SMART (Stormwater Management and Road Tunnel) in

Kuala Lumpur (Malaysia), 94, 121
smart cities, 92, 101, 104, 178–179
Australia's Smart Cities Plan, 178
society
creating societal value, 172–177
John Stuart Mill on, 23
prehistoric and early, 24
South Kensington Station subway to museums, 74–75
South Korea, Women's University (Seoul), 138–139
space (spaces)
contemporary thinking, 55–56
design, 59–83, 136, 137, 141
disruptive, 193–199
governance and use of see governance
investing in/financing/funding, 171–191
legislation on use of see legislation and regulations
natural inclination not to use, solutions, 136, 137
outer, travel, 192–193, 195, 197, 198
private see private space
public open see public open spaces
valued see valued spaces
Space X, 195, 198
Spain, Madrid Rio project, 35, 187–188
spatial dialogue, 13, 18, 96, 101–102, 110
Spatial Explorations 2000, 99–100
spatial planning, 28–29, 36, 98–99, 100, 107
Netherlands (incl. Subsurface Spatial Planning Vision), 17, 28–29, 37, 88, 151
object of, 16–18
sprinklers, 143
Stockholm metro, 77, 133–134
Stonehenge tunnel solution, 26
storm(s), 119
hurricanes and cyclones, 86, 121, 123–124, 124, 197
thunderstorms, 118
see also wind
STORM (Self-organizing Thermal Operational Resource Management) project, 89
Stormwater Management and Road Tunnel (SMART) in Kuala Lumpur (Malaysia), 94, 121
streets and roads, 18, 26, 50–51, 129–130
stresses, 116, 117, 118
chronic, 118, 120, 125
STRONG (Structuurvisie Ondergrond), 151–152
Structuurvisie Ondergrond (STRONG), 151–152
subsurface, 1–20, 23–30, 99–110
in case studies, 104–108
characterisation, 23–24
definitions/meanings, 13–14
ecosystem services see ecosystem
integration (with surface) into planning and, 65–66, 70, 78, 79, 104, 108, 109, 117

layered approach to use see layered approach
managing and regulating, 1, 50, 164–167, 168
as natural habitats, 43–46
oversight, 151–152, 167
threatening/as a liability, 117–118
SubTropolis facility (Kansas City), 90, 162
subway
    pedestrian, South Kensington Station to museums, 74–75
    rail see rapid transit and transportation systems
supporting ecosystem services, 28
surface (urban)
    extension to below surface, 16
    integration of subsurface and, into planning, 65–66, 70, 78, 79, 104, 108, 109, 117
surrogate streets, 129–130
sustainability (and sustainable development), 23, 24, 27, 35–39, 40
    cities and communities, 93–94
    food production systems, 86
    infrastructure, 182, 183, 189
    UN sustainable development goals (SDGs), 85–96, 110
Sweden
    Denmark, link to (Øresund), 47, 48, 180
    Stockholm metro, 77, 133–134
Switzerland
    Cargo sous terrain project, 155, 183–184
    Deep City Project at École Polytechnique Fédérale de Lausanne, 109
    Gotthard Base Tunnel, 98, 164
    Large Hadron Collider and, 11, 155
    Sechseläutenplatz underground car park in Zürich, 145
    Waferfab factory (Sargans), 37–38
symbiosis, industrial, 91, 92, 163, 196
synchronisation of operating hours, 80
System Exploration Environment and Subsurface (SEES), 101–104

T-Centralen, see Stockholm metro
tax increment financing, 179
taxi companies/drivers, 187
    Uber and, 193, 195
temperature (thermal considerations), 14, 38, 122, 141
    underground hotel in Coober Pedy, 160
    see also climate change; geothermal energy; heat; thermal energy storage and extraction
Terneuzen–Ghent shipping canal (Netherlands), 163–164
terrorism, 147–148
Thailand, Bangkok mass rapid transit system (MRT), 121
Thames Tideway scheme, 60
The Hague

Grote Marktstraat, 135
Laakhaven underground car park, 145
thermal energy storage and extraction, aquifer (ATES), 5–6, 8, 14, 61, 88, 101, 104, 107, 117
    see also temperature
three-dimensional development, 29, 37, 55, 68, 69, 81, 100
three-dimensional models, data presentation in, 109
three-layer approach to subsurface use, 99–101, 159
thunderstorms, 118
Tokyo, 95, 121–122
    earthquake (1923), 120
    metro, sarin attacks, 147
    water management system, 95, 121–122
Tokyo Declaration, 55
top subsurface/layer, 13, 17, 18
    deep vs, 13–14, 17, 18
topsoil removal, 164
Toronto, 155
    parks and recreation, 144–145, 145–146
    PATH pedestrian system, 71, 75–79, 80, 108, 146
tort, 157–159, 167
trains see railways; rapid transit and transportation systems
transalpine railway tunnels see Alps
Transbay Transit Center (San Francisco), 31–32, 62
transport
    of people see travel
    by pipelines see pipelines
travel and transport
    high-speed travel by Hyperloop, 92, 194–196
    interplanetary, 192–193, 195, 197, 198
    by rail see railways; rapid transit and transportation systems
trees, 7, 62, 131, 132, 175, 177
tubes (metro) see rapid transit and transportation systems
Tunisia (Magmata and Chenini), 43
tunnels and tunnelling, 26–27, 55–56
    19th C., 47–48
    transalpine see Alps

Uber, 193, 195
UK see United Kingdom
UN see United Nations; United Nations (UN)
Underground (the) see rapid transit and transportation systems
undesirables, 145, 146
unemployment, preventing, 89
United Kingdom
    climate action, 94
    Glasgow, 25, 104, 105–106, 109
    London see London
    Millennium Ecosystem Assessment, 28, 29, 39
    Stonehenge tunnel solution, 26
United Nations (UN)

Index

Ban Ki-Moon (Secretary-General), 3
Kofi Annan (Secretary-General), 27–28
Office for Disaster Risk Reduction (UNISDR), 115–116, 124–125
sustainable development goals (SDGs), 85–96, 110
sustainable food production, 86
United States (USA)
    Boston see Boston
    investments in infrastructure, 184
    Kansas City see Kansas City
    New York see New York
    Portland (Oregon), Pioneer Courthouse Square, 79
    San Francisco see Bay Area; San Francisco
    Seattle, Alaskan Way viaduct, 175–176
urban areas
    architecture see architecture
    challenges, 118–120
        meeting them, 120–124
    design see design
    mass migration from rural to, 2, 3, 94, 194
    planning see planning
    resilience, 115–127
urban frontier, final, 1–21
urban tissue, new, 18–19, 56, 59–83
    connectivity, 18, 91–92, 196
urbanism (20th C.), 49–56
USA see United States
users (people), 129–149
    building for, 129–149
    perceptions see perceptions
Utudjian, Édouard, 53–55, 56, 61, 67, 68, 69, 81

valued spaces, 129–149
    capturing crated value, 177–182
ventilation, 141, 142, 143
vertical greenery systems, 177
vertical zoning, 106, 107
Victoria and Albert Museum–South Kensington Station subway, 74–75
Viikinmaki waste water treatment plant (Helsinki), 46
Vision of the Subsurface (Municipality of Zwolle), 104
Voorburg, Sijtwende development, 179

Waferfab factory (Sargans, Switzerland), 37–38
waste water (incl. sewage) treatment
    Dokhaven (Rotterdam), 33–34
    Lee Tunnel (London), 60–61
    Sha Tin (Hong Kong), 46
    Viikinmaki (Helsinki), 46
water
    aquifers see aquifers
    clean, 87–88
    drinking, 17, 25, 36, 87, 88, 123, 125
    management systems, 6, 95, 96, 119–120, 122
    sprinkler and mist system, 143
    waste see waste water
    see also drought; groundwater; rainfall
waterfronts
    Boston and Charlestown, 185
    Rio de Janeiro, 174–175
    Seattle, 175–176
way-finding, 143–144
    signage, 73, 77, 144
Willems Rail Tunnel (Rotterdam), 159–160, 175
wind, 118
    power from (turbines or wind farms), 91–92, 136
    proofing/protection, 124
    see also storms
Women's University (Seoul, South Korea), 138–139
Words into Action report, 124–125
work, decent, 89–91
World Bank, 177, 183
World Urban Campaign, 3, 93
Wuhan, 16

yaodong, 43–46, 124

ZA Architects, Arina Ageeva of, 197
zero hunger, 86–87
Zocalo (Mexico City), Earthscraper, 96–97, 120, 139–140
zoning, 37, 73, 100, 107, 166
    maps, 6
    vertical, 106, 107
Zurich, Sechseläutenplatz underground car park, 145
Zwolle (Municipality of), Vision of the Subsurface by, 104